Windows Script Host

ISBN 0-13-028701-6

90000

9 780130 287014

PRENTICE HALL PTR MICROSOFT® TECHNOLOGIES SERIES

NETWORKING

- IP Solutions for Windows 2000
  Ammann
- Microsoft Technology: Networking, Concepts, Tools
  Woodard, Gattuccio, Brain
- NT Network Programming Toolkit
  Murphy
- Building COM Applications with Internet Explorer
  Loveman
- Understanding DCOM
  Rubin, Brain
- Web Database Development for Windows Platforms
  Gutierrez

PROGRAMMING

- Windows 2000 Kernel Debugging
  McDowell
- Windows Script Host
  Aitken
- The Windows 2000 Device Driver Book, Second Edition
  Baker, Lozano
- Win32 System Services: The Heart of Windows 98 and Windows 2000, Third Edition
  Brain, Reeves
- Programming the WIN32 API and UNIX System Services
  Merusi
- Windows CE 3.0: Application Programming
  Grattan, Brain
- The Visual Basic Style Guide
  Patrick
- Windows Shell Programming
  Seely
- Windows Installer Complete
  Easter
- Windows 2000 Web Applications Developer's Guide
  Yager
- Developing Windows Solutions with Office 2000 Components and VBA
  Aitken
- Multithreaded Programming with Win32
  Pham, Garg
- Developing Professional Applications for Windows 98 and NT Using MFC, Third Edition
  Brain, Lovette
- Introduction to Windows 98 Programming
  Murray, Pappas
- The COM and COM+ Programming Primer
  Gordon
- Understanding and Programming COM+: A Practical Guide to Windows 2000 DNA
  Oberg
- Distributed COM Application Development Using Visual C++ 6.0
  Maloney
- The Essence of COM, Third Edition
  Platt
- COM-CORBA Interoperability
  Geraghty, Joyce, Moriarty, Noone
- MFC Programming in C++ with the Standard Template Libraries
  Murray, Pappas
- Introduction to MFC Programming with Visual C++
  Jones
- Visual C++ Templates
  Murray, Pappas
- Visual Basic Object and Component Handbook
  Vogel
- Visual Basic 6: Error Coding and Layering
  Gill
- ADO Programming in Visual Basic 6
  Holzner
- Visual Basic 6: Design, Specification, and Objects
  Hollis
- ASP/MTS/ADSI Web Security
  Harrison

BACKOFFICE

- Microsoft SQL Server 2000 Optimization Guide
  Fields
- BizTalk: Implementing Business-To-Business E-Commerce
  Kobielus
- Designing Enterprise Solutions with Microsoft Technologies
  Kemp, Kemp, Goncalves
- Microsoft Site Server 3.0 Commerce Edition
  Libertone, Scoppa
- Building Microsoft SQL Server 7 Web Sites
  Byrne
- Optimizing SQL Server 7
  Schneider, Goncalves

ADMINISTRATION

- Tuning and Sizing Windows 2000 for Maximum Performance
  Aubley
- Windows 2000 Cluster Server Guidebook
  Libertone
- Windows 2000 Hardware and Disk Management
  Simmons
- Windows 2000 Server: Management and Control, Third Edition
  Spencer, Goncalves
- Creating Active Directory Infrastructures
  Simmons
- Windows 2000 Registry
  Sanna
- Configuring Windows 2000 Server
  Simmons
- Supporting Windows NT and 2000 Workstation and Server
  Mohr
- Zero Administration Kit for Windows
  McInerney
- Windows NT 4.0 Server Security Guide
  Goncalves
- Windows NT Security
  McInerney

CERTIFICATION

- Core MCSE: Windows 2000 Edition
  Dell
- Core MCSE: Designing a Windows 2000 Directory Services Infrastructure
  Simmons
- MCSE: Implementing and Supporting Windows 98
  Dell
- Core MCSE
  Dell
- Core MCSE: Networking Essentials
  Keogh
- MCSE: Administering Microsoft SQL Server 7
  Byrne
- MCSE: Implementing and Supporting Microsoft Exchange Server 5.5
  Goncalves
- MCSE: Internetworking with Microsoft TCP/IP
  Ryvkin, Houde, Hoffman
- MCSE: Implementing and Supporting Microsoft Proxy Server 2.0
  Ryvkin, Hoffman
- MCSE: Implementing and Supporting Microsoft SNA Server 4.0
  Mariscal
- MCSE: Implementing and Supporting Microsoft Internet Information Server 4
  Dell
- MCSE: Implementing and Supporting Web Sites Using Microsoft Site Server 3
  Goncalves
- MCSE: Microsoft System Management Server 2
  Jewett
- MCSE: Implementing and Supporting Internet Explorer 5
  Dell
- Core MCSD: Designing and Implementing Desktop Applications with Microsoft Visual Basic 6
  Holzner
- MCSD: Planning and Implementing SQL Server 7
  Vacca
- MCSD: Designing and Implementing Web Sites with Microsoft FrontPage 98
  Karlins

PRENTICE HALL PTR MICROSOFT® TECHNOLOGIES SERIES

Windows Script Host

Peter G. Aitken

PH PTR

Prentice Hall PTR, Upper Saddle River, NJ 07458
www.phptr.com

Library of Congress Cataloging-in-Publication Data

Aitken, Peter G.
Windows script host / Peter Aitken.
p. cm. – (Prentice Hall series on Microsoft technologies)
Includes bibliographical references and index.
ISBN 0-13-028701-6
1. TCP/IP (Computer network protocol) 2. Computer networks–Management. I. Title.

TK5105.585 .A45 2001
005.7'1376–dc21 00-066541

Acquisitions Editor: *Jill Pisoni*
Production Editor: *Rose Kernan*
Cover Design: *Nina Scuderi*
Cover Design Direction: *Jerry Votta*
Manufacturing Manager: *Alexis Heydt*
Composition: *PreTeX, Inc.*

Prentice-Hall, Inc.
Upper Saddle River, NJ 07458

Prentice Hall books are widely used by corporations and government agencies for training, marketing, and resale.

The publisher offers discounts on this book when ordered in bulk quantities. For more information, contact Corporate Sales Department, phone: 800-382-3419; fax: 201-236-7141; email: corpsales@prenhall.com or write Corporate Sales Department, Prentice Hall PTR, One Lake Street, Upper Saddle River, NJ 07458.

Printed in the United States of America

10 9 8 7 6 5 4 3 2 1

ISBN 0-13-028701-6

Prentice-Hall International (UK) Limited, *London*
Prentice-Hall of Australia Pty. Limited, *Sydney*
Prentice-Hall Canada Inc., *Toronto*
Prentice-Hall Hispanoamericana, S.A., *Mexico*
Prentice-Hall of India Private Limited, *New Delhi*
Prentice-Hall of Japan, Inc., *Tokyo*
Pearson Education Asia Pte. Ltd.
Editora Prentice-Hall do Brasil, Ltda., *Rio de Janeiro*

CONTENTS

Introduction xix

Who This Book Is For xix

What You Need xx

Resources xx

ONE Windows Script Host Fundamentals 1

Background 1

- Unix Scripting 2
- The DOS Batch Language 2
- Windows Scripting 3

How WSH Works 3

- What Can WSH Do? 3
- WSH Operation 4

Scripting Technology 5

- Two Scripting Utilities 6

WSH Languages 9

WSH and Objects 10

Overview 10

TWO The WSH Object Model 11

Objects 11

- Object References 12
- Object Properties 13

Object Method s14

Collections 17

- The WshCollection Object 17

The FileSystemObject 18
The Dictionary Object 19
The Wscript Object 22
Obtaining Host Information 24
Script Interactivity 25
Terminating a Script 26
Setting a Timeout 26
Working with Objects 27
The WshShell Object 30
The WshEnvironment Object 31
The WshSpecialFolders Object 32
Working with Shortcuts 35
Displaying Popup Messages 39
Working with the Registry 42
Running Programs 46
The WshNetwork Object 49
Obtaining User Information 49
Working with Printers 51
Managing Network Drives 53
Overview 55

THREE Creating, Running, and Scheduling Scripts 56
Creating Your Scripts 56
Online Documentation 57
Running Scripts 58
Script Shortcuts 59
Scheduling Scripts 60
Overview 64

FOUR Working with Script Arguments, .WSH Files, and Web Scripting 65
Script Arguments 65

WSH Files 68
WSH and Web Scripting 70
Overview 71

▼ FIVE Testing and Debugging Your Script s72

Catching Script Errors 72
- Syntax Errors 72
- Run-Time Errors 74
- Bugs 75

Debugging Your Scripts 76
- The Script Debugger 76
- Using the Debugger 77

Overview 82

▼ SIX VBScript: Syntax, Data Storage, and Operators 83

Introduction to VBScript 83
Comparison with Visual Basic 84
Syntax Fundamentals 84
Comments 85
Line Continuations 85
- Data Storage 86

Object References 89
Determining Data Type 89
Arrays 90
- Static Arrays 90
- Dynamic Arrays 92
- Variant Arrays 94

Operators 94
- Assignment Operator 94
- Arithmetic Operators 95
- String Operators 95

Comparison Operators *96*
Logical Operators *97*
Operator Precedence and Parentheses *98*
Overview *99*

▼ SEVEN VBScript: Program Control and Procedures 100

Conditional Statements *100*
If. . .Then. . .Else *101*
Select Case *102*
Loop Statements *104*
For. . .Next *104*
For Each. . .Next *105*
Do. . .Loop *106*
While. . .Wend *108*
Infinite Loops *108*
Procedures *109*
Types of Procedures *109*
Defining a Procedure *110*
Passing Arguments to Procedures *110*
Variables in Procedures *112*
Calling Procedures *113*
Overview *114*

▼ EIGHT VBScript: Working with Text, Numbers, Dates, and Times 115

Text Manipulation *115*
Asc *116*
Chr *116*
Filter *117*
InStr, InStrRev *119*
InStrRev *119*
Join *119*
LCase, UCase *120*

Left, Mid, Right *120*
Len *121*
LTrim, RTrim, Trim *121*
Mid (function) *121*
RegExp *121*
Right *126*
RTrim *126*
Space *126*
Split *126*
String *126*
StrComp *127*
Trim *127*
UCase *127*
Working With Numbers *127*
Using Dates and Times *128*
Date and Time Representation *129*
Getting the Current Date and Time *129*
Creating Dates and Times *129*
Adding and Subtracting Dates and Times *130*
Getting Date and Time Information *131*
Formatting Dates and Times *133*
Overview *134*

NINE VBScript: User Interaction, Error Handling, And Miscellaneous Topics 135

Interacting with the User *135*
The MsgBox Function *135*
InputBox *137*
Error Handling *138*
Other Topics *140*
Eval *141*
Execute and ExecuteGlobal *141*
Overview *142*

TEN JScript: Basic Syntax, Data Storage, and Operators 143

Introduction to JScript *143*
- Comparison with Java *144*
- Syntax Fundamentals *144*
- Comments *145*

Data Storage *145*
- Constants *145*
- Variables *147*
- Data Types and Coersion *148*
- Object References *149*
- Arrays *150*

JScript Operators *151*
- The Assignment Operators *151*
- The Arithmetic Operators *152*
- The Increment and Decrement Operators *152*
- The Comparison Operators *153*
- The Logical Operators *154*
- String Operators *155*
- Conditional Expressions *155*
- Operator Precedence and Parentheses *156*

Overview *156*

ELEVEN JScript: Conditional Statements, Loops, and Functions 157

Conditional Statements *157*
- If. . .Else *157*
- Switch *160*

Loop Statements *161*
- For *161*
- While *162*
- Do. . .While *163*
- The Continue Statement *163*

The With Statement 164

Functions 164

Defining a Function 165

Variables in Functions 166

Calling a Function 167

OverView 168

TWELVE JScript: Strings, Numbers, Math, Dates, and Times. 169

The String Object 169

The Split Method 172

Working with Regular Expressions 172

The Number Object 174

The Math Object 176

Dates and Times 176

Overview 180

THIRTEEN JScript: Built-in Objects, User Interaction, and Error Handling 181

JScript Objects 181

The Boolean Object 182

The Enumerator Object 182

The Function Object 183

The VBArray Object 184

User Interaction 186

Error Handling 188

The Error Object 188

Try. . . Catch 188

The Throw Statement 190

Overview 191

FOURTEEEN WSH 2.0 and WSF Files 192

Using WSF Files 192
XML and WSF Files 193
The <script> Tag 193
The <job> and <package>Tags 194
The <object> Tag 195
The <reference> Tag 195
Importing Files 196
XML Compliance 197
XML Errors and Debugging 198
Overview 199

FIFTEEN File Access and Management 200

The Scripting Run-time Library 200
File Management 202
Copying and Moving Files 202
Copying and Moving Folders 204
Creating Folders 205
Deleting Files and Folders 205
Seeing if a Drive, Folder, or File Exists 205
Obtaining Object References 206
Working with the Drives Collection and Drive Object 206
Working with the Folders Collection and Folder Object 209
Working with the Files Collection and File Object 213
Other FileSystemObject Methods 217
File Access 218
The TextStream Object 218
A TextStream Demonstration 221
Overview 223

SIXTEEN Creating Windows Script Components 224

Defining a Class 224
Creating Class Instances 225

Defining Class Properties 225
Defining Class Methods 226
Defining Private Class Information 228
Procedural Class Properties 228
Defining a Default Class Property 231

Using a Class in Multiple Scripts 232

A Class Example 233

Overview 235

SEVENTEEN Database Access with Scripting 236

Database Fundamentals 236

Database Technologies 239

Active Data Objects 240

Creating a Connection 241

Creating a Connection String 243
Recordsets 245

Creating a Recordset 247

Working with Recordsets 251

Accessing Field Data 251
Moving through a Recordset 252
Modifying Recordset Data 255

Overview 258

EIGHTEEN Scripting Microsoft Office Components 259

The Office Object Model 259

The Word Object Model 261

The Document Object 261
Manipulating Document Content 263
Other Document Properties and Methods 270

The Excel Object Model 271

The Workbook Object 272
The Worksheet Object 274

Validating Object References 285

Overview 285

▼ NINETEEN Messaging With WSH 286

Scripts and Messaging 286
Some E-mail Background 288
Scripting CDO 289
 Sending a Message with CDO 289
 Reading Mail with CDO 292
Scripting Microsoft Outlook 294
 The NameSpace Object 295
 Manipulating Folders and Items 295
 Working with Mail Messages 297
Overview 306

▼ TWENTY Using WSH For Administrative Tasks 307

Mapping Network Drive s307

Automating LogOn Scripts 310

Updating File s312

Creating Folders 315

Overview 318

▼ TWENTY-ONE A Script Programmer's Library 319

Installing Files from a CD 319
Obtaining Information about a Database 324
Printing from a Script 329

Appendix A VBScript Constants 332

Color Constant s332

Comparison Constants 332

Date and Time Constants 333

Date and Time Format Constants 333

Miscellaneous Constants 334

MsgBox Constants 334

String Constants 335

Appendix B VBScript Keywords 336

Appendix C ASCII Character Codes 338

Appendix D VBScript Error Codes 341

Appendix E JScript Reserved Words 343

Current Reserved Words 343

Future Reserved Words 343

Words to Avoid 344

Appendix F JScript Error Codes 345

Appendix G WSH Resources on the Internet 347

Index 349

INTRODUCTION

The Windows Script Host, or WSH, is a wonderful tool that is available to all users of the Windows operating system. In a nutshell, WSH is used to create scripts that automate operating system-related tasks. Which tasks are these? Anything you do with the Windows operating system, as opposed to an application program, falls into this category. Examples include copying and deleting files, logging onto network drives and printers, and executing programs. But WSH is not limited to operating system tasks - thanks to Microsoft's Component Object Model, scripts can also control many applications programs, such as Word and Excel. Almost anything you can do sitting at your computer's keyboard, you can also program a script to do for you.

So, what's the big deal? There are two factors:

- Saving time. With a couple of clicks, you can execute a script that carries out a complex series of action that would take a considerable time to perform manually.
- Preventing errors. Once tested and debugged, a script will carry out a precise sequence of actions error-free every time. Few people can say the same thing about their keyboard skills!

Either of these factors by itself would make a strong argument for scripting. Together, they are overpowering. Any Windows user who has gone beyond casual computing is a candidate to benefit from using WSH. Network administrators and other computer professionals can derive even more benefit.

Who This Book Is For

The intended audience for this book is anyone who wants to automate repetitive or time-consuming tasks under the Windows operating system. This includes both computer users, for whom the computer is a tool, as well as network professionals and systems administrators, who are responsibile for maintaining computer systems used by others. I assume no prior knowledge on the part of the reader beyond a reasonable familiarity with Windows. Specifically, no programming experience is needed. If, however, you do have some programming experience, certain parts of the book will likely go faster for you.

What You Need

The requirements for using this book are quite simple: a computer running Windows 95, 98, ME, NT 4.0, or 2000. As you will learn in Chapter 1, WSH is installed along with some of these operating systems, but must be installed separately with others (Windows 95 and NT). Details on obtaining the free install are also included in Chapter 1.

Resources

You will find my Web page for this book at this URL:

`http://www.pgacon.com/scripthost.htm`

This page lets you download a compressed archive containing all of the book's scripts, and there is also a link for reporting any errors, problems, or suggestion. I will also post a list of corrections and updates as they become available. Additional Internet resources for the Windows Script Host programmer can be found in Appendix 7.

Peter G. Aitken
Chapel Hill, North Carolina
January 2001

ONE

Windows Script Host Fundamentals

The Windows Script Host, or WSH for short, is one of the most powerful and useful parts of the Windows operating system. Strangely enough, it is also one of least well known, and is used by only a small percentage of Windows users. This strange set of circumstances is due in large part to the fact that Microsoft has not publicized the WSH in the same way that other parts of Windows, such as its Web capabilities, have been publicized. It is also because DOS and Windows users, unlike the Unix community, have no history of a powerful scripting language and therefore usually don't even think to look for one. Trust me — once you learn how to use WSH, you'll wonder how you ever got along without it! In this first chapter we take an introductory look at WSH: what it is, how it works, and what you can do with it. Then we create a real, working script that you can put to use on your system right away.

Background

Computers are supposed to make your life easier, right? Generally they do, but this does not mean computers are immune from errors. Many errors could be avoided by automating the task at hand so that it runs with little or no need for user intervention. This general idea applies not only to the typical application programs that you run, such as word processing and graphics, but also to the computer's operating system itself. If some of the operating system tasks can be automated, particularly those tasks that are repetitive and need to be performed regularly, that will be an additional increase in efficiency. Almost from the very beginning, when JCL (Job Control Language) and REXX were developed for mainframe computers, this has been a concern of operating system designers. Let's take a brief and incomplete look at the history of scripting languages.

Unix Scripting

The Unix operating system, in its various implementations, has been around for a long time, and recently has experienced a sort of renaissance with the popularity of the open source code Linux version. From its beginnings, Unix provided a powerful scripting language that could be used to automate a wide variety of tasks. First came CScript, and then the more powerful and better known Perl and Tcl, both of which are full-featured programming languages with support for variables, iteration, regular expressions, and looping (I'll explain these terms soon). The things that could be done with these languages left many non-Unix users green with envy.

The DOS Batch Language

When the DOS operating system was first introduced along with the first PCs, back in the early 1980s, it was provided with an extremely elementary scripting ability in the form of batch files. Batch files were simple text files that contained a combination of operating system commands and simple programming constructs. When you ran a batch file the effect was the same as if you had typed those commands at the command prompt. Likewise, if a batch file named autoexec.bat was present, it would be run automatically each time the system was booted.

Batch files were widely used to automate a variety of tasks, but they were extremely limited when compared with the scripting capabilities of Unix. These limitations are as follows:

- No support for looping or iteration (although some inelegant kludges could be used to implement limited functionality)
- Very limited variable support
- No regular expressions
- No direct support for structured programming (procedures)

Many DOS users managed to get a lot out of batch files, despite their inherent limitations. Not having experience with a "real" scripting language, they didn't know what they were missing!

Windows Scripting

In the early days of the Windows operating system, the term "Windows scripting" was a contradiction in terms because there was no Windows scripting — not as part of the operating system at least. The old DOS batch file capabilities were carried over into Windows, but given the additional features and capabilities of the new operating system the limitations of batch files were even more problematic. The Perl scripting language was available as a third party product, but only a small percentage of users knew about it. This shortcoming continued until the mid 1990s, when Windows 95 was the latest version of the operating system. At this time, Microsoft introduced the Windows Script Host as a powerful, full-featured scripting language for command scripting with Windows 95. Finally, after too many years, users of PCs with the Microsoft Windows operating system had a true command scripting language at their disposal. There was no more need for Unix envy!

The initial release of WSH was configured as an add-on to Windows 95, rather than being an integral part of the operating system. In other words, you had to download the WSH files and install them before you could write scripts. With Windows 98, Windows NT 4.0 (with the NT option pack), Windows ME, and Windows 2000 the WSH is included as part of the operating system.

Downloading WSH

If you are running Windows 95 and do not already have the WHS components installed, you can download them from http://msdn.microsoft.com/scripting/.

How WSH Works

I think you'll agree that WSH sounds intriguing, but you probably want to know more of the details. What can WSH do? How does it work? How do I create and run scripts? Most of this book is devoted to answering these and other questions in detail, but it's a good idea to have an understanding of the overall picture before getting to those details. That's what we do in this section.

What Can WSH Do?

An obvious question to ask at the start is what can be done with WSH? To be honest, it might almost be easier to list the things you *cannot* do with WSH! It is a very powerful and flexible tool, and in effect provides you with most of the functionality of a full-featured programming language combined with the capabilities that are built into the Windows operating system. If you have some familiarity with the old DOS batch files, it is definitely a mistake to think of WSH as simply a souped-up version of batch files. You might as well think of a Ferrari 360GT as a souped-up tricycle! Here are just some of the tasks that can be easily and efficiently performed using WSH:

- File management tasks, such as moving, copying, deleting, and renaming files and folders
- Reading data from, and writing data to, text files
- Scheduling scripts to run at specified times
- Administering user logins, operating system settings, and file shortcuts
- Automating the administration of Microsoft SQL Server and Internet Information Server
- Accessing the capabilities of the programs in Microsoft Office
- Working with information stored in databases
- Leveraging the power of ActiveX components
- Automating messaging tasks

This is only a partial list, but I think you get the idea. WSH was designed from the outset to impose as few limitations as possible, and to put the maximum power and convenience in the hands of the users.

WSH Operation

At the heart of WSH is a set of *scripting engines*. These are the same scripting engines that are used by the Microsoft Internet Explorer browser to execute client-side scripts, and by Microsoft Internet Information Server (Microsoft's Web server software) to execute Active Server Page scripts. WSH provides a different environment in which these scripting engines can run, an environment designed for local user execution of scripts.

You may have noticed that I said "engines." Is there more than one scripting engine for WSH? There is indeed. WSH was designed from the outset to support different scripting languages, with each language supported by a separate scripting engine. As supplied by Microsoft, WSH supports two languages (as detailed in the next section) but the WSH specification is open to the development of other engines by third-party vendors. As an analogy, think of a mail-order computer store that has telephone representatives who can speak English, Spanish, and Chinese. Depending on the language you want to speak, your order will be taken by a different person (analogous to a scripting engine), but regardless of who takes your order, your order will be packed and shipped by the same people in the warehouse (analogous to WSH).

All WSH scripts are stored as plain text files, in a file whose extension depends on the specific scripting language in use. When you execute a script, here's what happens, in a somewhat simplified form:

1. Based on the extension of the script file, WSH searches the Windows registry for information on the scripting engine that is associated with the script language.
2. Using the information obtained in (1), an instance of the scripting engine is created. At the same time, an instance of the script object (the host) is also created.
3. WSH establishes two-way communication between itself and the scripting engine.
4. The script file is read and its commands carried out.

Scripting Technology

It would be an error to think of WSH as some sort of independent "extra" that has been added to the Windows operating system. There is much integration within the operating system, and nothing is truly independent. When you create and use scripts, there are really several technologies coming into play:

- Windows Script Host provides the full-system scripting environment and object model that provides access to system and application functionality.
- The VBScript and JScript engines permit script authors to take advantage of the power of these two modern and full-featured scripting languages.
- COM (Component Object Model) is a standard for creation of reusable software components that expose an automation interface, and therefore can be controlled by scripts. COM is central to many aspects of Windows and Windows applications.
- Windows Script Components (previously called Server Scriptlets) supply the capability to provide COM objects in script code, which in turn permits the creation of reusable script objects.

You can see from these descriptions that the term "Windows Script Host," technically speaking, refers to only part of the picture. From the perspective of the script programmer, however, these distinctions are largely irrelevant, just like the details of a car's engine and transmission are irrelevant to most drivers. For the remainder of this book I use the term "Windows Script Host," or WSH, in the broad sense of referring to the full range of technologies that are utilized by scripts.

Two Scripting Utilities

The WSH actually offers two scripting utilities. Under the surface they are essentially identical. They differ in the interface between the utility and the user. Cscript is the command line WSH scripting utility, which communicates with the user by means of the DOS command line. In Windows, of course, this is a "DOS box," which is identified on the Start menu as "MS-DOS Prompt." Wscript is the Windows interface version of the script utility, which communicates by means of screen windows.

Let's take a look at these two approaches to scripting, using a very simple script (Listing 1-1). Use any text editor, such as Notepad, to create a file containing the code shown in the listing. Save the file using the name List0101.vbs. You can use another name if you prefer, as long as you be sure to use the .VBS extension.

LISTING 1–1 *A simple script to display a screen message.*

```
' List0101.vbs
' A very simple script!
Wscript.echo "Welcome to the Windows Scripting Host!"
```

Let's take a quick look at the code in this very simple script. The first two lines are *comments*, which are not executed by WSH but serve only as a way for the programmer to include comments and notes in a script file. The third line is the only line of executable script code in this file. It uses the `Wscript.echo` command to display text on the screen.

Create a scripts folder.

It is easier to keep your scripts organized if you keep them all in one place. For example, you might create a folder named C:\Windows\Scripts to keep your scripts.

Once the script file has been created, here's how to run it using the Cscript command line utility:

1. Open an MS-DOS window by selecting MS-DOS Prompt from the Windows Start menu.
2. At the prompt, enter the command to change to the folder where your script file is stored. For example, if your script file is in the folder C:\Windows\Scripts, then the command will be

```
cd c:\windows\scripts
```

3. Enter the following command to start the Cscript utility and execute your script:

```
Cscript list0101.vbs
```

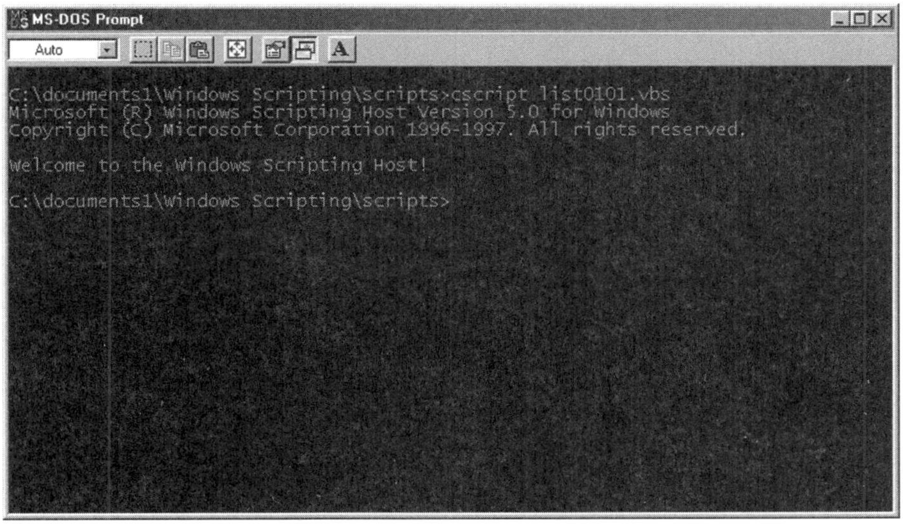

FIGURE 1–1 *The output when the sample script is run with Cscript.*

4. Examine the output, which is shown in Figure 1-1.

When you examine the output of the script, you'll note several things (your output may look slightly different depending on the folder where you put the script file).

1. The first line is where you entered the command to run the script.
2. The second and third lines are the version and copyright notices displayed by the Cscript utility.
3. The fourth line is the output created by the script.
4. The fifth and last line is the command prompt, which returns after the script terminates.

Now let's try out the Wscript utility. You could run it using the same steps as just described, replacing the Cscript command in step 3 with Wscript. However, it does not make a lot of sense to use the MS-DOS command line to run a Windows interface program. Here's a better way to run a script using Wscript:

1. Open the Windows Explorer.
2. Navigate to the folder where the script file List0101.vbs is located.
3. Double-click the name of the script file.

Script file actions

How does Windows know to run a script file with Wscript when you double-click the file name in Explorer? Windows keeps a list of file extensions and the actions that are associated with them. When WSH is installed, the action associated with opening a file with a .vbs or .js extension is set to "execute with Wscript." A file is opened in Explorer by double-clicking it or by selecting Open from its context (right-click) menu. Other actions are available on a file's context menu, such as Edit, which, for script files, opens the file in Notepad for editing. You can view and edit the actions for various file extensions as follows:

1. Open My Computer.
2. Select Folder Options from the View menu.
3. In the dialog box, select the File Types tab.

The output of the script as created by Wscript is shown in Figure 1-2. You can see that this is a lot more appropriate for the Windows environment, consisting of a dialog box with the message and an OK button.

Now let's take a look at another script, the one in Listing 1-2. This script does exactly the same thing as the one in Listing 1-1, but it is written in a different scripting language — JScript rather than VBScript. The two scripts look quite similar, but you'll note some differences:

1. The JScript comment is enclosed between /* and */ rather than being preceded by an apostrophe.
2. The text to be displayed by the WScript.Echo command is enclosed in parentheses as well as double quotes.
3. Statements in JScript end with a semicolon.
4. JScript scripts are saved in files with the .JS extension.
5. It is not obvious from the listing, but JScript is case sensitive. Thus, `WScript.Echo` must be entered exactly as shown; if you try `Wscript.echo` or some other capitalization variant, it will not work.

FIGURE 1–2 *The script file output produced by Wscript.*

LISTING 1–2 *Another version of the simple script.*

```
/* List0102.js
A very simple script! */
WScript.Echo("Welcome to the Windows Scripting Host!");
```

If you want to try this JScript example, follow the instructions for the VBScript example that were given earlier. Since the file will have the .JS extension, the scripting engine will know which language it contains and process it appropriately. The output will be exactly the same as it was for Listing 1-1 whether you use Cscript or Wscript.

Two JScript comment styles

JScript supports two styles of comments. As mentioned in the text, anything between /* and */ is a comment. This style can span multiple lines. Also, a single line that begins with // is a comment. To use this style with multiple lines, each line must begin with //.

WSH Languages

As you have seen, WSH as provided by Microsoft has support for two different scripting languages: VBScript and JScript. VBScript is based on Microsoft's Visual Basic and Visual Basic for Applications languages, which are used in the Visual Basic programming environment and the Microsoft Office applications suite, respectively. VBScript is not identical to Visual Basic but is very similar, with most syntax and language elements in common. JScript is Microsoft's implementation of the JavaScript language. Both JScript and JavaScript are, as the names imply, based on the Java language, although there are significant differences.

Do you need to know Visual Basic or Java to use WSH or to get the most out of this book? Definitely not. If you do happen to know either of these languages then you will certainly pick up VBScript and JScript more quickly, but that's all. You'll find all of the information you need to master both of these languages in this book.

Which language should you use? From a practical standpoint, it does not really matter as neither of the languages is really better than the other. I believe that VBScript is a little easier to learn and use, but that is a personal opinion, and other experienced WSH programmers may feel differently. If you are just going to write scripts for yourself and some friends, you can probably get away with learning just one of the languages. If, however, you will be doing WSH development at the professional level, I strongly suggest that you develop at least a reasonable familiarity with both languages. Even though you may write all your own scripts in your preferred language, you never know when you may be called on to modify or debug a script that someone else has written in the other language.

WSH and Objects

WSH development is closely based on the concept of *objects*. An object is a self-contained tool that has been designed to perform a specific task. The Windows operating system itself makes use of objects in most of the things it does, as do most Windows applications programs such as Excel and PhotoShop. Most of the scripts you write will use objects to carry out their tasks. The objects that are available to a script fall into three general categories:

- Objects provided by WSH itself
- Objects that are part of the Windows operating system
- Objects that are part of applications programs, such as Microsoft Office (ActiveX objects)

The beauty of working with objects is that the code required to perform most of the actions you need to do has already been written, tested, and tucked inside an object ready for you to use it when needed. For example, one of the objects that is part of WSH is the `FileSystemObject`. This object already "knows" how to perform all the file management tasks that a script might need, such as copying and renaming files and folders. When your script needs to perform a file management task, all you need do is write the VBScript or JScript code to send the proper commands to the **`FileSystem`**`Object`. You'll learn a lot more about working with objects in Chapter 2, and the details of the various objects available to a script will be presented as needed throughout the book.

Overview

The Windows Scripting Host is Microsoft's answer to the command scripting needs of the millions of users of the Windows operating system. Compared with other operating systems, such as Unix, scripting is a relatively new addition to Windows. It is, however, a very powerful addition, providing multiple language support, a powerful object model, access to existing ActiveX objects, and a powerful and flexible syntax. WSH puts you in command of your operating system and can simplify many tasks and save you time as well.

TWO

The WSH Object Model

Most of the more interesting things you can do with WSH involve the use of objects. As you learned in Chapter 1, some of these objects are part of WSH itself, while others are ActiveX objects that are part of other applications programs, such as Microsoft Office. This chapter covers those objects that are part of WSH itself. The chapter starts with an explanation of what objects are and also covers the `Collection` *object, which is used in some areas of WSH programming.*

Objects

As you create WSH scripts, you will unavoidably be involved with objects. What exactly is an object, and how do you use them?

The best way to think of objects is as tools. The people who created WSH realized that there were many tasks that scripts would commonly need to perform, and that it was a good idea to include this functionality as part of WSH rather than requiring that programmers do it themselves. A good example is dealing with the disk drives and files on a computer — something that many scripts need to do but that is potentially very complicated. The functionality for a specific task, such as dealing with a disk file, has been created, tested, and packaged in a reusable software component that you can easily utilize in your scripts. These components are called objects.

WSH offers a fairly wide range of objects, and the details of using each type of object will, of course, differ from case to case. The general syntax for working with objects is, however, standardized. First, you need a *reference* to the object in order to refer to it in your script code. Once you have a reference, you manipulate an object by means of its *properties* and *methods*. This section provides you with an introduction to working with object references, properties, and methods, enough for you to get started working with WSH. You'll learn more details in later chapters as needed.

Object References

An object reference is nothing more than a name assigned to the object. When you use this name in code, you are referring to the object. There are two types of object references: ones that already exist as part of WSH, and ones you create in your script code.

Objects that exist as part of WSH can simply be referred to in code without any preparation. Of course, you need to know the reference name, and you will learn the names of WSH's built-in objects later in this chapter as well as in other parts of the book. For example, there is an object named `WScript.Arguments` that lets you access any arguments that were passed to the script when it was executed. To access this object in your script code simply use its reference, `WScript.Arguments`. You'll learn more about this object in Chapter 4.

To create an object reference in a script, you first need a variable that will hold the reference. You'll learn more about variables in Chapters 6 (VBScript) and 10 (JScript), but the basics are as follows. In VBScript, use the `Dim` keyword followed by the variable name (which is up to you, as long as you follow the rules that are explained in Chapter 6):

```
Dim myObject
```

In JScript, the `var` keyword is used:

```
var myObject;
```

Now that you have the variable, you need to make it refer to an object. In VBScript you use the `Set` keyword along with the `CreateObject` method, passing the name of the object to be created as an argument to the method. This VBScript code, for example, creates an instance of the Microsoft Excel application and sets the variable `myObject` to refer to it:

```
Set myObject = WScript.CreateObject("Excel.Application")
```

In JScript the code is similar except that the `Set` keyword is not used:

```
myObject = WScript.CreateObject("Excel.Application");
```

It is often convenient to combine these two techniques to create a reference to an object that is part of WSH. Suppose, for example, that your script will use the `WScript.Arguments` object a lot. You can save typing and also make your code less cluttered by creating a reference to the object and then using your reference rather than the built-in one. In VBScript you would do this as follows:

```
Dim wsa
Set wsa = WScript.Arguments
```

In JScript here's what the code would look like:

```
var wsa;
wsa = WScript.Arguments;
```

In either case, your script can now use the variable `wsa` to refer to the `WScript.Arguments` object.

Confusing object names?

Some built-in objects have two-part names, such as `WScript.Arguments`. This may seem confusing to you — it looks like an object name followed by a property or method name. It's not, however. It means "the object named `Arguments` that belongs to `WScript`."

Object Properties

Properties are the way objects store information. To refer to an object property, you use the object name (its reference) and the property name separated by a period:

```
ObjectName.PropertyName
```

If you want to retrieve the value of a property, you would write code like this, which sets the variable X equal to the `Value` property of the object named `MyObj`:

```
X = MyObj.Value
```

To set the value of this property, the code would be as follows:

```
MyObj.Value = 123
```

Many object properties are read-only, which means that you can retrieve their value but cannot change it. Let's look at an example, using the `WScript.Arguments` object. This object has a property `Count` that returns the number of arguments passed to the script. An argument in this case is a bit of information passed to the script when it is executed by either Cscript or Wscript (you'll learn more about script arguments in Chapter 4). For example, if you execute a script with the following command line:

```
Cscript myscript.vbs one two three
```

you are passing three arguments: The first one is "one," the second one is "two," and so on. The code in Listings 2-1 and 2-2 shows how to access the number of arguments by means of the `WScript.Arguments.Count` property or, in the case of JScript, `WScript.Arguments.length`. The scripts display a message indicating the number of arguments passed to the script.

LISTING 2–1 *VBScript code to access the WScript.Arguments.Count property.*

```
' List0201.vbs
' Demonstrates object properties and the
' WScript.Arguments object.

Dim wsa

Set wsa = WScript.Arguments
WScript.Echo "The script was passed " & wsa.count &
   arguments."
```

LISTING 2–2 *JScript code to access the WScript.Arguments.length property.*

```
// List0202.js
// Demonstrates object properties and the
// WScript.Arguments object.

var wsa;

wsa = WScript.Arguments;
WScript.Echo("The script was passed " + wsa.length + "
   arguments.");
```

Object Methods

Methods are the way that objects carry out actions. The syntax for calling a method is similar to that for accessing a property, using the object name and the method name separated by a period. One difference is that many methods take arguments, which supply information that the method needs to carry out its task:

`ObjectName.MethodName ArgumentList`

Methods come in two types. Some methods perform an action, and that's all. Other methods perform an action and return information to the program. Typically the information that is returned provides some feedback about the action that was just carried out, such as whether or not it was successful.

You have already seen an example of the first type of method, namely `WScript.Echo`, which displays a message on the console (if the script is running in Cscript) or in a dialog box (if running in Wscript). You call, or invoke, a method by simply referring to it in your script code. In VBScript, for example,

```
WScript.Echo "Hello"
```

And in JScript,

```
WScript.Echo("Hello");
```

When a method returns data to the calling program, you usually need to make use of the information. Typically this involves assigning the return value to a variable, and then making use of the stored value as required. For example, the `WshShell` object has the `PopUp` method that displays a dialog box on the screen with a message and buttons for the user to select. The method's return value is a number indicating which of the buttons the user selected. The scripts in Listings 2-3 and 2-4 show how to call this method and retrieve its return value. Figure 2-1 shows the popup dialog box displayed by both scripts.

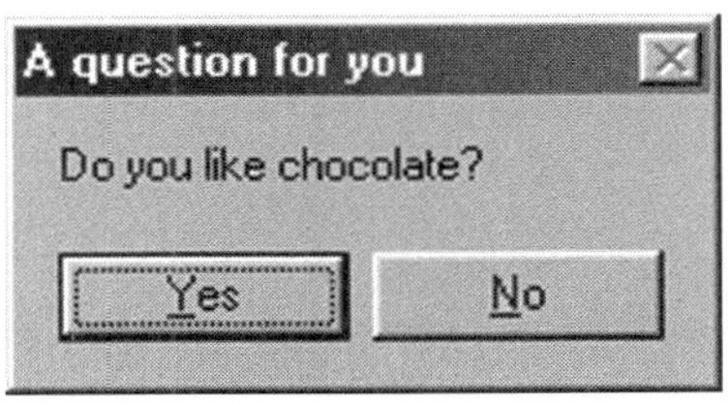

FIGURE 2–1 *The popup dialog box displayed by the WshShell. Popup method.*

Before you look at these listings, you need to know how VBScript and JScript deal with long lines of code. When a code line gets too long, WSH does not care, but it can be inconvenient to view and edit the code — not to mention impossible to print it in the listings! In VBScript you can extend a single line of code over two or more lines by using the line continuation character, an underscore ('_'). At the point where you want to break the line of code, type a space followed by an underscore and hit Enter to start a new line. In JScript, no special character is needed since the end of the line is marked by a semicolon (';') — simply hit Enter to continue a line of code on the next line. You can break a line anywhere except inside quoted text — in other words, inside double quotes. In both VBScript and JScript it is a good idea (although not required) to indent the continued line or lines with respect to the first part of the line, to make the code easier to read. In Listings 2.3 and 2.4, the line of code that starts with `button =` is extended over two lines.

LISTING 2-3 *Using the return value of a method (VBScript).*

```
' List0203.vbs
' Demonstrates using the return value
' from a method.

Dim button
Dim WshShell

Set WshShell = Wscript.CreateObject("Wscript.Shell")
button = WshShell.Popup("Do you like chocolate?",  , _
    "A question for you", vbYesNo)
WScript.Echo "Button " & button & " was selected."
```

LISTING 2-4 *Using the return value of a method (JScript).*

```
/* List0204.js
 Demonstrates using the return value
 from a method. */

var button
var WshShell

WshShell = WScript.CreateObject("Wscript.Shell");
button = WshShell.Popup("Do you like chocolate?",
    10, "A question for you", 4);
WScript.Echo("Button " + button + " was selected.");
```

In these listings you may have noticed that the VBScript code passes something called `vbYesNo` as the last argument to `WshShell.Popup`, whereas the JScript code passes the value 4. `vbYesNo` is a constant, a name assigned to a fixed numerical value — in this case 4. VBScript provides a whole range of constants such as this, and you'll find a list of them in Appendix 1. Their advantage is that it is easier to remember a mnemonic constant than a numerical value since the constant names are related to their function — in this case, displaying Yes and No buttons. JScript does not provide predefined constants.

Default properties and methods

Most objects have a default property or method; typically this is the property or method that programmers need most often. You can refer to an object's default property or method by using the object name alone or by using the usual ObjectName.PropertyName syntax.

Collections

WSH and its associated objects make frequent use of *collections*. A collection, represented by the `Collection` object, is a way to keep track of several data elements of the same type. Usually the data elements in a collection are objects, but this is not always the case. While different collections will hold different types of data elements, each collection has a standard set of methods and properties that is always the same. There may be minor differences between collections based on what they hold, but even so having a fairly standard collection syntax makes the WSH programmer's life a lot easier.

Collections almost always have a Courier property that returns the number of items in the collection. If the `Count` property is 0, then you know the collection is empty. To reference an individual item in the collection, use the following syntax to access the `Item` property:

```
CollectionName.Item(n)
```

In this example, *CollectionName* is the name of the collection and *n* is an integer specifying the position of the item in the collection. The value of *n* can range from 0, for the first item in the collection, up to `Count-1` for the last item. If you try to retrieve a collection element that does not exist, an error occurs. Because `Item` is the default property for collections, you can omit the property name and use the collection name by itself. The following therefore is equivalent to the previous code:

```
CollectionName(n)
```

Some collections associate a name with each element in the collection, in addition to a position number. You can retrieve individual items in the collection using either the name or the position number. For example,

```
CollectionName(name)
```

You'll learn more about collections as the need arises.

The WshCollection Object

Many of the collections you will use in WSH are specifically `WshCollection` objects. You cannot use this object in your scripting code to store information, but within WSH, certain objects provide information in the form of `WshCollection` objects. For example, the `WshNetwork` object, covered later in this chapter, has the `EnumNetworkDrives` and `EnumPrinterConnections` methods, which each return a collection containing all of the available network drives or printer connections. This object has three properties, listed in Table 2-1, and no methods. You will see examples of using these collections in Listings 2-29 through 2-32.

TABLE 2-1 *Properties of the WshCollection object.*

Property	Description
Count	Returns the number of items in the collection.
Item(*n*)	Returns the *n*th item in the collection. *n* can range from 0 to `Count-1`.
Length	Returns the number of items in the collection, the same as `Count`. This property is provided for compatibility with JScript conventions.

The FileSystemObject

The `FileSystemObject`, or FSO for short, is one of the most important objects in the WSH object hierarchy. As the name implies, you use this object for working with the file system. Working with the file system is generally divided into two areas:

- *File management*, which consists of creating folders, copying and moving files, and similar tasks
- *File access*, which refers to reading data from, and writing data to, files

The `FileSystemObject` and its subsidiary objects provide all the capabilities you will ever need for file management and access. The entire file system of a given computer is organized hierarchically, with individual parts of the file system represented by specific objects:

- The `FileSystemObject` represents the entire file system.
- The `FileSystemObject` contains a `Drives` collection, which contains one `Drive` object for each drive, both local and network, on the system.
- Each `Drive` object has a `RootFolder` property that references a `Folder` object, which represents the root folder on the drive.
- Each `Folder` object has a `Folders` collection containing a `Folder` object for each subfolder within the folder.
- Each `Folder` object also has a `Files` collection containing a `File` object for each file within the folder.

The hierarchy is represented schematically in Figure 2-2. This sounds and looks more complicated than it really is. Once you start working with the `FileSystemObject` and its subobjects, I think you'll agree that it is a well-designed and easy-to-use system. Because this is an important topic with lots of information to cover, I have devoted an entire chapter to it. You'll learn all the file system details in Chapter 15.

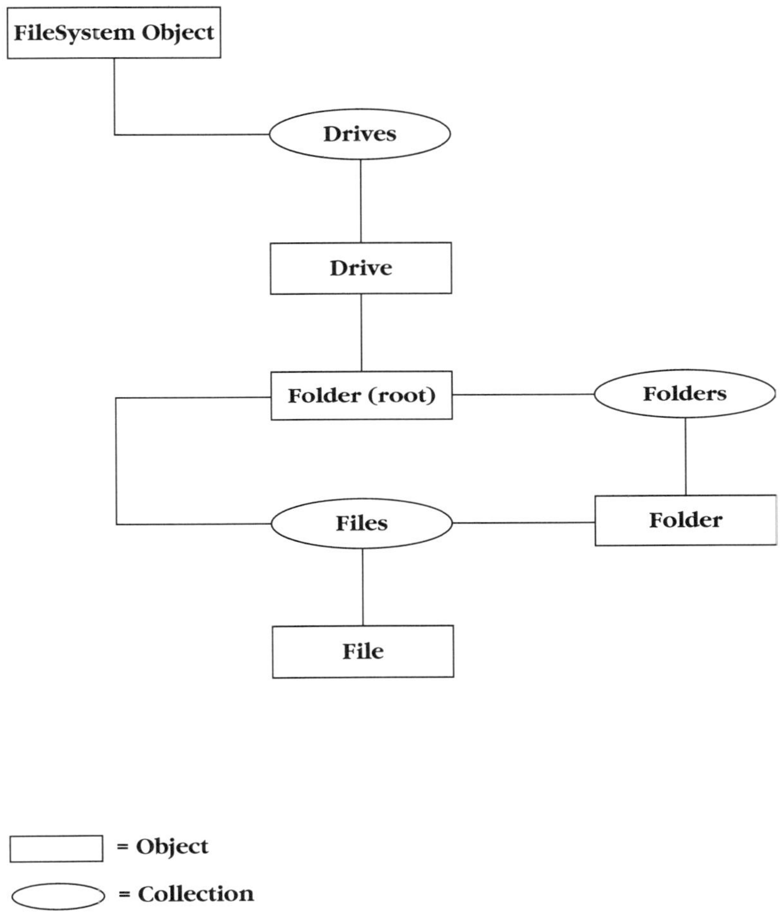

FIGURE 2–2 *Objects and collections in the FileSystemObject hierarchy.*

The Dictionary Object

The `Dictionary` object provides WSH with a specialized and very useful type of data storage. Specifically, this object lets you create associative arrays. An array is a way to store multiple data items under the same name. With regular arrays, supported by both VBScript and JScript, each item in the array is identified by a numerical index (you'll learn about regular arrays in Chapters 6 and 10). In contrast, an associative array lets you identify elements of the array with plain English names (or Spanish, Polish, or Norwegian if you prefer!)

Let's look at an example. Suppose you need to keep track of information related to each of the 50 states. Using regular arrays, you would create an array with 50 elements, indexed 1 though 50. Then you would arbitrarily decide that array element 1 will hold information for Maine, element 2 for New Hampshire, and so on. The relationship between the array index and the related information is purely arbitrary.

With a `Dictionary` object, however, you can create an array in which each data element is identified by a meaningful name — in this case, the name of the state. Clearly this arrangement is more intuitive and easier to use. When working with a dictionary object, each data element is referred to as an *item* and the identifying name for each item is its *key*. Obviously, the same key cannot be used more than once in a given dictionary.

The `Dictionary` object has a set of properties and methods that you use to work with the data stored there. These properties and methods are summarized in Tables 2-2 and 2-3.

TABLE 2-2 *Dictionary object properties.*

Property	Description
CompareMode	Specifies the way comparisons are done for key values. The default setting of 0 provides binary comparisons, in which upper- and lowercase letters do not match. A setting of 1 provides text comparisons in which the case of letters does not matter. You can set this property only when the dictionary is empty.
Count	Returns the number of items in the dictionary.
Item(*key*)	Returns or sets the item with the specified key. If the specified key does not exist, then the return value is undefined (the special value `Empty`). When setting an item, if *key* exists the associated item is changed; if *key* does not exist a new item is added to the dictionary.
Key(*key*)	Modifies the specified key. If *key* does not exist in the dictionary, an error occurs.

TABLE 2-3 *Dictionary object methods.*

Method	Description
Add(*key, item*)	Adds the specified item to the dictionary, using the specified key. If *key* already exists in the dictionary, an error occurs.
Exists(*key*)	Returns True if the specified key already exists in the dictionary, False otherwise.
Items()	Returns an array containing all the items in the dictionary, in the order they were entered.
Keys()	Returns an array containing all the key values in the dictionary, in the order they were entered.
Remove(*key*)	Removes the item associated with *key* from the dictionary. If the specified key does not exist, an error occurs.
RemoveAll()	Removes all items from the dictionary.

The basics of using the Dictionary object are as follows:

1. Create an instance of the Dictionary object.
2. Set the Compare property if the default binary comparison mode is not suited to your needs.
3. Add items to the dictionary, modify them, and remove them as dictated by the needs of your script.

Listings 2-5 and 2-6 demonstrate how to create and use a Dictionary object.

LISTING 2-5 *Creating and using a Dictionary object (VBScript).*

```
' List0205.vbs
' Demonstrates the Dictionary object.

Dim EmployeeOfMonth
Dim i
Dim ItemArray
Dim KeyArray

' Create an instance of the Dictionary.
Set EmployeeOfMonth = WScript.CreateObject("Scripting.Dictionary")

' Set compare mode.
EmployeeOfMonth.CompareMode = 1

' Add some data.
EmployeeOfMonth.add "January", "John Henry"
EmployeeOfMonth.add "February", "Arlene Walker"
EmployeeOfMonth.add "March", "Mimi Chang"
EmployeeOfMonth.add "April", "Roosevelt Jones"
EmployeeOfMonth.add "May", "Juanita Gomez"
EmployeeOfMonth.add "June", "Mario Camponi"

' Modify an entry due to a name change.
EmployeeOfMonth.Item("March") = "Mimi Smith"

' Display all entries.
KeyArray = EmployeeOfMonth.Keys
ItemArray = EmployeeOfMonth.Items
WScript.Echo "Employees of the month"
For i = 0 to EmployeeOfMonth.Count - 1
    WScript.Echo KeyArray(i) & ": " & ItemArray(i)
Next
```

LISTING 2-6 *Creating and using a Dictionary object (JScript).*

```
/* List0206.js
 Demonstrates the Dictionary object. */

var EmployeeOfMonth;
var i;
var ItemArray;
var KeyArray;

// Create an instance of the Dictionary.
EmployeeOfMonth = WScript.CreateObject("Scripting.Dictionary");

// Set compare mode.
EmployeeOfMonth.CompareMode = 1;

// Add some data.
EmployeeOfMonth.add("January", "John Henry");
EmployeeOfMonth.add("February", "Arlene Walker");
EmployeeOfMonth.add("March", "Mimi Chang');
EmployeeOfMonth.add("April", "Roosevelt Jones");
EmployeeOfMonth.add("May", "Juanita Gomez");
EmployeeOfMonth.add("June", "Mario Camponi");

// Modify an entry due to a name change.
EmployeeOfMonth.Item("March") = "Mimi Smith";

// Display all entries.
ItemArray = (new VBArray(EmployeeOfMonth.Items())).toArray();
KeyArray = (new VBArray(EmployeeOfMonth.Keys())).toArray();
WScript.Echo("Employees of the month");
for (i in ItemArray)
    WScript.Echo(KeyArray[i] + ": " + ItemArray[i]);
```

The Wscript Object

`Wscript` is the root object of those objects that are specifically part of WSH. It is always available when a script is running, so you never need to create an instance. The `Wscript` object lets you retrieve information about the running script's environment and arguments, as well as allowing you to create new objects or retrieve them from files. Also, as you have already seen, the `Wscript` object lets you echo information to the screen (with `Wscript.Echo`). Note that this object is available regardless of whether the script is running in Wscript or Cscript.

The `Wscript` object has a variety of methods and properties. It's hard to imagine a script that does not use at least one of these! The properties are described in Table 2-4, and the methods in Table 2-5. Note that all of the properties except `Interactive` and `TimeOut` are read-only. Some demonstration scripts are presented following the tables.

TABLE 2-4 *Properties of the Wscript object.*

Property	Description
Application	Returns a reference to the `Wscript` object. Used when you need to make a copy of the object or pass it as an argument to a method or function.
Arguments	Returns a collection that contains the arguments that were passed to the script. You'll learn how to use this property in Chapter 4.
FullName	Returns the fully qualified path of the script host that is running the script; for example, c:\windows\cscript.exe.
Interactive	Specifies whether the script runs in interactive or batch mode.*
Name	Returns the name of the scripting host; for example, Windows Scripting Host.
Path	Returns the path to the folder where the scripting host program is located.
ScriptFullName	Returns the full path and file name of the script that is executing; for example, c:\scripts\MyScript.vbs.
ScriptName	Returns the file name of the script that is executing; for example, myscript.vbs.
TimeOut	Specifies the timeout setting for the script (WSH 2.0 only).*
Version	Returns the version of the scripting host program.

* These are undocumented properties.

TABLE 2-5 *Methods of the Wscript object.*

Method	Description
CreateObject (*ProgId*)	Creates an instance of the object specified by *ProgID* and returns a reference to it.
DisconnectObject(*object*)	Disconnects event handling from an object that was created with `CreateObject` or `GetObject`.
GetObject (*path, ProgID*)	Returns a reference to an ActiveX object contained in a file specified by *path*, or creates a new instance of an object specified by *ProgID*.
Echo (*argument*)	Displays a message in a popup window (if the script is running in Wscript) or at the command prompt (Cscript).
Quit (*errorcode*)	Terminates script execution with the specified numerical error code.
Sleep (*milliseconds*)	Suspends execution of the script for the specified number of milliseconds (WSH 2.0 only).

Obtaining Host Information

Using the Wscript object's properties to obtain information about the host is perfectly straightforward, but when and why would you need this information? One situation has to do with the difference between Cscript and Wscript as regards the output of the Echo method. Perhaps your script uses Echo for a lot of its output, and you want to be sure this output appears in popup windows rather than at a command prompt. In other words, you want to prevent your script from running in Cscript at all. By retrieving the Wscript.FullName property and determining whether it contains the string "Cscript.exe," you can display a message to the user and terminate the script if it is running in Cscript. Listings 2-7 and 2-8 show how to do this.

LISTING 2-7 *Using Wscript properties (VBScript).*

```
' List0207.vbs
' Using the Wscript.FullName property to
' prevent the script from running in Cscript.

Dim s

s = Wscript.FullName

if instr(1, s, "Cscript.exe", vbTextCompare) <> 0 then
    MsgBox "Please run this script using Wscript."
    Wscript.Quit
end if

' Remainder of script code goes here.
```

LISTING 2-8 *Using Wscript properties (JScript).*

```
/* List0208.js
 Using the Wscript.FullName property to
 prevent the script from running in Cscript. */

var s;
var shell;

shell = WScript.CreateObject("WScript.Shell");

s = WScript.FullName;
s = s.toLowerCase();

if (s.indexOf("Cscript.exe") != -1)
{
    shell.Popup("Please run this script using Wscript.");
    WScript.Quit();
}
/* Remainder of script code goes here. */
```

Script Interactivity

The term *interactivity* refers to the way a script interacts with the user. In interactive mode, calls to `Wscript.Echo` display information to the user and, if the script is running in Wscript, require the user to respond. In batch mode, calls to `Wscript.Echo` are ignored. This means that scripts can run unattended, which is sometimes a desirable feature.

The documented method for setting a script to run in either interactive or batch mode is to use an option on the command line, //B for batch mode and //I for interactive mode. Thus, to run the script MyScript.vbs in batch mode you would enter the following at the command prompt:

```
Wscript myscript.vbs //B
```

You'll learn more about script command line options in Chapter 3. However, there is an undocumented property of the `Wscript` object that lets you set a script's interactivity in code. Set `Wscript.Interactive` to True to have the script run interactively; set this property to False to run the script in batch mode.

The scripts in Listings 2-9 and 2-10 demonstrate the use of this property. The `WScript.Interactive` property is set to False (represented by the constant False in VBScript and the value 0 in JScript) and the `WScript.Echo` method is called three times. Then the `WScript.Interactive` property is set to True (represented by the constant True in VBScript and the value −1 in JScript) and the `Echo` method called again. You'll see that only the final message is echoed to the screen. Change the script by deleting the line where the `Interactive` property is set to False, and run it again — you will see all four messages echoed.

LISTING 2–9 *Controlling script interactivity (VBScript).*

```
' List0209.vbs
' Demonstrates the undocumented
' Wscript.Interactive property.

WScript.Interactive = False

WScript.Echo "First message."
WScript.Echo "Second message."
WScript.Echo "Third message."

WScript.Interactive = True

WScript.Echo "Final message."
```

LISTING 2–10 *Controlling script interactivity (JScript).*

```
/* List0210.js
 Demonstrates the undocumented
 Wscript.Interactive property. */

WScript.Interactive = 0;

WScript.Echo("First message.");
WScript.Echo("Second message.");
WScript.Echo("Third message.");

WScript.Interactive = -1;

WScript.Echo("Final message.");
```

Although using the `WScript.Interactive` property has its uses, it is unfortunately not as flexible as you might wish. It affects only the output of the `Echo` method and has no effect on other methods of displaying output to the user, such as VBScript's `MsgBox` function. Therefore, for many scripts, it is impossible to truly run them in batch mode with no user interaction whatsoever. However, sometimes you really would not want to. When a script displays information to the user, there is often a good reason. Sometimes the script needs input from the user or requires the user to carry out some other action, such as inserting a diskette in a drive. Suppressing such messages clearly would not be a good idea.

Terminating a Script

Normally, a script executes from the beginning to the end, starting with the first line of executable code and terminating after the final line of executable code has been run. At times, particularly with more complex scripts, you may need to terminate script execution before the final line of code is reached. You can force a script to terminate at any time by calling the `Wscript.Quit` method. This method takes an optional argument, a numerical code that is returned to the process that called the script. In advanced uses, this return value can be used to signal an error condition if the script did not run properly. Traditionally, a return value of 0 is used to signal normal script termination. If you call the `Quit` method with no argument, it returns the value of 0.

Setting a Timeout

By default, WSH will permit a script to run as long as it wants to. Sometimes this is fine, but situations do exist in which you may want to limit the time a script can execute. This is particularly true when a successful execution of the script is dependent on external circumstances over which you may not have any control. A successful network connection, modem dial-up, and similar scenarios fall into this category. By setting a timeout limit for the script, you prevent the possibility that the script will sit and wait for some external event that may never happen.

You can set a script timeout using a command line option passed to the script engine. By specifying //T:*n* when the script is run, you specify a timeout value of *n* seconds. For example, the following command executes the specified script with a timeout value of 12 seconds:

```
Wscript //T:12 MyScript.vbs
```

With version 2.0 of WSH there is an undocumented property that permits you to set the timeout in code. This can be somewhat more flexible than setting a timeout by the command line, because it permits your script to set and cancel the timeout as required based on the immediate circumstances. For example, this line of code sets the timeout to 12:

```
WScript.Timeout = 12
```

Working with Objects

Creating and manipulating objects is one of the most powerful techniques available to the script developer. WSH has three methods, available through the `Wscript` object, for working with objects. These are not the only ways a script can deal with objects, as we will see, but they are very important.

To create a new instance of an object, use the `CreateObject` method. This method requires as its argument the programmatic ID of the object that you wish to create. You'll learn the IDs of many important objects throughout this book. For example, to create an instance of the Microsoft Excel application, the programmatic ID is `Excel.Application`. Once you have created an instance of an object and obtained a reference to it, you can then manipulate the object as permitted by the object's properties and methods.

The `GetObject` method works slightly differently from `CreateObject`. `GetObject`'s primary use is to create an object based on an existing disk file. For example, if you call `GetObject` and pass it the name of a Microsoft Excel file, the result will be to create an instance of the Excel application and to load that file into it. In contrast, `CreateObject` would simply start an instance of Excel without loading any file.

In theory, the `GetObject` method is supposed to be able to return a reference to a running instance of an object. This means, for example, that if the Microsoft Excel program is already running and your script calls `GetObject` and passes it the programmatic ID for Microsoft Excel, the method will return a reference to the copy of Excel that is already running rather than creating a new instance. However, the method does not seem to work this way. Rather, it always creates a new instance of the specified object even if there is an instance already in existence. I am not sure whether this is an error in the Microsoft documentation or an error in implementation of the method, but the bottom line seems to be that there is currently no way to obtain a reference to a running instance of an object from within a script.

Listings 2-11 and 2-12 demonstrate how to create and manipulate an instance of Microsoft Excel. You need to have Excel installed on your system for these scripts to work properly. The scripts do the following:

1. Create a new instance of the `Excel.Application` object.
2. Make the application visible. Applications started by script code are hidden by default. This step is not necessary, as Excel is perfectly happy to operate while hidden, but it lets you see what's going on.
3. Add a new workbook. Unlike when it is run by the user, Excel does not automatically create a new, blank workbook when it is started by script automation.
4. Put some data in cells of the workbook.
5. Save the workbook as c:\testwsh.xls.
6. Quit Excel.

There are two things you should note about these scripts. First, if you run the script a second time you will get an error message because the file you are trying to save already exists. There are ways to avoid this in your scripts, but I will postpone that until we cover Excel in more detail. For now you can simply change the file name or delete the originally saved file. Second, in the file specification in the JScript code you'll see that a double backslash is used, c:\\testwsh.xls. This is because in JScript the \ character has a special meaning, so to insert a single backslash in text you must use two. You'll learn about JScript's special characters in Chapter 10.

LISTING 2-11 *Creating and manipulating an instance of Excel (VBScript).*

```
' List0211.vbs
' Creating and manipulating a new object.

Dim xlApp
Dim NewWorkbook

' Create an instance of Excel.
Set xl = Wscript.CreateObject("Excel.Application")

' Make it visible.
xl.Visible = True

' Add a new workbook.
Set NewWorkbook = xl.Workbooks.Add

' Put some data in the cells.
xl.Cells(1,1).Value = 1
xl.Cells(1,2).Value = 2

' Save the workbook.
NewWorkbook.SaveAs("c:\testwsh.xls")

' Quit Excel.
xl.Quit
```

LISTING 2-12 *Creating and manipulating an instance of Excel (JScript).*

```
/* List0212.js
Creating and manipulating a new object. */

var xlApp;
var NewWorkbook;

// Create an instance of Excel.
xl = WScript.CreateObject("Excel.Application");

// Make it visible.
xl.Visible = -1;

// Add a new workbook.
NewWorkbook = xl.Workbooks.Add;

// Put some data in the cells.
xl.Cells(1,1).Value = 1;
xl.Cells(1,2).Value = 2;

// Save the workbook.
NewWorkbook.SaveAs("c:\\testwsh2.xls");

// Quit Excel.
xl.Quit();
```

When you use `WScript.GetObject` to open an object contained in a file, it is important to note that the reference returned is to the object and not to the associated application. Look, for example, at this VBScript code:

```
Set xl = GetObject("c:\testwsh.xls")
```

In JScript the code would be

```
xl = GetObject("c:\\testwsh.xls");
```

This code results in the variable xl referring to an `Excel.Workbook` object, and not to an instance of Excel.

The object-related methods we have been looking at, `CreateObject` and `GetObject`, are part of WSH itself; specifically they are methods of the `Wscript` object. The VBScript and JScript languages have their own statements for obtaining object references. In JScript, `ActiveXObject` creates a new instance of an object and returns a reference to it:

```
var obj = new ActiveXObject(ProgID);
```

This has the same result as the following:

```
var obj = WScript.CreateObject(ProgID);
```

In VBScript, the `CreateObject` function does the same thing. These two lines of code perform the same action:

```
Set obj = CreateObject(ProgID)
Set obj = WScript.CreateObject(ProgID)
```

VBScript also has a `GetObject` function that has the same syntax as the `WScript.GetObject` method. It differs in that it appears to be able to return a reference to a running instance of an object. Thus, this code returns a reference to a running instance of Word:

```
Set wdApp = GetObject(, "Word.Application")
```

If, however, there is no instance of Word running, an error occurs.

The WshShell Object

The `WshShell` object is used to gain access to the Windows shell and registry, as well as to environment variables. You can use `WshShell` to create shortcuts, display popup messages, access special Windows folders, and run other programs. Tables 2-6 and 2-7 describe the properties and objects of this object; in the following sections they are explained in more detail and examples are given.

TABLE 2-6 *WshShell object properties.*

Property	Description
Environment	Returns the `WshEnvironment` object, which provides access to Windows Environment variables.
SpecialFolders	Returns the `WshSpecialFolders` object, which provides access to the special system folders.

TABLE 2-7 *WshShell object methods.*

Method	Description
CreateShortcut (*path*)	Creates a new `WshShortcut` object pointing to path and returns a reference to it. If the title of the shortcut ends with .url, a `WshURLShortcut` object is created.
Expand Environment Strings (*string*)	Returns the environment settings corresponding to the environment variable names in *string*. Names must be enclosed in %%, for example, %TEMP%.
PopUp	Displays a message in a popup window. See the section Displaying Popup Messages later in this chapter for details.
RegDelete (*key*)	Deletes a registry key or value.
RegRead (*key*)	Returns the value of a registry key or value.
RegWrite (*key, value, type*)	Sets a registry key or value.
Run (*command, style, wait*)	Executes a program.

The WshEnvironment Object

The WshEnvironment object provides your scripts with access to Windows environment variables. You obtain this object from the Environment property of the WshShell object. Environment variables are system variables that are used to hold information such as PATH, which is the set of folders that Windows searches for executable programs. Some environment variables are defined by the Windows operating system, while others are set by specific applications.

The WshEnvironment object has three properties and one method, detailed in Table 2-8. Listings 2-13 and 2-14 demonstrate how to use the WshEnvironment object to access the settings for two of the more important variables: PATH, which specifies the path for executable programs, and WINDIR, which identifies the folder where Windows is installed. The output of these scripts is shown in Figure 2-3.

TABLE 2-8 *Properties and methods of the WshEnvironment object.*

Property or method	Description
Item(*name*) or Item(*n*)	Returns the setting of the environment variable identified by *name* or with index *n*. This is the default property. If there is no environment variable matching name a blank string is returned. *n* can range from 0 to count-1.
Count	Returns the number of environment variables.
Length	Returns the number of environment variables. The same asCount, provided for compatibility with JScript standards.
Remove(*name*)	Deletes the specified environment variable.

FIGURE 2-3 *Displaying the value of environment variables.*

LISTING 2–13 *Reading environment variables (VBScript).*

```
'List0213.vbs
'Reading environment variables.

Dim shell
Dim env
Dim vars

' Create instance of WshShell object.
Set shell = Wscript.CreateObject("Wscript.Shell")

' Get reference to WshEnvironment object.
Set env = shell.Environment

vars = "Environment settings:" & vbCRLF
vars = vars & "Path: " & env("PATH") & vbCRLF
vars = vars & "Windows directory: " & env("windir")

Wscript.Echo vars
```

LISTING 2–14 *Reading environment variables (JScript).*

```
//List0214.js
//Reading environment variables.

var shell;
var environment;
var vars;

// Create instance of WshShell object.
shell = WScript.CreateObject("Wscript.Shell");

// Get reference to WshEnvironment object.
env = shell.Environment

vars = "Environment variables:\n";
vars = vars + "Path: " + env("PATH") + "\n";
vars = vars + "Windows directory: " + env("windir") + "\n";
WScript.Echo(vars);
```

The WshSpecialFolders Object

The Windows operating system makes use of a number of special folders that are used for storing specific kinds of information. These include shortcuts to recently used documents, document templates, fonts, and user favorites. Some special folders are user specific, while others apply to all users. The `WshSpecialFolders` object, which is actually a collection, has three prop-

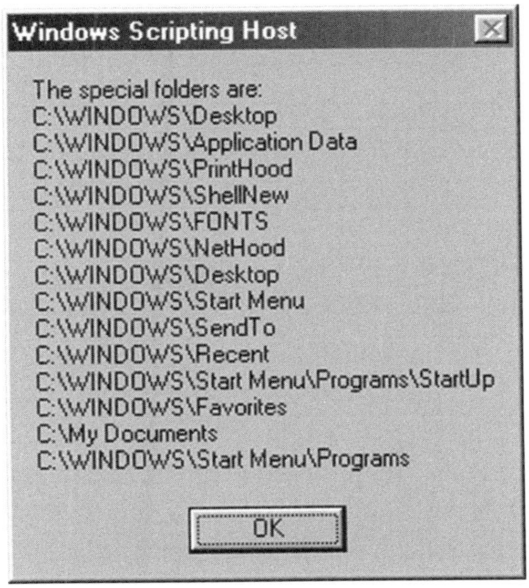

FIGURE 2–4 *Output of script enumerating the special folders.*

erties that let you retrieve these folders (this object has no methods). These properties are described in Table 2-9, and the names and functions of the various special folders are listed in Table 2-10. Listings 2-15 and 2-16 show how to access the special folders collection, with the output shown in Figure 2-4.

Note that you can only read the names of the special folders using the `WshSpecialFolders` object, not change them. Most of the folder names are actually stored in the registry and can be modified using the WSH registry access techniques covered elsewhere in this chapter. I advise against modifying any of the special folder settings, however, unless you are sure that you know what you are doing.

TABLE 2-9 *Properties of the WshSpecialFolders object.*

Property	Description
Item(*name*) or Item(*n*)	Returns the path of the special folder identified by *name* or with index *n*. This is the default property. If there is no special folder matching *name* a blank string is returned. *n* can range from 0 to `count-1`.
Count	Returns the number of special folders.
Length	Returns the number of special folders. The same as `Count`, provided for compatibility with JScript standards.

TABLE 2-10 *Windows special folders.*

Folder name	Contains
AllUsersDesktop	Contains shortcuts that appear on the Desktop for all users.*
AllUsersStart Menu	Contains shortcuts that appear on the Start menu for all users.*
AllUsersPrograms	Contains shortcuts that appear on the Start, Programs menu for all users.*
AllUsersStartup	Contains shortcuts that appear on the Start, Programs, Startup menu for all users.*
AppData	User-specific folder for storage of application-specific information (the Application Data folder).
Desktop	Contains Desktop folders and shortcuts.
Favorites	User-specific folder containing shortcuts that appear on the Favorites menu.
Fonts	Contains fonts.
MyDocuments	User-specific folder that is the default location for the user's documents.
NetHood	User-specific folder that serves to hold network connections.
PrintHood	User-specific folder containing printer links.
Programs	User-specific folder containing shortcuts that appear on the Start, Programs menu.
Recent	User-specific folder containing shortcuts that appear on the Start, Documents menu.
SendTo	User-specific folder containing shortcuts that appear on the Send To menu.
StartMenu	User-specific folder containing shortcuts that appear on the Start menu.
Startup	User-specific folder containing shortcuts that appear on the Start, Programs, Startup menu.
Templates	User-specific folder that contains document templates.

* Windows NT only.

LISTING 2–15 *Accessing the Windows special folders (VBScript).*

```
' List0215.vbs
' Accessing the Windows special folders.

Dim shell
Dim folders
Dim i
Dim list

Set shell = WScript.CreateObject("WScript.Shell")
Set folders = shell.SpecialFolders

list = "The special folders are: " & vbCRLF
for i = 0 to folders.count - 1
    list = list & folders(i) & vbCRLF
next

WScript.Echo list
```

LISTING 2-16 *Accessing the Windows special folders (JScript).*

```
// List0216.js
// Accessing the Windows special folders.

var shell;
var folders;
var list;

shell = WScript.CreateObject("WScript.Shell");
folders = shell.SpecialFolders;

list = "The special folders are: \n";
for (var i = 0; i < folders.length; i++)
    list = list + folders(i) + "\n";

WScript.Echo(list);
```

Working with Shortcuts

Windows supports two kinds of shortcuts, both of which can be manipulated using WSH. The `WshShortcut` object represents a regular Windows shortcut, as found on the Desktop, on the Start menu, and so on. It's difficult to imagine using Windows without using shortcuts, so the script programmer needs to know how to use this object. The `WshURLShortcut` object represents a shortcut to a URL and is a lot simpler than a `WshShortcut` object.

Windows shortcuts

A Windows shortcut can refer to an executable program, in which case selecting the shortcut causes the program to start. A shortcut can also refer to a file. In this case, selecting the shortcut starts the application that is associated with the file and loads the file. Finally, a shortcut can refer to a folder. Selecting such a shortcut displays the folder in Windows Explorer.

THE WSHSHORTCUT OBJECT

A `WshShortcut` object can represent a program, a file, or a folder. A shortcut can be placed on the Desktop, on the Start menu, on the Quick Launch toolbar, and so on. To create a `WshShortcut` object, call the `WshShell.CreateShortcut` method. This object has several properties and one method, which are detailed in Table 2-11.

TABLE 2-11 *The properties and method of the WshShortcut object.*

Property or method	Description
Arguments	Specifies the arguments to be passed to the program that the shortcut points to.
Description	The shortcut's description.
FullName	The full path of the shortcut itself (not the item it points to). Read-only. Shortcuts have the .lnk extension.
HotKey	A string representing the shortcut's hotkey. Hotkeys for shortcuts always begin with Ctrl+Alt, for example, Ctrl+Alt+H.
IconLocation	Path and 0-based index of the shortcut's icon. For example, c:\windows\system\shell32.dll,5 specifies the 6th icon in the file c:\windows\system\shell32.dll.
TargetPath	Path to the shortcut's target: a folder, program, or file.
WindowStyle	Specifies the window style for the target to use. Possible settings are detailed in Table 2-12. Some programs do not support this argument, in which case it will be ignored.
Working Directory	The directory from which to start the target.
Save*	Saves the shortcut to the location specified by the `FullName` property.

*This is the object's one method.

TABLE 2-12 *Window Styles for the WshShortcut object's WindowStyle property.*

Constant	Value	Window effect
SW_HIDE	0	Hidden
SW_SHOWNORMAL	1	Displays the window and gives it the focus (the default).
SW_SHOWMINIMIZED	2	Minimizes the window and gives it the focus.
SW_MAXIMIZE	3	Maximizes the window and gives it the focus.
SW_SHOWNOACTIVATE	4	Displays the window but does not give it the focus.
SW_MINIMIZE	6	Minimizes the window without giving it the focus.

To create a shortcut, call the `WshShell` object's `CreateShortcut` method, passing it the name of the shortcut you want created. This method returns a reference to the new shortcut. You then must set the `WshShortcut` object's properties as desired and then use its `Save` method to save it to the desired location. This location is often obtained from the `WshSpecialFolders` collection, as we will see in the example. A shortcut does not become permanent until it is saved.

Let's look at an example. The code in Listings 2-17 and 2-18 creates a shortcut to the script file c:\scripts\MyScript.vbs and places the shortcut on the Start menu.

LISTING 2–17 *Creating a shortcut and placing it on the Start menu (VBScript).*

```
' List0217.vbs
' Creating a shortcut and placing it on the Start menu.

Dim StartMenu
Dim shortcut
Dim shell

Set shell = WScript.CreateObject("WScript.Shell")
' Get the start menu path.
StartMenu = shell.SpecialFolders("StartMenu")

' Create a new shortcut.
Set shortcut = shell.CreateShortcut(StartMenu & "\MyScript.lnk")

' Set the shortcut description and target.
shortcut.Description = "MyScript"
shortcut.TargetPath = "c:\scripts\MyScript.vbs"

' Save the shortcut.
shortcut.Save
```

LISTING 2–18 *Creating a shortcut and placing it on the Start menu (JScript).*

```
// List0218.js
// Creating a shortcut and placing it on the Start menu.

var StartMenu;
var shortcut;
var shell;

shell = WScript.CreateObject("WScript.Shell");
// Get the start menu path.
StartMenu = shell.SpecialFolders("StartMenu");

// Create a new shortcut.
shortcut = shell.CreateShortcut(StartMenu + "\\MyScript.lnk");

// Set the shortcut description and target.
shortcut.Description = "MyScript";
shortcut.TargetPath = "c:\\scripts\\MyScript.vbs";

// Save the shortcut.
shortcut.Save();
```

THE WSHURLSHORTCUT OBJECT

The `WshURLShortcut` object is used to represent a shortcut to a URL (uniform resource locator) on the Internet or another location. When a user clicks on this type of link, the target of the URL is automatically accessed, whether it be a Web page, a file on a network computer, or whatever. The `WshURLShortcut` object is a lot simpler than the `WshShortcut` object, having only two properties and one method. They are explained in Table 2-13.

TABLE 2-13 *Properties and method of the WshURLShortcut object.*

Property or method	Description
FullName	The full path of the shortcut itself. Must end in .url.
TargetPath	The full URL or path of the shortcut's target.
Save	Saves the shortcut to the location specified by its FullName property.

You create a `WshURLShortcut` object in the same way as you create a `WshShortcut` object, by invoking the `WshShell.CreateShortcut` method. This method knows which type of shortcut to create by the file extension: .lnk for regular shortcuts, .url for URL shortcuts. The scripts in Listings 2-19 and 2-20 show how to create a URL shortcut to Microsoft's web page and save it on the Desktop.

LISTING 2–19 *Creating a URL shortcut and saving it on the Desktop (VBScript).*

```
' List0219.vbs
' Creating a URL shortcut and saving it on the desktop.

Dim shell
Dim desktop
Dim shortcut

Set shell = WScript.CreateObject("WScript.Shell")
desktop = shell.SpecialFolders("Desktop")

' Create a new shortcut.
Set shortcut = shell.CreateShortcut(desktop & "\Microsoft.url")

' Set the shortcut target.
shortcut.TargetPath = "http://www.microsoft.com"

' Save the shortcut.
shortcut.Save
```

LISTING 2–20 *Creating a URL shortcut and saving it on the Desktop (JScript).*

```
// List0220.js
//Creating a URL shortcut and saving it on the desktop.

var shell;
var desktop;
var shortcut;

shell = WScript.CreateObject("WScript.Shell");
desktop = shell.SpecialFolders("Desktop");

// Create a new shortcut.
shortcut = shell.CreateShortcut(desktop + "\\Microsoft.url");

// Set the shortcut target.
shortcut.TargetPath = "http://www.microsoft.com";

// Save the shortcut.
shortcut.Save();
```

Displaying Popup Messages

Many times, your scripts will need to display information to users as well as get input from them. The `Wscript.Echo` method works for displaying information, although it is rather limited. It is not particularly flexible but, more important, it has no way to input a response from the user beyond "OK." In addition, it works differently depending on whether you are using Cscript or Wscript to execute the script.

For much greater flexibility, use the `WShell` object's `Popup` method. This method displays a popup dialog box with a message, title, and buttons as specified by the script code. The syntax is

```
reply = WshShell.Popup(text, wait, title, flags)
```

The *text* argument is required and specifies the text that will be displayed in the popup dialog box. The *wait* argument is optional and specifies the number of seconds the dialog will wait for the user to respond before closing automatically. The default value of 0 causes the dialog to wait as long as needed. The optional *title* argument specifies the text displayed in the dialog box's title bar. The default is "Windows Scripting Host." The optional *flags* argument controls the display of icons and/or buttons in the dialog box. Possible settings and their meanings are explained in Table 2-14. If this argument is omitted, the dialog box is displayed with an OK button and no icon.

TABLE 2-14 Settings for the Popup method's *flags* argument.

VBScript constant	Value	Display
vbOKOnly	0	An OK button.*
vbOKCancel	1	OK and Cancel buttons.*
vbAbortRetryIgnore	2	Abort, Retry, and Ignore buttons.**
vbYesNoCancel	3	Yes, No, and Cancel buttons.*
vbYesNo	4	Yes and No buttons.**
vbRetryCancel	5	Retry and Cancel buttons.*
vbCritical	16	The "stop" icon.
vbQuestion	32	A question mark icon.
vbExclamation	48	An exclamation point icon.
vbInformation	64	An information icon (an "i" in a balloon).

* The dialog box can be canceled by pressing Esc or Alt+F4.
** The dialog box cannot be canceled from the keyboard.

If you want to display nondefault buttons along with an icon, simply add the corresponding arguments together. For example, a *flags* argument of 33 (`vbOKCancel + vbQuestion`) displays OK and Cancel buttons along with a question mark icon.

The value returned by this method identifies the way the dialog box was closed. The possible return values are described in Table 2-15.

TABLE 2-15 *Return values of the Popup method.*

VBScript constant	Value	Meaning
vbOK	1	The OK button was selected, or a dialog box displaying only an OK button was canceled. from the keyboard.
vbCancel	2	The Cancel button was selected, or a dialog box with a Cancel button was cancel from the keyboard.
vbAbort	3	The Abort button was selected.
vbRetry	4	The Retry button was selected.
vbIgnore	5	The Ignore button was selected.
vbYes	6	The Yes button was selected.
vbNo	7	The No button was selected.
none	–1	The timeout expired.

The use of a timeout can be useful, particularly when you want the script to be able to run unattended. In this case there must be a default action to take in the event of a timeout. This is illustrated in the scripts in Listings 2-21 and 2-22, which ask the user if he or she wants to delete all temporary files. In the event of a timeout, the script deletes nothing. These scripts do not actually contain the code to delete files, but show you how to use the Popup method in your scripts. The dialog box displayed by these scripts is shown in Figure 2-5.

LISTING 2–21 *Using the Popup method (VBScript).*

```
' List0221.vbs
' Using the Popup method.

Dim shell
Dim reply

Set shell = WScript.CreateObject("Wscript.Shell")
reply = shell.Popup("Delete all temporary files?", _
    3, "File Cleanup", vbYesNo + vbQuestion)

if reply = vbYes Then
    ' Code to delete files goes here.
    shell.Popup("Files deleted.")
else
    shell.Popup("Files were not deleted.")
end if
```

LISTING 2–22 *Using the Popup method (JScript).*

```
// List0222.js
// Using the Popup method.

var shell;
var reply;

shell = WScript.CreateObject("WScript.Shell");
reply = shell.Popup("Delete all temporary files?",
    3, "File Cleanup", 36);

if (reply == 6)
     // Code to delete files goes here.
    shell.Popup("Files deleted.");
else
    shell.Popup("Files were not deleted.");
```

FIGURE 2–5 A dialog box displayed by the Popup method.

Working with the Registry

The registry is a very important but poorly understood aspect of Windows. Windows itself as well as various applications programs keep all kinds of information in the registry. For the most part, you do not want to modify the information in the registry unless you are sure you know what you are doing, because inappropriate changes can have unexpected and serious effects on the operating system and your programs. You can still use the registry to store information, and this can be particularly useful for saving script information between sessions. Certain types of actions that may be performed by scripts, such as software installations, may also require use of the registry.

To use the registry, you need to understand the basics of how it is organized. The information in the registry is organized hierarchically. At the top of the hierarchy are six *root keys* that divide the registry information into broad categories:

HKEY_CLASSES_ROOT. File types, associations, and COM objects

HKEY_CURRENT_USER. User-specific settings for software, hardware, and Internet connections

HKEY_LOCAL_MACHINE. Settings that apply to all users

HKEY_USERS. Settings for all registered users

HKEY_CURRENT_CONFIG. Current hardware and software configuration

HKEY_DYN_DATA. Driver and performance information

Each root key contains subkeys that further divide the data, and each subkey may contain data values and/or additional levels of subkeys. At the lowest level, the final subkey contains one or more *values*, which are best thought of as names identifying individual registry entries. Each value can have data associated with it, or the entry for that value can be blank. We see

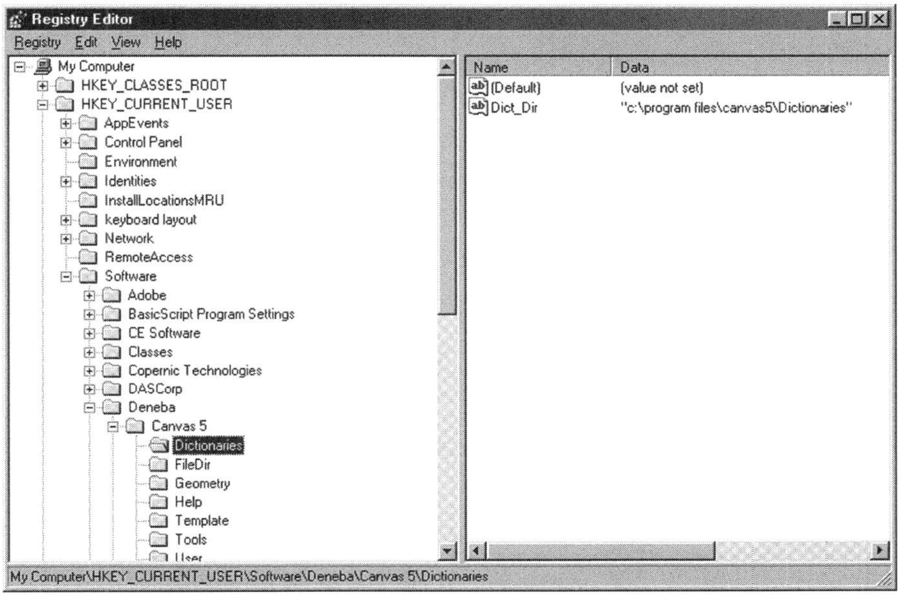

FIGURE 2–6 *Viewing the registry hierarchy in the Windows Registry Editor.*

that each piece of information, or value, in the registry is identified by its value, one or more subkeys, and finally the root key that it is under. Each subkey also has a default value associated with it. Figure 2-6 shows some registry data displayed in the Windows Registry Editor. The left panel shows the hierarchy of keys and subkeys, and the right panel shows the values and data for the individual entries associated with the open subkey. You can see, for example, that the open subkey has two values: the default value, whose data is not set, and the Dict_Dir value, whose data is "c:\program files\canvas5\dictionaries."

Exploring the registry

You can explore the registry using a Windows program called RegEdit (for Registry Editor). Select Run from the Start menu and enter RegEdit. You can examine the registry hierarchy, view keys and their values and, if desired, make changes. You can also make a backup copy of the registry by selecting Export from the Registry menu. Making a backup can be good insurance if you are going to make changes whose effects you are not sure of.

When referring to keys and values in your script code, you use the following notation:

```
AAAA\BBBB\....\XXXX\VVVV
```

Here, AAAA is the top-level key, BBBB is the second-level key, and so on down to XXXX, which is the lowest-level key, and VVVV, which is the value. To save time and improve clarity, you can use the following shortcuts to refer to some of the top-level keys:

HKEY_CLASSES_ROOT: HKCR

HKEY_CURRENT_USER: HKCU

HKEY_LOCAL_MACHINE: HKLM

Here's an example of referring to a specific key and its value:

```
HKCU\Software\Microsoft\Windows\Current Version\MSID
```

By convention, if a string ends with a backslash it refers to a subkey alone (without the value), and if it does not end in a backslash it refers to a key with a value. Thus we know in the preceding that HKCU\Software\Microsoft \Windows\Current Version\ is the key and MSID is the value.

To read a registry value, use the `WshShell.ReadReg` method. The syntax is

```
data = WshShell.ReadReg(key)
```

Key is a string specifying the key or the value to retrieve. If you pass a key (ending with a backslash), the method returns that key's default value. If you pass a value, the method returns the data associated with that value. If the key or value does not exist, an error occurs.

To write data to the registry, use the `WshShell.RegWrite` method. The syntax is

```
WshShell.RegWrite(key, data, type)
```

Key is a string specifying the key or the value to write data to. If you pass a value (ending with a backslash), the method saves the data as that value's default value. If you pass a value that already exists, the new data overwrites the existing data associated with that value. If the key or value does not exist, it is created.

Type is an optional argument specifying the way the data will be interpreted. Possible settings are as follows:

- REG_SZ. Store the data as a string. If you pass numeric data, it will be converted to a string. For example, the number 99 will be stored as the string "99." This is the default data type.
- REG_EXPAND_SZ. An expandable string that refers to an environment variable. Expandable strings must be enclosed in %%. This, if you pass the string %WINDIR%\regedit.exe, the %WINDIR% part will be interpreted as an environment variable and when the registry value is retrieved the data will be expanded appropriately (for example, the preceding might be returned as c:\windows\regedit.exe).

- REG_BINARY. A binary value. To use this data type, the data you pass must be a numeric value and not a string.
- REG_DWORD. A numeric value. If you pass a string it will be converted to the corresponding numeric value.

In my experience you will rarely, if ever, need to use any of these data types other than the default REG_SZ.

To delete a registry entry, use the `WshShell.RegDelete` method. The syntax is

```
WshShell.RegDelete(key)
```

Key is a string specifying the key or value to delete, as described previously. I recommend that you never delete registry entries except those you have added yourself. Because of the importance of the registry to the proper functioning of Windows and applications programs, it is all too easy to create problems.

Windows 9x versus Windows NT

In Windows 9x, if you delete a subkey then its entire branch — any subsidiary subkeys and values — will be deleted as well. In Windows NT, you can delete a subkey only if it has no child subkeys.

The code in Listings 2-23 and 2-24 shows how to add a registry entry, read its value, and delete it.

LISTING 2-23 *Working with registry entries (VBScript).*

```
' List0223.vbs
' Working with registry entries.

Dim shell
Dim key

Set shell = WScript.CreateObject("WScript.Shell")

key = "HKCU\Software\Aitken\UserName"

' Create the registry entry with the data "Peter"
shell.RegWrite key, "Peter"

' Retrieve and display the value.
WScript.Echo shell.RegRead(key)

' Delete the registry entry. Note that this deletes
' the value "UserName" only. To delete the subkey
' "Aitken" you would call:
' shell.regDelete "HKCU\Software\Aitken\"
shell.RegDelete key
```

LISTING 2–24 *Working with registry entries (JScript).*

```
// List0224.js
// Working with registry entries.

var shell;
var key;

shell = WScript.CreateObject("WScript.Shell");
key = "HKCU\\Software\\Aitken\\UserName";
// Create the registry entry with the data "Peter"
shell.RegWrite(key, "Peter");

// Retrieve and display the value.
WScript.Echo(shell.RegRead(key));

// Delete the registry entry. Note that this deletes
// the value "UserName" only. To delete the subkey
// "Aitken" you would call:
// shell.regDelete "HKCU\\Software\\Aitken\\";
shell.RegDelete(key);
```

Running Programs

The `Run` method of the `WshShell` object is used to run external programs. Sometimes this process is called *spawning* a program. This method also gives your script control over the program's window style (when supported) and the loading of document files. The syntax for this method is

```
retval = WshShell.Run(command, windowtype, wait)
```

Command is a required argument specifying the command line to run, including parameters to pass if required. *Windowtype* is an optional argument specifying the style of the program's window. Some programs ignore this argument. Possible values for this argument were presented earlier in Table 2-12. *Wait* is an optional argument that specifies whether the script will wait for the spawned program to terminate. If this argument is set to True, the script will not continue executing past the call to the `Run` method until the spawned program terminates. If False, which is the default, the script continues as soon as the program is spawned.

This method's return value is 0 if *wait* is False or omitted. If *wait* is True then the return value of the method is the return value of the spawned program.

There are some factors to consider when creating the command line to pass to the Run method. The most essential part is the name of the program to run, such as notepad.exe. If the program is in the system search path, which includes the Windows directory, you can specify only the program name. Otherwise, however, you must include the full path to the executable, such as

```
c:\program files\microsoft office\office\excel.exe
```

This will not work as is, however, because of the spaces in the folder names. If you pass this command line to the Run method, it will be interpreted, because of the spaces in the folder names, as a request to run the program "c:\program" and pass it the two command line arguments "files\microsoft" and "office\office\excel.exe." To avoid this problem the program path and name must be enclosed in double quotes so the Run method can distinguish between the program name and any arguments you are including. In VBScript you can accomplish this by using Chr$(34), which returns the double quote character, or by using a double-double quote. Here are examples of both methods:

```
shell.Run Chr$(34) & _
    "c:\program files\microsoft office\office\excel.exe" & Chr$(34)
```

```
shell.Run """c:\program files\microsoft office\office\excel.exe"""
```

In JScript you use \" to represent the double quote, so you would write the following:

```
shell.Run("\"c:\\program files\\microsoft office
\\office\\excel.exe\"");
```

You can also use the Run method to open data files, provided that the file type is associated with a particular application. For example, look at this VBScript code:

```
shell.Run "c:\documents\sales.doc"
```

On systems with Microsoft Office installed, this will start Microsoft Word and load the specified file because files with the .doc extension are associated with the Word application. You can also start an application and open a specific file by passing the file name as an argument on the command line.

Let's look at an example. The scripts in Listings 2-25 and 2-26 start the Microsoft Word and Excel programs and load the specified data files, column01.doc and report.xls. Note that two different approaches are used. Word is started by passing a command line that contains the program name and the file name, while Excel is started by passing only the file name.

LISTING 2–25 *Starting Word and Excel from a script (VBScript).*

```
' List0225.vbs
' Running external programs.

Dim shell
Dim program
Dim filename

Set shell = WScript.CreateObject("WScript.Shell")
program = Chr(34) & _
    "c:\program files\microsoft office\office\winword.exe" _ & Chr(34)
filename = "c:\documents\column01.doc"
shell.Run program & " " & filename
shell.Run "c:\documents\report.xls"
```

LISTING 2–26 *Starting Word and Excel from a script (JScript).*

```
// List0226.js
// Running external programs.

var shell;
var program;
var filename;

shell = WScript.CreateObject("WScript.Shell");
program = "\"c:\\program files\\microsoft office\\office\\winword.exe\"";
filename = "c:\\documents\\column01.doc";
shell.Run(program + " " + filename);
shell.Run("c:\\documents\\report.xls");
```

Saving Time

Using scripts to start programs and load files can be very useful. Suppose, for example, that you are working on a long-term project that requires you to start Word, Excel, and PowerPoint and load specified data files every morning. You can easily write a script to perform these tasks, and then use the Task Scheduler (covered in Chapter 3) to run the script every time the computer is started. Each morning, flip on your computer and go have a cup of coffee. By the time you come back your system will be booted with all programs open and ready to use.

The WshNetwork Object

The WshNetwork object is used to obtain and work with network connections. You can use this object to determine which network connections are available, to establish or break specific connections, to map network drives, and to map/unmap network printers. In today's typical computing environment, where networked systems are common, this object is a valuable tool for the script developer.

Before using the WshNetwork object you must create an instance of it. This is accomplished using the standard format that you learned earlier in this chapter. In VBScript this is

```
Dim myNet = Wscript.CreateObject("Wscript.Network")
```

And in JScript you would write as follows:

```
var myNet = Wscript.CreateObject("Wscript.Network");
```

Once you have an instance of the WshNetwork object, you can use its methods and properties, which are described in Tables 2-16 and 2-17. Details on using these properties and methods are covered following the tables.

Obtaining User Information

The properties of the WshNetwork object are all read-only. This means you can use them to obtain information about the system and the current user, but not to set this information. On a system with multiple user logins, for example, you can use this information to permit a script to run only for certain users. This is demonstrated in Listings 2-27 and 2-28.

TABLE 2-16 *Properties of the WshNetwork object.*

Property	Description
ComputerName	Returns the network name of the current system.
UserDomain	Returns the current user's domain name. This is the Windows networking domain and is not related to Internet domain names.
UserName	Returns the current user's user name.

TABLE 2-17 *Methods of the WshNetwork object.*

Method	Description
AddPrinterConnection	Maps a remote printer as a local resource. See below for details.
EnumNetworkDrives	Returns a `WshCollection` collection containing all currently mapped network drives.
EnumPrinterConnections	Returns a `WshCollection` collection containing all currently mapped printers.
MapNetworkDrive	Maps a network drive as a local drive. See the topic Managing Network Drives later in this chapter for details.
RemoveNetworkDrive	Removes a drive mapping.
RemovePrinterConnection	Removes a printer mapping.
SetDefaultPrinter	Specifies the default printer.

LISTING 2–27 *Permitting a script to run only for a specified user (VBScript).*

```
' List0227.vbs
' Running a script only for the administrator.

Dim myNetwork

set myNetwork = Wscript.CreateObject("Wscript.Network")

If myNetwork.UserName <> "Administrator" Then
      Wscript.Echo "This script can be run by the administrator only."
      Wscript.Quit
End If

' Remainder of script code goes here.
```

LISTING 2–28 *Permitting a script to run only for a specified user (JScript).*

```
// List0228.js
// Running a script only for the administrator.

var myNetwork;

myNetwork = WScript.CreateObject("WScript.Network");

If (myNetwork.UserName != "Administrator") {
      WScript.Echo("This script can be run by the administrator only.");
      Wscript.Quit; }

// Remainder of script code goes here.
```

Working with Printers

A networked computer is likely to have one or more printers available to it over the network. To use a network printer, that printer must be *mapped* by the system. Depending on the user's profile, a given printer may already be mapped. Using the `WshNetwork` object, your scripts can determine which printers are mapped as well as mapping and unmapping printers. You can also set the default printer, which is the location to which print jobs are sent by default.

A network printer will have a remote name, sometimes referred to as the UNC (Universal Naming Convention) path, which identifies it on the network. When you map a printer, it is assigned a local name that is used to refer to the printer on that system. A printer named LaserJet6 on a computer named Server1 will have the UNC name \\Server1\LaserJet6. The local name must be the name of an unused printer port, such as LPT2:. It is important to note that the `WshNetwork` object will not let you determine what unmapped printers are available on the network, but will only let you connect to a printer if you know its remote name.

Using mapped printers

Be aware that before a computer can actually use a mapped network printer, that printer's drivers must be installed on the system. In other words, mapping a network printer as shown here is not in itself sufficient to be able to print to that printer.

To map a network printer, use the `AddPrinterConnection` method. The syntax is

```
WshNetwork.AddPrinterConnection(localname, remotename,
updateprofile, _ username, password)
```

Localname is the local name for the printer. This is the name by which the printer will be available locally (for example, LPT1). If the local name is already in use, an error occurs. *Remotename* is the UNC path to the remote (for example, \\Server1\LaserJet1). If the UNC path cannot be found, an error occurs. *Updateprofile* is an optional argument. Set to True to have the printer connection saved in the user's profile (so it will be automatically reestablished each time the user logs on). The default is False. *Username* is an optional argument for the user's name if you are mapping the printer using someone else's credentials. *Password* is an optional argument giving the password, if required.

To enumerate the mapped printers, use the `EnumPrinterConnections` method. This method takes no arguments and returns a collection containing two entries for each mapped printer. The first entry for a given printer contains the local name, and the second entry contains the remote name.

To remove a printer mapping, use the `RemovePrinterConnection` method. The syntax for this method is

```
WshNetwork.RemovePrinterConnection(name, force, updateprofile)
```

Name is the name of the printer. If the printer was connected using `AddPrinterConnection`, you must use the local name. Otherwise you can use the UNC path of the printer. If the specified printer cannot be found, an error occurs. *Force* is an optional Boolean argument. If True, the connection will be closed even if a user is currently connected to the printer. The default is False. *Updateprofile* is an optional Boolean argument. If True, the change will be saved in the user's profile. The default is False.

To specify the default printer, use the `SetDefaultPrinter` method. The syntax is

```
WshNetwork.SetDefaultPrinter(name)
```

Name is the local name of the printer that you want to make the default.

Let's look at an example. The scripts in Listings 2-29 and 2-30 map a network printer with the UNC name \\Desktop\hp3100 to the local name LPT2:. Then a list of mapped printers is displayed; this list will contain the just-mapped printer as well as any others on the current system. Finally, the printer LPT2: is disconnected.

LISTING 2–29 *Working with network printers (VBScript).*

```
' List0229.vbs
' Mapping network printers.

Dim net
Dim printers
Dim i
Dim msg

Set net = WScript.CreateObject("WScript.Network")

net.AddPrinterConnection "LPT2:", "\\Desktop\hp3100"

Set printers = net.EnumPrinterConnections

if printers.Count = 0 then
    Msgbox "No network printers found."
else
    msg = "There are " & printers.Count / 2 & " network printer(s):" _
        & vbCRLF
    for i = 0 to printers.Count - 1
        msg = msg & printers(i) & vbCRLF
    next
    Msgbox msg
end if

net.RemovePrinterConnection "LPT2:"
```

LISTING 2–30 *Working with network printers (JScript).*

```
// List0230.js
// Mapping network printers.

var net;
var printers;
var i;
var msg;
var shell;

net = WScript.CreateObject("WScript.Network");
shell = WScript.CreateObject("WScript.Shell");

net.AddPrinterConnection("LPT2:", "\\\\Desktop\\hp3100");

printers = net.EnumPrinterConnections();

if (printers.length == 0)
    shell.Popup("No network printers found.");
else {
    msg = "There are " + printers.length / 2 + " network printer(s):\n";
    for (i = 0; i < printers.length; i++)
        msg = msg + printers(i) + "\n";
    shell.Popup(msg); }

net.RemovePrinterConnection("LPT2:");
```

Managing Network Drives

Managing network drives in your scripts is very similar to the process of managing network printers. In fact, it is a bit simpler as there is no need to install drivers before using a network drive, nor is there a default drive to be concerned with. To map a network drive, use the `MapNetworkDrive` method. The syntax is:

```
WshNetwork.MapNetworkDrive(localname, remotename,
updateprofile, _ username, password)
```

Localname is the local name for the drive. This is the name by which the drive will be available locally (for example, H:). If the local name is already in use, an error occurs. *Remotename* is the UNC path to the remote drive (for example, \\Server1\Drive_C). If the UNC path cannot be found, an error occurs. *Updateprofile* is an optional argument. Set to True to have the drive mapping saved in the user's profile (so it will be automatically reestablished each time the user logs on). The default is False. *Username* is an optional argument for the user's name if you are mapping the drive using someone else's credentials. *Password* is an optional argument giving the password, if required.

To remove a drive mapping, use the `RemoveNetworkDrive` method. The syntax is

```
WshNetwork.RemoveNetworkDrive(name, force, updateprofile)
```

Name is the local name of the drive. If the specified drive cannot be found, an error occurs. *Force* is an optional Boolean argument. If True, the connection will be closed even if a user is currently using the drive. The default is False. *Updateprofile* is an optional Boolean argument. If True, the change will be saved in the user's profile. The default is False.

To enumerate the mapped network drives, use the `EnumNetworkDrives` method. This method takes no arguments and returns a collection containing two entries for each mapped drive. The first entry for a given drive contains the local name, and the second entry contains the UNC name.

The scripts in Listings 2-31 and 2-32 show how to map, list, and remove network drives. A remote drive named \\laptop\laptop_c is mapped to the local name H:, using the password "saturday." The mapped drives are then enumerated and listed, and finally the drive mapping to H: is removed.

LISTING 2–31 *Mapping network drives (VBScript).*

```
' List0231.vbs
' Mapping network drives.

Dim net
Dim drives
Dim i
Dim msg

Set net = WScript.CreateObject("WScript.Network")

net.MapNetworkDrive "H:", "\\laptop\laptop_c",,, "saturday"

Set drives = net.EnumNetworkDrives

if drives.Count = 0 then
    Msgbox "No network drives found."
else
    msg = "There are " & drives.Count / 2 & " network
drives:" & vbCRLF
    for i = 0 to drives.Count - 1
        msg = msg & drives(i) & vbCRLF
    next
    Msgbox msg
end if

net.RemoveNetworkDrive("H:")
```

LISTING 2-32 *Mapping network drives (JScript).*

```
// List0232.js
// Mapping network drives.

var net;
var drives;
var i;
var msg;
var shell;

net = WScript.CreateObject("WScript.Network");
shell = WScript.CreateObject("WScript.Shell");

net.MapNetworkDrive("H:", "\\\\laptop\\laptop_c",,, "saturday");

drives = net.EnumNetworkDrives();

if (drives.length == 0)
    shell.Popup("No network drives found.");
else {
    msg = "There are " + drives.length / 2 + " network
drives:\n";
    for (i = 0; i < drives.length; i++)
        msg = msg + drives(i) + "\n";
    shell.Popup(msg); }

net.RemoveNetworkDrive("H:");
```

Overview

This has been a very important chapter, and admittedly it is rather long! Much of the power of the WSH model comes from the objects it exposes, and gaining some familiarity with these objects is important for every WSH programmer. Whether it be system information, network operations, data storage, or user interaction, the WSH object model is likely to provide just what you need.

T H R E E

Creating, Running, and Scheduling Scripts

When learning any new development technology, some of the most important questions are the basic "how to" nuts and bolts questions. How do I create a script? Do I need a special editor? What are my options for running a script? Can I schedule a script to run automatically at preset times? These fundamental questions are the topics of this chapter.

Creating Your Scripts

There are no special tools required to create scripts. Since scripts are plain text files, any text editor can do the job. You can use NotePad, the simple text editor that comes with Windows. You can also use any of the various freeware or shareware text editors that are available on the Web, or one of the specialized programmer's editors that are available commercially. Another choice is the editor that comes as a part of Microsoft Visual Studio. The bottom line is that it does not matter — you should choose your script editor based on availability and your own preferences. Fancy editors have some advantages such as more sophisticated search and replace capabilities, but the end result is the same.

Online Documentation

There can be do doubt that there is a lot of information related to scripting. Even the most experienced script developer cannot keep every little detail in his or her head and needs a place to turn to for reference information. Most people find that an online source of reference information is the most convenient. Microsoft makes a variety of information available, both on the Web and as downloadable files that you can install on your system and access even if you are not connected to the Web.

The Scripting Start Page is located at http://msdn.microsoft.com/scripting/. On this page you will find information about latest developments in scripting, new products, and other news. You'll also find links to additional script related pages, including

- JScript documentation (online and downloadable)
- VBScript documentation (online and downloadable)
- Windows Script components
- The Script debugger

The Windows Scripting Clinic is located at http://msdn.microsoft.com/voices/scripting.asp. This is a very useful column, published approximately monthly, that discusses various scripting-related topics. You can read the current as well as previous columns at this site.

The MSDN (Microsoft Developers Network) Library at http://msdn.microsoft.com/library/ is an extensive searchable database of information on all Microsoft development technologies, including scripting.

The page at http://msdn.microsoft.com/library/backgrnd/html/wsh_object.htm provides a useful overview of the WSH object model.

The Windows Scripting Host FAQ (Frequently Asked Questions) is a non-Microsoft site located at http://www.ntfaq.com/wsh.html. It provides answers to common questions with particular reference to using WSH on Windows NT.

The scripting technologies Start page provides the latest news about new scripting products as well as links to other related pages: http://msdn.microsoft.com/scripting/default.htm?RLD=452.

The public Usenet newsgroup microsoft.public.scripting.wsh, which can be obtained from the news server msnews.microsoft.com, is a discussion group where script programmers ask and answer questions and share ideas.

Please be aware that while the URLs I give here are current as I write this, there is no guarantee that things won't change in the future. Microsoft is pretty good about redirecting people to moved and changed web sites, but if you cannot find any of the information that I describe I suggest you use the Search function at http://msdn.microsoft.com.

Running Scripts

You have already learned how to run scripts from the command line, and while this works fine when you are developing and testing a script, it rarely is a good choice for the end user. In this section we look at other ways to execute scripts, but first we need to look at some of the options available when a script is run.

To employ a script option, you specify the option on the command line, preceded by a double slash. The options for Cscript and Wscript are almost identical and are explained in Table 3-1 with differences noted as applicable.

TABLE 3-1 *Command line options for Cscript and Wscript.*

Option	Description
//B	Runs the script in batch mode (non-interactive).
//I	Runs the script in interactive mode. This is the default.
//Logo	Displays a banner at startup (Cscript only). This is the default.
//Nologo	Suppresses banner display at startup. Cscript only.
//S	Saves the current command line options, making them the defaults for all scripts run by the current user.
//T:*n*	Sets a time limit of *n* seconds for the script. The default is no time limit.
//H:Wscript or //H:Cscript	Sets the default WSH executable that will run scripts. This is the engine that will be used if, for example, the user double-clicks a script file name in Windows Explorer. The initial default is Wscript.
//?	Displays information about the script engine's options.
//E:vbscript or //E:jscript	Specifies the scripting engine to use. By default this is determined by the extension of the script file.
//D	Turns the debugger on (WSH 2.0 only).
//X	Launches the script in the debugger (WSH 2.0 only).
//Job:ID	Launches the specified job from a .WS file (WSH 2.0 only).

The general syntax for running a script from the command line is as follows, depending on which executable you want to use:

```
Cscript scriptfilename arguments options
Wscript scriptfilename arguments options
```

Actually, the arguments (which are passed to the script) and the options (which control the operation of WSH) can be mixed, as the options are distinguished by the leading double slash. Let's look at some examples:

```
Cscript script1.vbs //Nologo //T:6 d:\data
```

This command line uses Cscript to run script1.vbs, with logo display suppressed and a timeout limit of 6 seconds. The string "d:\data" is passed to the script as an argument.

```
Wscript script2.js //B
```

This command line uses Wscript to run script2.js in batch mode.

```
Cscript //H:Cscript
```

This command line does not run a script, but sets the default WSH executable to Cscript.

```
Cscript script1.vbs //Nologo //T:6 //S
```

This command line runs the specified script with no logo and a timeout of 6 seconds, and saves those options as the defaults for future scripts.

Script Shortcuts

You can create a shortcut for a script file, just as you can for any Windows file. The shortcut can be placed on the Desktop, in the taskbar, or on the Start menu, permitting the user to run it like any other Windows program. Here's how:

1. Open Windows Explorer.
2. Navigate to the folder where the script file is located.
3. Right-click the script file name, and select Create Shortcut from the popup menu. A shortcut will be placed in the same folder with the name Shortcut to *XXXX*, where *XXXX* is the name of the script file.
4. If desired, rename the shortcut by right-clicking it and selecting Rename from the popup menu.
5. Place the shortcut in the desired location as follows:

    - To place it on the Desktop, drag it from the Explorer window and drop it on the Desktop.
    - To place it on the Quick Launch toolbar, drag it from the Explorer window and drop it on the toolbar.
    - To add it to the Start menu, click the Start button, and then click Settings and Taskbar and Start menu. Display the Start menu Programs tab in the dialog box, click the Add button, and follow the steps to add the shortcut to the Start menu.

The Quick Launch Toolbar

The Quick Launch toolbar is a feature of Windows 98, Windows 2000, and Windows ME. Windows 95 or NT users will have it only if Internet Explorer with Active Desktop has been installed. This toolbar is by default displayed on the Taskbar, immediately to the right of the Start button. It displays small program icons that let you launch frequently needed programs with a single click. If it is not displayed on your system, right-click the Taskbar, select Toolbars from the popup menu, then select Quick Launch.

Scheduling Scripts

With some scripts, it can be advantageous to run them automatically at regular intervals or at specified times. System maintenance scripts typically fall into this category, but they are not the only types of scripts that you may want to schedule. You can use the Windows Task Scheduler to schedule tasks, or, if you are running Windows NT, you use the AT command.

USING THE TASK SCHEDULER

The Task Scheduler is a standard component of Windows 98/ME and Windows 2000, and will be installed on Windows 95 if Internet Explorer version 4.0 or greater has been installed (based on installation options). If you are running Windows 95, you can determine if the Task Scheduler is installed by opening the My Computer folder on your Desktop. If there's a Scheduled Tasks folder visible, as shown in Figure 3-1, then it is installed. The Task Scheduler also displays as a small icon in the System Tray. If it is not, you can

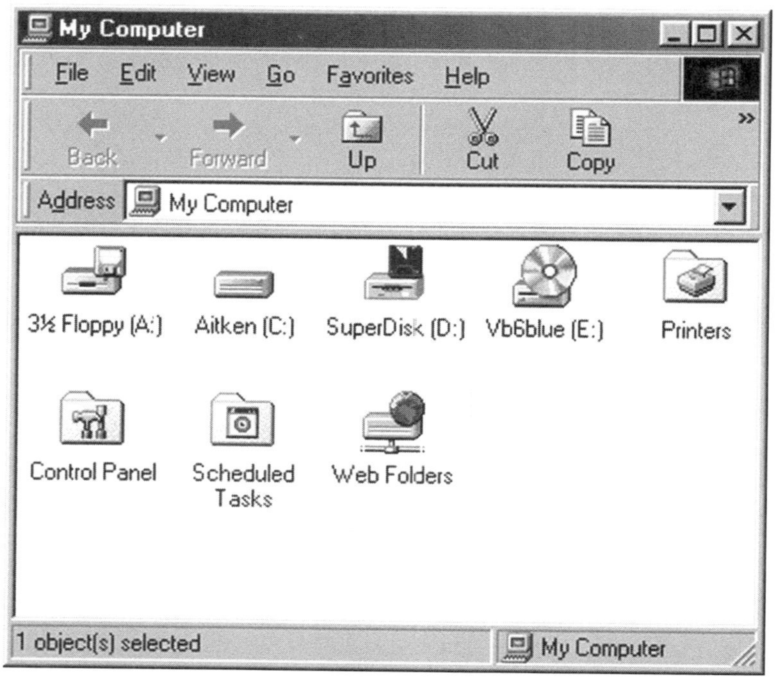

FIGURE 3–1 *Determining if the Task Scheduler is installed.*

obtain it by installing Internet Explorer and specifying Task Scheduler as one of the install options, or obtain it from the Microsoft Windows Update page.

To schedule a script, follow these steps:

1. Open the Task Scheduler by double-clicking its System Tray icon, or by opening My Computer and double-clicking the Scheduled Tasks folder. The Task Scheduler window is shown in Figure 3-2. Your display may look somewhat different from this based on your View settings, but the window will have an entry for each scheduled task that already exists, as well as an "Add Scheduled Task" item.
2. Double-click the Add Scheduled Task entry. The Scheduled Task Wizard starts and displays its opening window. Click the Next button.
3. The next Scheduled Task Wizard window, shown in Figure 3-3, lets you select the program to run. Click the Browse button, navigate to the desired script file, select it, then click Open.
4. The next Scheduled Task Wizard window, shown in Figure 3-4, displays the name of the script you selected (in the figure it is CheckTempFiles) and presents you with options for how often the script is to run, such as daily, weekly, or when the computer starts. The When I Log On option runs a script each time the specified user logs on to the system. Select the desired schedule, then click the Next button.

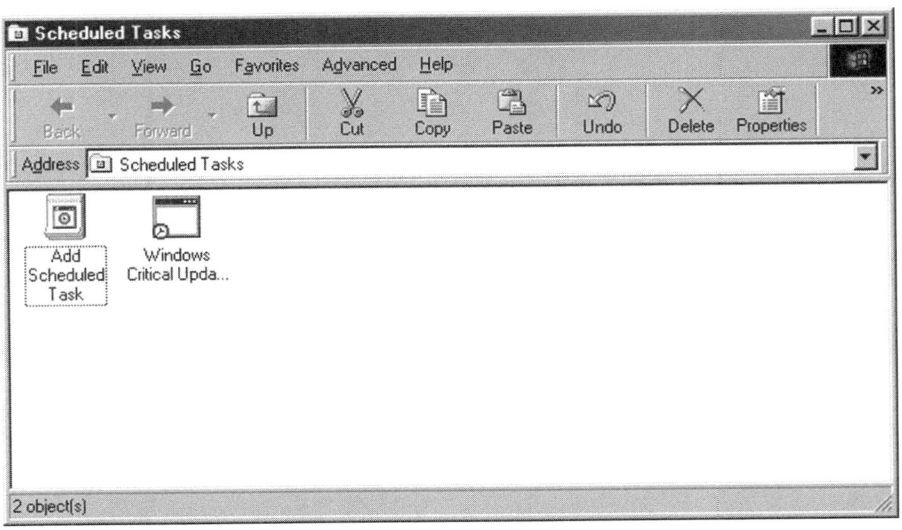

FIGURE 3–2 *The Task Scheduler window.*

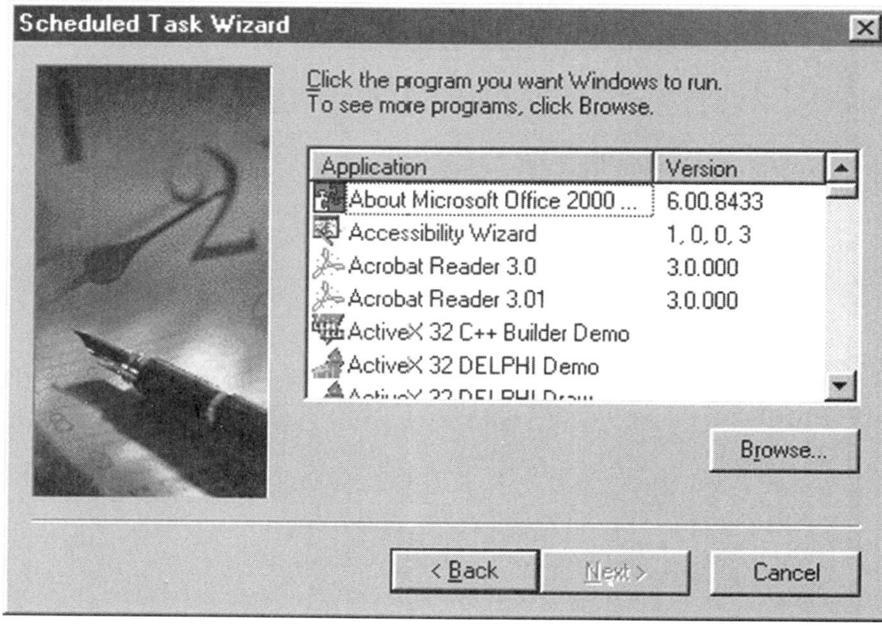

FIGURE 3–3 *Selecting a script to schedule.*

5. The next window lets you set the details of the schedule, based on the option selected in step 4. If you selected Daily, for example, you will be able to select the run time and whether the script runs every day or just on weekdays. If you selected Weekly, you will be able to select the day of the week for the script to run, as well as the start time. Make the desired settings here and click Next.
6. The final Scheduled Task Wizard window summarizes your schedule settings and offers you the option of displaying the advanced properties for the task. These properties are used to modify schedule settings and to set other options, such as whether the task will run on a laptop that is using batteries.

Once a script has been scheduled, it will run as specified without the user having to start it. You can access the script's advanced properties at any time by opening the Task Scheduler, right-clicking the entry for the script, and selecting Properties from the popup menu. One handy setting in the properties window is the Enabled option. By turning this option off you can temporarily "unschedule" the script without totally deleting it from the Task Scheduler.

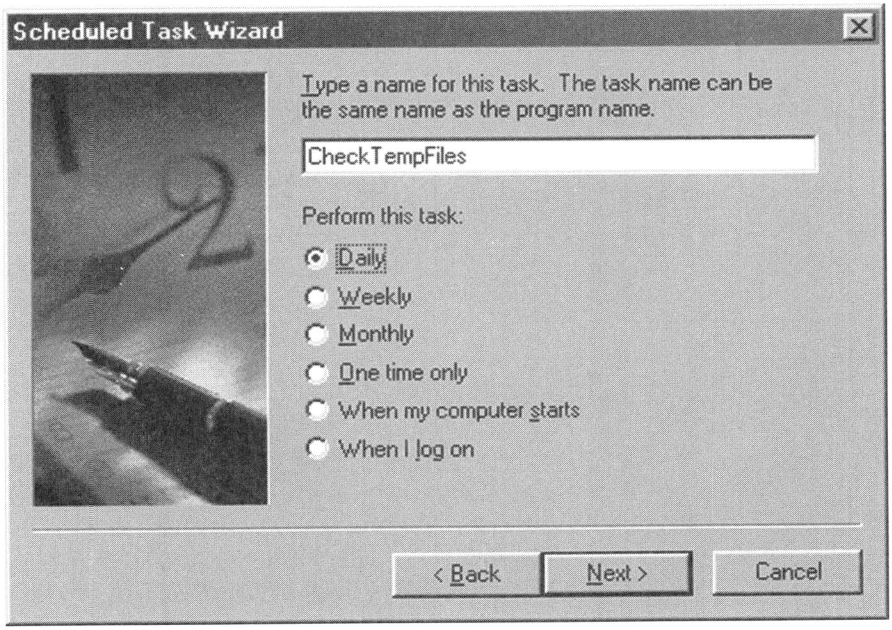

FIGURE 3–4 *Selecting the schedule for your script.*

USING THE WINDOWS NT AT COMMAND

Lacking the Task Scheduler, Windows NT requires users to rely on the AT command to schedule scripts. This command provides a way to control the NT Scheduler service, which in many ways does the same thing as the Task Scheduler while making it a lot more difficult for the user. I cannot cover all the details of the AT command here but can show you the basics of scheduling your scripts.

You run the AT command from the command prompt. Its simplified syntax, relevant for scheduling scripts to run on the local computer, is as follows:

```
at time /interactive /every:date[] /next:date[] command
```

The command arguments are as follows:

- *Time* specifies the time of day when the command is to run.
- /Interactive is an optional argument that specifies that the script will interact with the desktop of the user who is logged on at the time the script runs.
- /every:date[] is an optional argument specifying the day(s) of the week or month on which the command should be run. Days of the week are specified with the abbreviations M, T, W, Th, F, S, Su; days

of the month are specified by numbers 1–31. If omitted, the current day of the month is assumed.

- /next:date[] is an optional argument specifying the next date the script should run. Days are specified as described for the /every option. If omitted, the current day of the month is assumed. Note that you would not use the /every and /next options together in the same command.
- *Command* is the name of the script to run.

Let's look at some examples. The following command schedules a script to execute at 11:00 P.M. on the next 15th of the month:

```
at 23:00 /next:15 MyScript
```

This command schedules a script to execute every Monday and Friday at noon:

```
at 12:00 /every:M,F MyScript
```

It is sometimes useful to use a batch file to run the script, and schedule the batch file to run rather than scheduling the script directly. The AT command includes additional options for deleting tasks, listing scheduled tasks, and so on. You can refer to your Windows NT documentation for information.

Overview

WSH scripts are simple text files and can be created with any text editor. A specialized editor may make certain tasks easier but is certainly not a requirement. Scripts can be run in a variety of ways: from the command line, from Windows Explorer, as a shortcut on the Desktop or Quick Launch bar, or as a selection on the Start menu. You can select the method or methods that is most appropriate for your users. In addition, you can use the Windows Task Scheduler or the Windows NT AT command to schedule scripts to be run at specific times, which can be a very useful tool.

FOUR

Working with Script Arguments, .WSH Files, and Web Scripting

In this chapter we look at some other important aspects of Windows scripting. First, we look at script arguments. The ability to pass arguments to scripts greatly enhances their flexibility, permitting the same script to perform different actions each time it is executed. Next, we look at a special type of file that can be used to control script execution and options. These .wsh files are not required to run a script, but can be very useful in certain circumstances. Finally, we briefly explore the world of Web scripting. While this is not a book on the topic of Web scripting, it is still a good idea for you to understand how Microsoft scripting technology extends beyond the desktop scripting provided by the Windows Script Host.

Script Arguments

When you execute a script using either Wscript or Cscript, you have the option of passing one or more arguments to the script on the command line. The code in a script needs a way to determine if arguments were passed, how many arguments, and to retrieve the argument data. These tasks are done with the help of the `Arguments` collection, which is obtained as a property of the `WScript` object.

Arguments versus Options

Remember that script arguments are distinguished from script engine options by the fact that the latter are always preceded by //.

The `Arguments` collection, which is actually a `WshArguments` object, has three properties. The `Count` and `length` properties are the same, returning the number of arguments passed. You use `Count` with VBScript and `length` with JScript. The `Item` property is an array that contains one string for each argument passed to the script. Legal indexes for `Item` range from 0 to `Count-1`. For example, this VBScript code will display all of a script's arguments on the screen:

```
Dim i

for i = 0 to WScript.Arguments.Count - 1
    WScript.Echo WScript.Arguments.Item(i)
next
```

VBScript also permits the following syntax:

```
Dim arg

for each arg in WScript.Arguments
    WScript.Echo arg
next
```

In JScript, the code is similar:

```
var i;

for (i=0; i< WScript.Arguments.Count; i++)
    WScript.Echo(WScript.Arguments.Item(i));
```

When a script requires arguments (as opposed to the arguments being optional), your script code should always check to see that the proper number of arguments was in fact passed. Actually, this is the minimum checking that should be done — it is usually wise also to verify that the arguments are the correct type, such as numeric versus string. Other types of verification are also possible. A script that works with a folder name passed as an argument might want to check to see if the folder exists before doing anything else.

The scripts in Listings 4-1 and 4-2 show an example. These scripts are passed a folder name as a command line argument, and display the total number of bytes of the files in the folder. The code works as follows:

1. Verify that a single argument was passed to the script. If not, display a message describing how the script should be called (you should do this in all scripts that take arguments).
2. Verify that the argument refers to an existing folder. If it does not, display a message and then exit.
3. Calculate the total file sizes and display it.

This script makes use of the `FileScriptingObject`. Do not be concerned if the function of some of the code in these scripts is not clear — these topics will be covered in subsequent chapters.

LISTING 4-1 *Verifying command line arguments (VBScript).*

```
' List0401.vbs
' Demonstrates verification of command line arguments.
' Displays total bytes of files in a specified folder.

Dim fso
Dim foldername
Dim folder
Dim total
Dim file

' Check that there is a single argument.
if WScript.Arguments.Count <> 1 then
      MsgBox "Usage: Cscript (or Wscript) list0401.vbs foldername."
      WScript.Quit
end if

' Retrieve the argument.
foldername = WScript.Arguments.Item(0)
Set fso = WScript.CreateObject("Scripting.FileSystemObject")

' If the folder exists, sum the file sizes and display the result.
if (fso.FolderExists(foldername)) then
      Set folder = fso.GetFolder(foldername)
      for each file in folder.files
            total = total + file.size
      next
      MsgBox "The files in " & foldername & " total " & total & " bytes."
' If the folder does not exist, display a message and exit.
else
      MsgBox foldername & " does not exist."
end if
```

LISTING 4–2 *Verifying command line arguments (JScript).*

```
// List0402.js
// Demonstrates verification of command line arguments.
// Displays total bytes of files in a specified folder.

var fso;
var foldername;
var folder;
var total;
var file;
var e;

// Check that there is a single argument.
if (WScript.Arguments.length != 1) {
    WScript.Echo("Usage: Cscript (or Wscript) list0401.vbs
foldername.");
    WScript.Quit(); }

// Retrieve the argument.
foldername = WScript.Arguments.Item(0);
fso = WScript.CreateObject("Scripting.FileSystemObject");

// If the folder exists, sum the file sizes and display the result.
if (fso.FolderExists(foldername)) {
    folder = fso.GetFolder(foldername);
    total = 0;
    e = new Enumerator(folder.files)
    for (; !e.atEnd(); e.moveNext())
    {
        file = e.item();
        total = total + file.size;
    }

    WScript.Echo("The files in " + foldername + " total " + total + " bytes.");}
// If the folder does not exist, display a message and exit.
else
    WScript.Echo(foldername + " does not exist.");
```

WSH Files

When you start working with scripts, you may notice some files with the .wsh extension located in the folder where you keep your scripts. These are *script preference files* that are used by WSH to store information about how the script is to be executed. A .wsh file has the same name as the associated script. A script will have a .wsh file only if one or more options associated with that script has been changed from the default.

To view a script's options, or properties, locate the script file in Windows Explorer and right-click its name. Then select Properties from the popup menu. As shown in Figure 4-1, the properties dialog box will have a Scripts tab in it. In this dialog box you can set two script options: the script timeout value, and whether or not a logo is displayed by the scripting engine. If you change either of these options from their default value, and then close the dialog box, you will see that a .wsh file is written to the same folder as the script file.

You can run a script by selecting its .wsh file, just like selecting the script file itself. You can also create shortcuts to .wsh files. One advantage accorded by .wsh files is that they do not need to remain in the same direc-

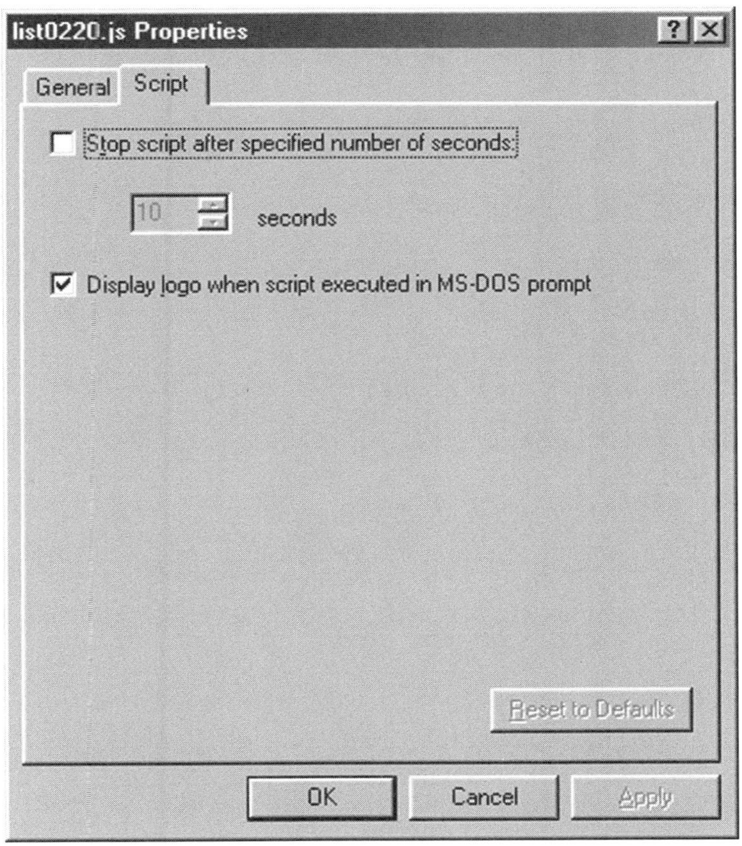

FIGURE 4–1 *Setting properties for a script file.*

tory as the script. You cannot, however, move the script file because the location of the script file is encoded in the .wsh file and if you move it, it will not be found when you try to execute it. You can get around this problem if desired by editing the .wsh file, as we will soon see.

A .wsh file is simply a text file containing information about the location of the script and the options set for it. Here is the content of a typical .wsh file:

```
[ScriptFile]
Path=C:\documents1\Windows Scripting\scripts\list0226.js

[Options]
Timeout=0
DisplayLogo=0
BatchMode=0
```

There are two sections to a .wsh file. The ScriptFile section contains the full path to the script file. If you want to move the script file to a different folder, you must edit the .wsh file so this section points to the new path. You can use any text editor to work with .wsh files. The Options section contains settings for three script file options; you learned about these options previously. A value of 0 means the option is turned off. For the Timeout option, a value > 0 specifies the timeout in seconds. For the other options, a value of 1 means the option is turned on.

WSH and Web Scripting

When the people at Microsoft were developing their scripting technologies, they had a lot more in mind than the desktop scripting provided by the Windows Script Host. They saw scripting as a solution for many needs in the world of computers, and the scripting technologies were designed with these various needs in mind. Most important, the same scripting engines that are used for the Windows script host are also used by Microsoft Internet technologies. How does this work?

One way that scripts are used on the Internet is called *client-side scripting*. Script code can be embedded inside a Web page, along with the standard HTML (Hypertext Markup Language) that defines the appearance of the page. When the Web page is viewed in a Web browser, the embedded script code is executed by the scripting engine. Script code can be used for many purposes in a Web page, including interacting with the user and validating data. This type of scripting is called client-side because the script executes on the client machine. Both VBScript and JScript are supported by the Microsoft technologies, just like with the Windows Script Host. A given Web page can actually have both VBScript and JScript code embedded in it, with sections of code marked off and identified by HTML tags.

The second way that scripts are used on the Internet is called *server-side scripting*. As you might guess, this name is used because the scripts are executed on the Web server rather than on the client machine. Microsoft refers to this technology as active server pages, or ASP. When a user navigates to an active server page (identified by the .asp extension) the script code embedded in the page is read and executed by the scripting engine on the server, with the output being a standard HTML page, which is then sent to the client for viewing in the browser. Active server pages are very flexible and powerful, with one common usage being to display dynamic information from a database file.

The bottom line here is that any investment of time spent learning Microsoft Windows Script Host will give you a leg up if you ever need to do any Internet-related programming that requires scripting technologies. Likewise, if you already have some experience with Internet scripting, you'll find it a lot easier to learn how to use the Windows Script Host. Further coverage of Web scripting technologies is not appropriate here; after all, this is a book on the Windows Script Host! If you do want to explore the Web scripting technologies further, there are plenty of books on the market that can help you.

Overview

This chapter explained some of the ways that you can increase the flexibility of your scripts. By passing arguments to a script, you can have the script perform different tasks each time it is run. Remember that any script that uses arguments should provide feedback to the user if the incorrect number or type of arguments is passed. .WSH files provide another type of flexibility by providing a way to make certain script options permanent, so they will take affect every time the script is run. Finally, this chapter presented a brief introduction to Web scripting. While this book does not delve further into this topic, it is a good idea for you to have at least a basic idea of how the various scripting technologies relate to each other.

FIVE

Testing and Debugging Your Scripts

There are numerous things that can go wrong when you are developing a script. These potential problems fall into two categories. Errors prevent the script from executing, while bugs cause the script to produce incorrect results or actions. This chapter shows you how to detect and fix errors and bugs in your scripts.

Catching Script Errors

Like just about any activity that is related to computers, the creation of scripts is a process with lots of opportunities for errors. Obviously, you need to detect these errors and fix them before the script can be considered finished. There are several different kinds of errors that a script can encounter, and you need to understand the differences in terms of what causes the errors and what you can do about them.

Syntax Errors

A syntax error occurs when your script code does not follow the rules of the scripting language you are using. Just like the sentence "I are going to the store" violates the syntax rules of English, there are many ways in which script code can violate the rules of VBScript or JScript. When a script is executed, the first thing that happens is that the script processor scans the script code and checks it for syntax. If a syntax error is encountered by Wscript, a dialog box pops up notifying you of the error. With Cscript, the error message is displayed at the command prompt. Here's an example: The following line of VBScript code is missing the terminating double quote on the message:

```
MsgBox "Hello
```

If you try to execute a script containing this line in Wscript, the message shown in Figure 5-1 will be displayed. The first four lines in this message box are of interest to the programmer. They provide the following information about the error:

- The full path of the script that caused the error
- The number of the line in the script where the error was found
- The character position where the error was found
- The nature of the error

Using this information, it is a fairly easy task to locate the cause of the error and fix it. Be aware, however, that the line number reported is not always precisely accurate, but it will always be close and can help you locate the error even when it is not on that precise line.

What happens if a script has more than one syntax error? Only one error is reported at a time — the one that occurs nearest the beginning of the script. After you have fixed the first error and try to run the script again, then the second error will be detected and reported. It's a step-by-step process, but because syntax errors are always caught and reported by the scripting engine, there is rarely any serious problem in getting rid of them.

About text editors

One feature I would want in any text editor used for creating scripts is an indication of the line and character where the cursor is located. When you are trying to track down a syntax error on, say, line 49, having this information makes the error a lot easier to find. Unfortunately, NotePad, the free Window editor, does not have this feature. Many other editors, including the one that is part of DevStudio, do have this feature.

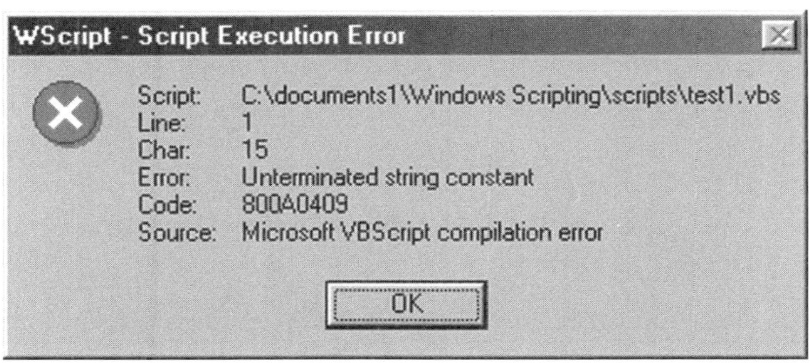

FIGURE 5–1 *A dialog box caused by a syntax error.*

Run-Time Errors

A run-time error is an error that does not cause any problems until the script executes, or *runs*. There is no syntax violation, so the mechanism for reporting syntax errors that was explained in the previous section does not apply. Here are some examples of things that will cause a run-time error:

- Trying to use `WScript.CreateObject` to create an object that does not exist
- Dividing by zero
- Trying to open a file that does not exist

Dealing with run-time errors is more complicated than dealing with syntax errors for several reasons. First, VBScript and JScript have quite different error-handling capabilities. Second, the two script languages will, in some cases, differ as to what constitutes an error. For example, dividing by zero is a definite error in VBScript, causing an Overflow error. In JScript, however, no error occurs because JScript supports the special value `#INF` to represent infinity, which of course is the result of dividing by zero. Finally, the possible causes of run-time errors are so varied that it is impossible to categorize them neatly and present easy solutions.

This does not mean that you can ignore errors! You could not ignore them even if you wanted to, as the default response of WSH to a run-time error is to stop running the script and display an error message. This message is similar to that displayed for a syntax error, with an example shown in Figure 5-2. You can tell a syntax error from a run-time error by the Source entry in the error dialog box. For a syntax error, this will say "Microsoft VBScript (or JScript) Compilation Error" while for a run-time error it will identify a different error source.

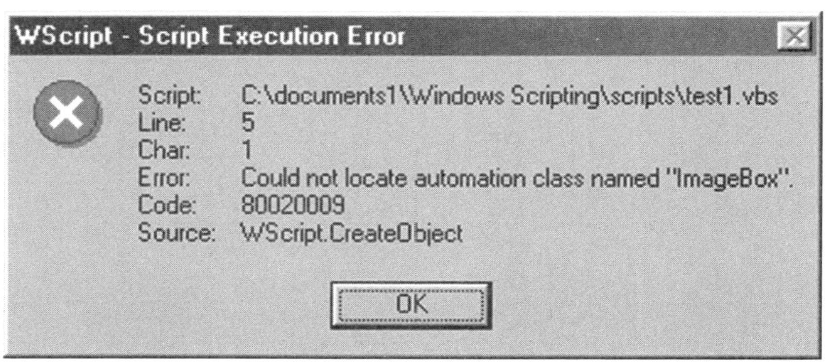

FIGURE 5–2 *WSH displays a message when a run-time error occurs.*

You may have noticed that I said that the "default" response of WSH is to halt the script and display an error message. This default response occurs only if you have not enabled error handling in your script code. With error handling, your script code deals with the error and the default error message is not displayed. With error handling, a script will not be halted by an error but can deal with it as appropriate for the specific error. You'll learn about error handling in Chapter 9 for VBScript, and Chapter 13 for JScript.

Despite the power of WSH error handling, let me finish this section with an old adage: An ounce of prevention is worth a pound of cure. Rather than handling an error, it is better to prevent it. There is no "secret technique" for error prevention, but rather it depends on a combination of good programming practices, common sense, and experience. As you become more familiar with the kinds of errors that can occur, you will soon start to think of ways to avoid them. You cannot avoid all errors, but it is worth the effort to avoid as many as possible.

Bugs

The final type of error a script programmer will have to deal with is called a *bug*. Sometimes this sort of problem is also called a logic error. A bug does not prevent the script from executing, nor does it cause any kind of message to be displayed. Rather, a bug is an error in the script code that prevents the script from doing its intended task properly. For example, a script written to copy files onto a network server for backup may copy the wrong set of files. Or, a script that performs numerical calculations may provide incorrect results. There are as many possible bugs as there are tasks for scripts to perform, and unfortunately they can be difficult to track down and fix.

Why are bugs so difficult to deal with? The main reason is that, unlike with syntax and run-time errors, WSH is no help with bugs. As far as WSH is concerned, the script is working just fine. There is no way for WSH to know that you wanted to copy those files instead of these, or to divide instead of multiply. The script is doing exactly what you told it to do — the problem is that the code you wrote does not match your intentions!

There is only one way to detect bugs: test test test! Only by thorough testing of your script can you ensure that the script is bug free. Once you have determined that there is a bug in your script, then what? The process of getting rid of bugs is called *debugging*, and that's the topic of the next section.

Why are they called *bugs*?

Computer legend has it that several decades ago, in the early years of computing, a malfunctioning program was found to have been due to an insect that got into the computer and caused a short circuit. The first "bug" was a real bug, and the name stuck.

Debugging Your Scripts

Once you have determined that a script has one or more bugs, how can you fix it? Sometimes a careful examination of the code is all that is required, but more often than not you'll need to take additional steps. Sometimes you can track down the problem by displaying information from your script (for example, with the `WScript.Echo` command), at appropriate locations in your code. This is a fairly simple way to track the value of variables, to determine the order of statement execution, and so on. For more demanding debugging needs, you will turn to the Microsoft Script Debugger.

The Script Debugger

The Script Debugger is a free utility that Microsoft developed to assist in the debugging of Internet scripts. You will recall from earlier in this book that both the VBScript and JScript languages are used for Internet scripting as well as for the command line scripting provided by WSH. While WSH scripts are not the same as Internet scripts, there are methods that can be used to enable most WSH scripts to be executed and debugged using this utility.

Getting the Script Debugger

If you have Microsoft Internet Explorer installed on your system, you may already have the Script Debugger installed. To determine if you do, open Internet Explorer then open the View menu. If you see the menu command Script Debugger, then you are all set.

To install the Script Debugger, you must have Internet Explorer 4 or 5 on your system. Then go to http://msdn.microsoft.com/scripting/ and follow the links to download and install the utility.

Before you can use the Script Debugger to debug a WSH script, there are a few preparatory steps you must take. Use of the Script Debugger is based on making it appear as if your script is in fact an Internet script. In a Web page, script code is identified by HTML tags that mark the beginning and end of the script as well as identify the script language. For VBScript the tags look like this:

```
<SCRIPT LANGUAGE="VBScript">
script code goes here.
</SCRIPT>
```

For JScript the tags are identical except the "VBScript" is replaced by "JScript." To prepare your script for use in the debugger, all you need do is edit the script and add these two lines, one at the beginning and the other at the end of the script. Also, save the script as an HTML file. This requires nothing more than using your editor's Save As command to save the script file as *Scriptname*.html or *Scriptname*.htm (both the .html and .htm extensions are valid for HTML files).

So much for the easy part. There is a more serious limitation when using the Script Debugger in that the `WScript` object is not supported. This makes sense, when you think about it. The Script Debugger was designed to debug scripts that run inside the Internet Explorer browser, and such scripts do not use the `WScript` object. Therefore, WSH scripts that use the `WScript` object (and its subobjects) cannot be debugged unless the statements that refer to `WScript`-related objects are temporarily removed (or converted to comments). Sometimes this is not possible, and then you will not be able to use the debugger. However, for many scripts it can be a valuable tool. If the script uses only the `WScript.Echo` method, it can be replaced with calls to the `Alert` method, which is supported by the Internet Explorer scripting model.

Using the Debugger

Once you have prepared your script as described previously, here's how to use the debugger. First, open the script in Internet Explorer. You can do this two ways:

- Use Windows Explorer to navigate to the script HTML file, and double-click it.
- Open Internet Explorer, press Ctrl+O or select File, Open, then browse to locate the script HTML file.

When the script opens it will run. This is OK, but if for any reason you do not want the script to run right away, put the following line at the beginning of the script:

```
alert("Starting script")
```

For a JScript script, add a semicolon at the end. This statement will display the indicated message and pause the script until you click OK.

The second step is to start the Script Debugger. Again, there are two ways to do this:

- Select View, Script Debugger, Open from the Internet Explorer menu.
- In Windows Explorer, navigate to the location where the Script Debugger is installed (typically this is c:\program files\Microsoft script debugger) and double click the program name (msscrdbg.exe).

Other debuggers

If you have certain Microsoft development tools installed on your system, such as Visual Basic or Visual Studio, your installation may include another version of the Microsoft Debugger, one that can handle other programming languages as well as scripts. In this case, starting the debugger from the Internet Explorer menu may start this other debugger rather than the script debugger. That's OK; if you are familiar with the full-featured debugger you can certainly use it with your scripts. If you would rather use the Script Debugger, then use the second just method described to start the debugger.

When the debugger starts, it displays a blank screen. Select View, Running Documents from the menu and the Running Documents window will open, as shown in Figure 5-3. Click the + sign next to Microsoft Internet Explorer to display a list of scripts running. Unless there is something else going on, such as another copy of Internet Explorer running, this list should contain only the script that you started.

The final step is to double-click the name of your script file. This causes the Script Debugger to display the script code in the debugging window. You will see that the debugger uses color coding for different parts of your script: green for comments, blue for script code, brown for HTML tags, and so on. You cannot edit the script in the debugger.

To start your script in the debugger, select Break At Next Statement from the Debug window. Then switch back to the browser and click the Refresh button, which causes the browser to reload and reexecute the script. Because of the Break At Next Statement command, the script will break, or pause, at

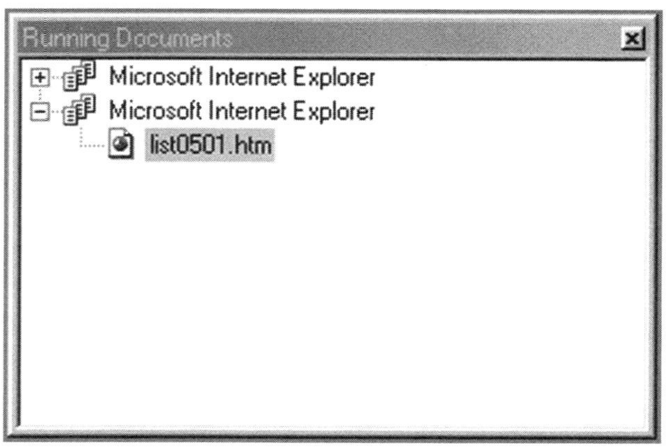

FIGURE 5–3 *The Running Documents window lists the scripts available for debugging.*

the first executable statement in the script. In the debugger window, this statement will be highlighted in yellow with an arrow in the left margin. At this point, your script is loaded in the debugger and you are ready to get to work with your debugging tasks. The process of debugging has four main components, which you will usually use in conjunction with each other:

- *Single stepping*: Executing your script one line at a time
- *Breakpoints*: Forcing script execution to pause at specified locations
- *Variable monitoring*: Examining the values of variables during script execution
- *The call stack*: Determining the order that execution has taken through your script's procedures

Let's look at these in turn.

SINGLE STEPPING

When you single step a script, it executes one line at a time. There are three variants of the single step command, with the differences between them applying only when your script contains procedures or functions. You can access these commands either from the Debug menu or via icons on the debugger's toolbar.

- *Step Into*: Executes the currently highlighted line of code and pauses at the next statement regardless of whether the next statement is located in a function.
- *Step Over*: Executes the currently highlighted line of code. If this line calls a function, executes the entire function and pauses at the first line of code after execution returns from the function.
- *Step Out*: Executes the currently highlighted line of code. If the line is inside a function, executes the remainder of the function and pauses at the first line of code after execution returns from the function.

The reason for having these three options for the single step command is that a script often will contain functions that have been thoroughly tested and debugged. If you are trying to track down a bug in single step mode, but know the bug is not within a particular function, you have the choice of skipping over the function rather than stepping through it one line at a time.

Single stepping through a script is rarely used by itself. Most often it is used in conjunction with monitoring of variables, to be discussed soon.

USING BREAKPOINTS

A breakpoint can be set on any line of executable code within a script. When execution reaches that line, it pauses and the line is highlighted. Note that execution always pauses before a line with a breakpoint set on it. In other words, that line will be the first one executed when script execution is resumed.

You can set breakpoints on as many lines of code as you like. To do so, simply move the cursor to the line of code and press F9 or select Toggle Breakpoint from the Debug menu. A line that has a breakpoint set is displayed in a different color with a small circle in the left margin. To remove a breakpoint from a line of code, follow the same procedure. To remove all breakpoints from a script, press Ctrl+Shift+F9 or select Clear All Breakpoints from the Debug menu.

Breakpoints are useful when you believe that the bug you are trying to track down is located in a specific section of code. By setting a breakpoint on the first line in that section, you can quickly execute the script up to that point and then use single step commands to examine the code in detail.

VARIABLE MONITORING

Whenever a script is in break mode, having been paused either by a breakpoint or by use of a single step command, you can monitor and modify the value of script variables. To do so, you need to display the Command Window by selecting Command Window from the debugger's View menu. To view the value of a variable,

- For VBScript scripts, type a question mark followed by a space and the name of the variable, then press Enter.
- For JScript scripts, type the name of the variable and press Enter.

Figure 5-4 shows the Command Window displaying the value of the variable *x* in a VBScript script. In this case the variable has been assigned the string "hello." If the variable has not yet been assigned a value, the Command Window will display "undefined."

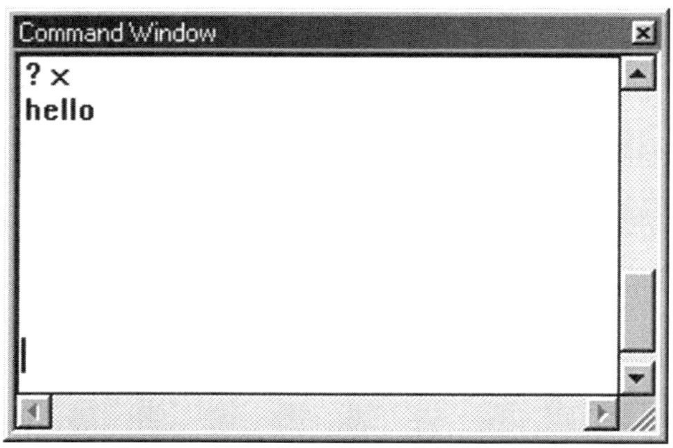

FIGURE 5–4 *Displaying the value of a variable in the Script Debugger's Command Window.*

You can also use the Command Window to change the value of a variable. This is done by typing an assignment statement into the Command Window, using the syntax of the script language in use. To change the value of *x* to "goodbye" in a VBScript script, you would type:

```
x = "goodbye"
```

In a JScript script you would type

```
x = "goodbye";
```

When the script resumes executing, the new value will be in effect. You can use the Command Window to change the value of object properties as well.

Because many if not most script bugs are caused by variables taking on inappropriate values, you will find that the Command Window is an invaluable debugging tool. By using this window to view and change variable values, you can determine which variables are involved and where in the script code they are being assigned the inappropriate values. Once you have gotten this far, it is usually a simple matter to modify the script to fix the bug.

THE CALL STACK

The Call Stack is used to keep track of function execution in your scripts. You display the Call Stack window by selecting Call Stack from the View menu. You interpret the information in this window as follows:

- The top entry in the list indicates where execution has paused. If execution is paused within a function, the function name is displayed. If execution is paused outside of a function, then VBScript Global Code is displayed (or, for JScript, JScript Global Code).
- If execution is paused within a function, the second entry in the list indicates where the function was called from. This can be another function or global code.
- Additional entries in the list identify other steps taken in reaching the location where execution is paused.

Look at the Call Stack displayed in Figure 5-5. This tells us the following:

- Execution is paused in the function named Func2
- Func2 was called from within a function named Func1.
- Func1 was called by global code (code not in any function).

The Call Stack is not that useful for debugging simple scripts, but for complex scripts with lots of intertwined function calls it can sometimes be the easiest way to pinpoint the problem.

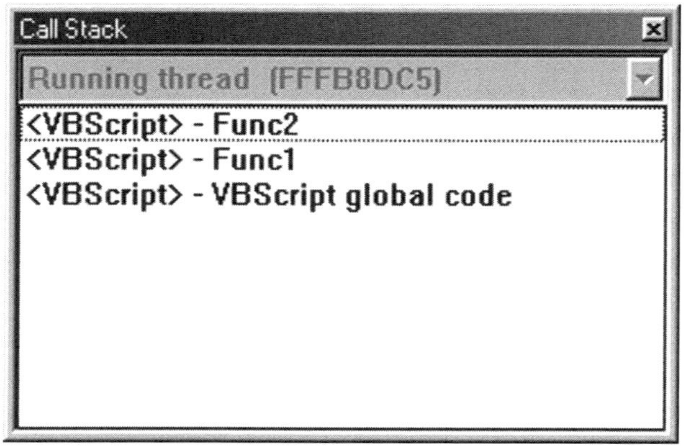

FIGURE 5–5 *Displaying function calls in the Call Stack window.*

Overview

Any script that you write presents the potential for errors. The types of errors you may encounter fall into three categories: syntax errors, run-time errors, and bugs. The methods you use to detect and fix these different types of errors may differ, but in all three cases it is equally important that you ensure your scripts are error free. At the least, distributing a script that includes errors will cause inconvenience and earn you a bad reputation among your end users. At the worst it can result in data loss and serious system problems, so you need to be careful.

SIX

VBScript: Syntax, Data Storage, and Operators

VBScript is one of the two languages supported by the Microsoft Windows Scripting Host. It is a powerful and flexible language but is still relatively easy to learn. This is the first of four chapters covering the syntax and statements of VBScript. In this chapter you will learn about the relationship of VBScript to the full Visual Basic development language. We also cover the fundamentals of the language syntax and look at the tools VBScript provides for storing and manipulating data.

Introduction to VBScript

VBScript got its name because it is the scripting edition of Visual Basic. As you may know, Basic was one of the first languages offered by Microsoft for the PC, and Visual Basic was the first programming language for Windows that made visual interface design accessible to the nonspecialist. Visual Basic is also an important part of the Microsoft Office suite of applications programs, which uses Visual Basic for Applications as its internal macro and programming language. Clearly, Microsoft has a lot riding on different variants of the Visual Basic language, and VBScript is its entry into the scripting arena.

Comparison with Visual Basic

If you are familiar with Visual Basic or Visual Basic for Applications, you may be wondering how VBScript relates to them. You'll be glad to know that all three languages have a lot in common. If you know one, you'll find the others very easy to learn. There are some differences, however. When comparing VBScript to the other varieties of Basic, you'll see that the differences consist mainly of features that are present in Visual Basic but absent in VBScript. Specifically, VBScript differs from Visual Basic as follows:

- Data types. Only a single data type, `Variant`, is available.
- File input/output. There are no intrinsic file access statements in VBScript. You must rely on the `FileSystemObject`.
- Built-in functions. VBScript lacks functions for financial calculations and Dynamic Data Exchange.
- Compiler features. VBScript lacks support for type libraries and include files.
- Error handling. VBScript does not support the `On Error Goto` statement.

These are the most important ways in which VBScript differs from Visual Basic. Admittedly it sounds rather negative, but it does not mean that VBScript is limited or crippled in some way. VBScript was designed for a specific purpose, and it has all the capabilities that it needs. A scripting language has somewhat different requirements from a full-featured programming language such as Visual Basic. Remember also that VBScript is used for Web scripting as well as desktop scripting, where safety and security concerns come into play. For its intended use, as a general-purpose scripting language, VBScript has all the needed features.

Syntax Fundamentals

VBScript syntax is relatively simple. There are lots of language details you will learn in the next few chapters, but here are some fundamental rules of syntax to get started:

- There is one VBScript statement per line. The end of a line is marked by a carriage return (pressing Enter).
- White space does not matter. That is, you can use blank lines and indentation freely to format your code.
- The language in not case sensitive.

- Execution begins with the first statement in the script file and continues in order to the last statement *unless* the order of execution is modified by statements in the file.

Comments

A *comment* is text in a script file that is ignored by the scripting engine. You can use comments to document your code, leave reminders for yourself, and so on. In VBScript, anything on a line following a single quote character (') is considered a comment. The single quote character can, but does not have to be, the first character on the line. Thus

```
' This is a comment
x = 234 ' This is a comment too.
```

The one exception is inside double quotes, where the ' character does not create a comment. In this code

```
name = "Smith's Dry Goods"
```

there is no comment because the ' is inside quoted text.

Commenting out code

The VBScript comment character can be useful during script development as a way of temporarily "removing" lines of code from a script. If you want to see how a script works with one or more lines removed, simply convert them to comments by placing a ' at the start of each line. If you decide to leave them in, just remove the comment character.

Line Continuations

As mentioned previously, VBScript syntax requires that each VBScript statement be placed on its own line. Strictly speaking this is true, but the designers of the Basic language realized that sometimes individual lines of code get so long that they are difficult to work with in an editor. The *line continuation character* lets you avoid this problem, breaking a single line of code over two or more lines in your editor. To break a line, simply type a space followed by an underscore at the place you want the break, and then hit Enter. For example,

```
Set MyShell = WScript.CreateObject _
    ("Scripting.FileSystemObject")
```

When separated in this way, the two or more lines are treated by the scripting engine as a single line. While not required, it is good practice to indent the second and subsequent continued lines, as shown in the example, to make it clear that they are continuations of the first one. The only place you cannot use the line continuation character is within a literal string (quoted text). The following would not be permitted:

```
Set MyShell = WScript.CreateObject ("Scripting. _
    FileSystemObject")
```

Data Storage

If there is anything that just about every script needs, it is a way to store data while the script is running. VBScript offers two general methods for storing data: *constants* for data that does not change during script execution, and *variables* for data that can change.

CONSTANTS

VBScript provides two types of constants for holding data that does not change during script execution. A *literal* constant is simply text or a number that is typed directly into your script code. In this code

```
InterestRate = 0.05
Name = "John Doe"
```

the 0.05 and the "John Doe" are literal constants. Literal numbers are typed directly, while literal text must be enclosed in double quotation marks.

A *symbolic* constant has a name, or symbol, that is used in the code. You create a symbolic constant using the `Const` keyword. This code creates a symbolic constant named INTEREST_RATE and assigns it the value 0.05:

```
Const INTEREST_RATE = 0.05
```

Now, any time you use the constant name in your code, it will be the same as using the literal constant 0.05. For example,

```
Payment = Balance * INTEREST_RATE
```

Constant names

The rules for naming symbolic constants are the same as the rules for naming variables, presented in the next section. I find it useful to make constant names all uppercase, using the underscore character as needed for clarity. This is not required, but by having constant names easily distinguished from variable names, I think the code is easier to read.

There are two advantages of using symbolic constants. First, by assigning a meaningful name to the constant, you make your code easier to read.

Second, if the constant is used in more than one location in the code, and you ever need to change it, you need make the change in only one location — where the constant is initially defined.

VBScript also provides some built-in symbolic constants that you can use in your code without having to define them. All of the built-in constants start with the letters "vb" for Visual Basic. For example, vbTrue and vbFalse represent the logical values True and False. Appendix 1 presents a complete list of VBScript's built-in constants.

VARIABLES

A *variable* is a named location where the script can store data. The value of a variable can be changed as often as needed. Unlike most other programming languages, VBScript has only a single type of variable, called `Variant`. Rather than having a variety of different variable types for different kinds of data (integers, real numbers, text, and so on) VBScript was designed with this one type that can hold any type of data you give it.

NAMING VARIABLES • To create a variable you must decide on a name for it. Variable names must be unique within a given script and must follow these rules (which apply to constant names as well):

- The first character must be a letter.
- The second and subsequent characters can be letters, numbers, or symbols but cannot include a space or the math symbols *, +, –, and /.
- The name can be no longer than 255 characters.
- The name cannot be the same as a VBScript keyword.

Since VBScript is not a case-sensitive language, the case of variable names does not matter. The names RATE, Rate, and rate will all refer to one and the same variable. I find it useful to follow the naming convention that uses a combination of upper and lowercase for variable names, as shown in these examples:

```
InterestRate
Count
NumberOfPages
```

If you use all uppercase for constants, as I suggested earlier, this will make you code easier to read. For example, it will be clear that InterestRate is a variable and INTEREST_RATE is a constant.

Use names that are meaningful. It may seem like extra typing at first, but it is worth it in the long run. If you need a variable to store, say, the number of files your script is working with, you could name the variable X or Q45 or Madonna, and the WSH would not care one bit. However, if you name it NumberOfFiles, your code will be a lot easier to read and maintain, especially when you come back to the script 6 months down the road to make some changes. Do yourself a favor — get in the habit of using meaningful variable names right from the start.

Some programmers like to use a prefix notation in which the variable name prefix identifies the type of data stored in the variable. Other programmers don't find this useful, but you can decide for yourself whether you want to use prefixes. Table 6-1 presents some standard prefixes and their meanings. Note that using these prefixes does not restrict the kind of data a variable can hold. It is only an aid for the programmer to identify the type of the data that the variable is being used for. However, realize that if you use a prefix and then store a different type of data in the variable, the incorrect prefix may cause confusion during program maintenance.

TABLE 6-1 *Variable type prefixes.*

Prefix	Data type	Example
b	Boolean (True/False)	bSaved
dtm	Date or time	dtmStartOfPeriod
err	Error code	errFileError
int	Integer (number with no fractional part such as 5).	intCount
fp	Floating point (number with a fractional part such as 5.123)	fpAverageCost
obj	Object reference	objShell
str	String (text)	strLastName

DECLARING VARIABLES AND THE OPTION EXPLICIT STATEMENT • Before you use a variable in your script, you should declare it using the `Dim` statement. The syntax is as follows:

```
Dim varname1, varname2, ...
```

You can declare as many variables as you like with a single `Dim` statement, although many programmers prefer a single variable per `Dim` statement to make the code more readable. If you declare a variable inside a function, it will be available anywhere in that function but nowhere else. If you declare a variable outside of any function, it will be available anywhere in the script.

You may have noticed that I said you "should" declare variables. VBScript does not require variable declaration, which means you can simply use variable names when and as needed with no prior declaration with the `Dim` statement. However, this is a bad idea — a *very* bad idea. Why is this?

If variable declaration is not required, then what happens when you misspell a variable name? Nothing. VBScript simply considers it to be a new variable, and the script runs without an error message. However, it is not going to run properly, since it will be using an incorrect value when the misspelled variable is referenced. You can (and should) avoid this problem by telling VBScript to require variable declaration. This is done by including the

Option Explicit statement at the beginning of the script. With this statement in effect, VBScript will generate an error if it encounters a variable that has not been declared using a Dim statement. This way, you are protected against the pesky errors that misspelled variable names could otherwise cause. I strongly recommend that you always use Option Explicit in your scripts.

Uninitialized variables

A variable that has been declared but has not had any data assigned to it is said to be *uninitialized*. The value of an uninitialized variable depends on how you treat that variable. If you treat it as a string (for example, trying to display it), the value is an empty string. If you treat it as a number, trying to add it to another variable, its value will be 0. If you treat it as an object reference, it will have the special value Nothing. You can determine if a variable has been initialized using the IsEmpty function, explained later in this chapter.

Object References

In addition to holding numeric and text data, VBScript variables can also be used to hold object references. You have seen this in previous chapters. When you create an instance of an object, such as the WScript.Shell object, you need a way to refer to the object in code. This is done by storing a reference to the object in a variable. This requires the use of the Set keyword, as shown here:

```
Set MyShell = WScript.CreateObject("WScript.Shell")
```

Once an object reference has been assigned to a variable, you then use that variable to access the object's properties and methods in code.

The Null value

VBScript has the special value Null to indicate that a variable does not contain valid data.

Determining Data Type

While VBScript supports only a single type of variable, that one type can hold various different kinds of data. There will be times when your script may need to know what kind of data is stored in a particular variable. VBScript provides a set of functions for this very task. They are explained in Table 6-2.

TABLE 6-2 *Determining the data type of a variable.*

Function	Description
IsArray(*varname*)	Returns True if the variable contains an array (variant arrays are explained later in this chapter).
IsDate(*varname*)	Returns True if the variable can be evaluated as a date.
IsEmpty(*varname*)	Returns True if the variable has not been initialized.
IsNull(*varname*)	Returns True if the variable contains the value `Null`.
IsNumeric(*varname*)	Returns True if the variable can be evaluated as a number.
IsObject(*varname*)	Returns True if the variable contains an object reference.

Arrays

Arrays are a very powerful and flexible way to store data. Using an array, you can keep multiple data items under the same name, using a numerical index to access individual data items. VBScript offers two types of arrays: static and dynamic.

Associative arrays

The arrays covered in this section use numbers as the index to retrieve specific data items. Remember that WSH also supports associative arrays, which identify data items using arbitrary text keys. Associative arrays are provided by the `Dictionary` object, covered in Chapter 2.

Static Arrays

A static array contains a fixed number of elements that does not change while the script is executing. When you first declare the array, you specify the number of elements it will contain. You declare a static array using the following syntax:

```
Dim ArrayName(n)
```

ArrayName is the name of the array, which follows the same naming rule as regular VBScript variables. *n* specifies the number of elements in the array. Here's an example:

```
Dim MyArray(100)
```

Because VBScript starts array indexes at 0, this array actually contains 101 elements, at indexes 0 through 100. Once an array has been declared, you access its elements using any expression to specify the index. For example,

What is an expression?

You'll see the term *expression* used frequently in programming. The term refers to anything in code that evaluates to a value. The value can be a number, some text, or an object reference. Here are some examples:

```
5               ' Evaluates to the value 5.
2+13            ' Evaluates to the value 15.
Count           ' Evaluates to whatever is stored in the variable Count
MyFunction()    ' Evaluates to whatever value is returned by the function.
```

Sometimes expressions are classified depending on the type of value they evaluate to:

Numeric expression: a numeric value
String expression: text
Logical expression: a True or False value
Object expression: an object reference

```
MyArray(0) = 45
x = 3
MyArray(x) = 25                          ' Same as MyArray(3)
MyArray(MyArray(0)) = 55                 ' Same as MyArray(45)
```

These arrays are one dimensional, meaning that they have a single index. You can also create multidimensional arrays that have two or more indexes by including the information about the additional indexes in the `Dim` statement. This statement creates a two dimensional array with 8 elements (0–7) in each dimension:

```
Dim ChessBoard(7, 7)
```

This array could be used, for example, to represent the squares of a chessboard. If you try to access an array element that does not exist, an error occurs. After the preceding declaration, for example, this statement would generate a run-time error because the second array index is out of bounds:

```
ChessBoard(2,8) = "White King"
```

You can determine the size of an array using the `UBound` function, which is one of VBScript's many built in functions. The syntax is as follows:

UBound(*arrayname*, *dimension*)

Arrayname is the name of the array, without parentheses. *Dimension* is an optional argument specifying which dimension you are interested in: 1 (the default) for the first dimension, 2 for the second, and so on. The function returns the highest legal index for the specified dimension of the array. If you pass a nonexistent dimension argument, a run-time error occurs. Table 6-3 presents some examples of using the `UBound` function.

TABLE 6-3 *Using the UBound function to determine array size.*

Array declaration	UBound call	Value of x
Array(50)	x = UBound(Array)	50
Array(10,20)	x = UBound(Array,2)	20
Array(100)	x = UBound(Array,2)	An error occurs because the array does not have a second dimension.

Here is an example of using the `UBound` function. This code determines the sum of all values stored in the first dimension of the array X, without knowing ahead of time how large the array is. This code makes use of the `For...Next` loop, a VBScript statement that will be covered in Chapter 7.

```
For i = 0 To UBound(X)
    total = total + X(i)
Next
```

The `UBound` function is particularly useful with dynamic arrays, which are covered next.

Dynamic Arrays

Unlike a static array, a dynamic array does not have a fixed size. You can change the number of array elements, and even the number of dimensions, while the script is running. The syntax for declaring a dynamic array is the same as for static arrays except that no indexes are specified — the parentheses are left blank:

```
Dim arrayname()
```

Before you can use a dynamic array, you must set its initial size using the `ReDim` statement:

```
ReDim arrayname(indexes)
```

The *indexes* argument specifies the number of dimensions and the number of elements, using the same syntax as you learned for declaring static arrays. Here are some examples:

```
Dim Array1()
Dim Array2()
Dim Array3()
...
Redim Array1(10)'   1 dimension, 11 elements 0-10.
Redim Array2(20)'   1 dimension, 21 elements 0-20.
ReDim Array3(4, 9)' 2 dimensions, 50 total elements.
```

After the initial size setting, you can change the array size as many times as needed. The syntax is

```
ReDim Preserve arrayname(indexes)
```

Indexes specify the new array size, as before. The optional `Preserve` keyword is used when you want the existing data in the array to be kept. If you do not use `Preserve` the array will be reinitialized and existing data lost when you execute `ReDim`. There are some limitations on the use of `Preserve`:

- If you make an array smaller, the data in the part of the array that is "trimmed off" will be lost.
- You cannot change the number of dimensions of the array when you use `Preserve`.
- If the array is multidimensional, you can change only the last dimension.

Dynamic arrays are very useful when you do not know how much data you will have. The example in Listing 6-1 uses a dynamic array to store names entered by the user, expanding the array as needed. Then all the names are printed. This script uses the `UBound` function, which you learned about in the previous section of this chapter. Note in this code that the first element of the array — with index 0 — is never used. This was done so that the NameCount variable would accurately reflect the number of names while also being used as the array index.

LISTING 6–1 *Working with dynamic arrays in VBScript.*

```
' List0601.vbs
' Working with dynamic arrays

Option Explicit

Dim Names()
Dim NameCount
Dim NewName
Dim Message
Dim i

NameCount = 0

' Loop to input names.
Do
    NewName = InputBox("Enter a name, a blank when finished:")
    If NewName = "" Then Exit Do
    NameCount = NameCount + 1
    ReDim Preserve Names(NameCount)
    Names(NameCount) = NewName
Loop While True

' Construct the output message.
Message = "You entered these names:"& vbCRLF

for i = 1 to UBound(Names)
    Message = Message & Names(i) & vbCRLF
Next

MsgBox Message
```

The `Erase` statement

You use the `Erase` statement to reinitialize arrays. The syntax is

```
Erase arrayname
```

When used with static arrays, `Erase` reinitializes all array elements. With dynamic arrays, this statement deallocates the array storage space. In both cases the effect is to return the array to its state immediately after it was declared.

Variant Arrays

In addition to the explicitly declared arrays that we have just covered, VBScript also permits you to store an array in a simple variant variable. There are not all that many programming situations where you would need this technique, but it can be useful to know. This technique involves using the `Array` function, one of the VBScript built-in functions. You pass this function a list of the values that you want in the array, and it returns a variant containing the array. Here's an example.

```
Dim VA
VA = Array("apple", "pear", "peach", "grape")
```

After this code executes, VA(0) evaluates as "apple," VA(1) as "pear," and so on. You can go back to using the variable to store a single value at any time. To determine whether a variable contains an array, use the `IsArray` function. The syntax is

```
IsArray(variablename)
```

The function returns True if the variable contains an array, False otherwise.

Operators

An operator is a symbol that instructs VBScript to manipulate or combine data. Adding or subtracting two numbers is a common example. VBScript operators fall into several categories.

Assignment Operator

The most fundamental operator is the assignment operator, represented by the equal sign. When the assignment operator is used in a statement, the value of the expression on the right side of the operator is assigned to the variable on the left side of the operator. For example, the statement

```
a = b + c + d
```

adds the values in variables b, c, and d and assigns the result to variable a.

Arithmetic Operators

The arithmetic operators perform mathematical operations. There are the common operations of addition, subtraction, multiplication, and division that everyone knows about, as well as a few more specialized operations. The arithmetic operators available in VBScript are summarized in Table 6-4.

TABLE 6-4 *The arithmetic operators.*

Operator	Description	Example
+	Addition	5 + 12 evaluates to 17
–	Subtraction	17 – 7 evaluates to 10
*	Multiplication	3 * 2.5 evaluates to 7.5
/	Division	63 / 3 evaluates to 21
\	Integer division	10 \ 3 evaluates to 3
^	Exponentiation (to the power of)	3 ^ 2 evaluates to 9
mod	Modulus (remainder after division)	33 mod 6 evaluates to 3

Please keep the following points in mind when using the arithmetic operators:

- For both regular and integer division, the divisor must not be equal to 0 or a run-time error occurs.
- Integer division does not round off the answer but simply discards any fractional part. Thus both 41\10 and 49\10 evaluate to 4.
- Exponentiation requires that if the number being raised is negative, then the exponent must be an integer. If not, no error occurs but the exponent is rounded off before the calculation is performed.
- If floating point numbers are used with `mod`, they are rounded to integers before the calculation is performed.

String Operators

There is a single string operation called *concatenation*. The operator for this is the & symbol. Concatenation combines two strings. For example, after this code

```
MyString = "Windows " & "Scripting"
```

the variable MyString contains "Windows Scripting". There are lots of other things you can do with strings, but they involve functions, not operators. You'll learn more in Chapter 8.

Comparison Operators

The comparison operators perform comparisons between two expressions. The result of a comparison is either True or False depending on whether the comparison is true or not. Table 6-5 lists the comparison operators that are most commonly used with numeric expressions.

TABLE 6-5 *The numerical comparison operators.*

Operator	Comparison
=	Is equal to?
>	Is greater than?
<	Is less than?
>=	Is greater than or equal to?
<=	Is less than or equal to?
<>	Is not equal to?

For example, the expression

```
x > y
```

asks the question "is x greater than y?" and returns either True or False depending on the values of the two variables.

These operators can also be used to perform string comparisons. Strings are compared character by character, with order determined by the ASCII value of characters (ASCII refers to the numerical codes that VBScript uses internally to represent letters and other characters). For the letters of the alphabet this results in the standard alphabetical order we are all used to, with "a" being considered to be less than "c." Because upper- and lowercase letters have different ASCII values, we have the strange situation where any uppercase letter is considered to be less than its lowercase counterpart. For example, "Z" is less than "a". Since this is usually not what you want when doing string comparisons, you can use the `UCase` function to convert the strings you are comparing to all uppercase. Then the comparison operators will perform an alphabetic order comparison as desired. For example,

```
"aardvark" < "Zebra"
```

will return False, but

```
UCase("aardvark") < UCase("Zebra")
```

will return True.

There is one special comparison operator that is used with object references. The `Is` operator is used to compare two object references and determine if they refer to the same object. The expression

```
obj1 Is obj2
```

returns True if obj1 and obj2 refer to the same object, False if they do not. You can use `Is` in conjunction with the `Nothing` keyword to determine if an object reference has been initialized. The expression

```
obj1 Is Nothing
```

evaluates as True if obj1 has not been initialized to refer to an object, False if obj1 refers to any object.

Logical Operators

The logical operators are used to manipulate logical (True/False) expressions. Most of the logical operators combine two logical expressions into a single logical value. There are plenty of examples of this in your daily life. Suppose you want to buy a stereo that has surround sound, at least 100 watts of power, and a CD player. Your decision could be stated logically like this:

```
BuyStereo = (surround sound?) and (100 watts?) and (CD player?)
```

In other words, BuyStereo will be True only if all three of the conditions are True. This makes use of the and operator. This and the other logical operators are described in Table 6-6.

TABLE 6-6 *The logical operators. X and Y are both assumed to be logical expressions.*

Operator	Example	Evaluation
And	X And Y	True if both X and Y are True; False otherwise.
Or	X Or Y	True if X or Y, or both of them, are True; False only if both X and Y are False.
Xor (exclusive Or)	X Xor Y	True if X and Y are different (one True and the other False); False if both are True or both are False.
Eqv (Equivalence)	X Eqv Y	True if X and Y are the same (both True or both False); False otherwise.
Imp (Implication)	X Imp Y	False only if X is True and Y is False; True otherwise.
Not	Not X	True if X is False, False if X is True.

The logical operators are often used in conjunction with the comparison operators. For example, the following expression evaluates as True only if x is equal to 4 and y is not equal to 2.

```
(x = 4) And (y <> 2)
```

Operator Precedence and Parentheses

If an expression contains more than one operator, it may not always be clear how the expression evaluates. Here is an example:

```
15 + 3 * 4
```

If the addition is performed first, it evaluates to 72 (15 plus 3 is 18, 18 times 4 is 72); but if the multiplication is performed first, the result is 27 (3 times 4 is 12, 12 plus 15 is 27). Such potentially ambiguous expressions are resolved by VBScript's rules of operator precedence. These rules specify the order in which operations are performed The precedence of the operators is given in Table 6-7. Operators with low precedence numbers are performed first.

TABLE 6-7 *VBA Operator precedence.*

Operator	Precedence
Exponentiation ^	1
Multiplication (*), division (/)	2
Integer division (\)	3
Modulus (Mod)	4
Addition (+), subtraction (-)	5
String concatenation (&)	6

Returning to the original example, you can see that because multiplication has a higher precedence than addition, the expression will evaluate to 27. For operators that have the same precedence level, such as multiplication and division, the order of execution is always left to right.

You can modify the order of execution by using parentheses in an expression. Parts of an expression within parentheses are always evaluated first regardless of operator precedence. Thus

```
(15 + 3) * 4
```

evaluates to 72 because the parentheses force the addition to be performed before the multiplication. You can use as many parentheses in an expression as you like, as long as they always come in pairs; each left parenthesis must have a matching right parenthesis. When parentheses are nested (one set inside another set), execution starts with the innermost set and proceeds outward.

Overview

Almost every script works with data of one kind or another, and as this chapter showed you, VBScript has a wide range of data storage and manipulation tools suitable for just about any circumstance. By having only a single data type, the `Variant`, VBScript avoids some of the confusion that can arise in other languages when dealing with multiple data types. Perhaps the most important single lesson you should take from this chapter is to use the `Option Explicit` statement at the start of every script so that VBScript will not permit you to use a variable without declaring it. This simple step will save you plenty of headaches that would otherwise be caused by misspelled variable names.

SEVEN

VBScript: Program Control and Procedures

Unless programmed otherwise, the code in a script will execute in top-down order, from the first statement to the last. This is OK for simple scripts, but as your script programs become more sophisticated you'll find that this simple flow of execution is not adequate. It is not sufficient simply to write the code that performs the required tasks — you must also control which code is executed, when it is executed, and how many times it is executed. Conditional statements control the order of code execution. Defined blocks of code may be executed, or not executed, based on variable conditions in the program as it is executing. Loop statements repeat blocks of code zero, one, or more times as required. Procedures let you separate code into discrete, named sections that can be executed by a single function call whenever needed. These VBScript program control capabilities are the topic of this chapter.

Conditional Statements

Conditional statements are used to control the execution of other VBScript statements. Using conditional statements, you can specify that certain code in your program either is or is not executed, depending on conditions in the program — hence the term *conditional*. VBScript offers two conditional statements.

If. . .Then. . .Else

The `If...Then...Else` statement executes a block of one or more VBScript statements only if a specified logical expression is True. Optionally, a second block of statements is executed only if the expression is False. The syntax is as follows:

```
If condition Then
    block1
Else
    block2
End If
```

Condition is a logical expression. If *condition* evaluates as True, the statements in *block1* are executed. If *condition* is False, the statements in *block2* are executed. The `Else` keyword and the second block of statements are optional; you can write an `If` statement like this:

```
If condition Then
    block1
End If
```

In this case, no statements are executed when *condition* is False. If you have only a single statement to be executed when *condition* is True, you can place it on the same line as the `If` keyword and omit the `End If`:

```
If condition Then statement
```

For more flexibility, you can use the `ElseIf` keyword in an `If` statement to test multiple conditions. The syntax is as follows:

```
If condition1 Then
    block1
ElseIf condition2 Then
    block2
ElseIf condition3 Then
    block3
....
Else
    block4
End If
```

There is no limit to the number of `ElseIf` blocks. The various conditions are tested one at a time, starting at the top. As soon as one is found that is True, the associated block of statements is executed and execution exits the `If` statement. If no true condition is found, the block following the `Else` keyword is executed. Note that at most one block of statements will be executed regardless of how many of the conditions are true. Note also that the `Else` keyword and its associated block of statements are again optional.

The script in Listing 7-1 illustrates use of the `If...Then...Else` statement. It prompts the user to enter a number then uses an `If...Then...Else` statement to display a message indicating whether the number if less than, equal to, or greater than 0.

LISTING 7–1 *Demonstrating the* `If...Then...Else` *statement.*

```
' List0701.vbs
' Using the If...Then...Else statement.

Option Explicit

Dim reply
Dim msg

reply = InputBox("Enter any number:")

If reply < 0 then
    msg = "Your number is less than 0."
Elseif reply = 0 then
    msg = "Your number is 0."
Else
    msg = "Your number is greater than 0."
End If

MsgBox msg
```

When you have multiple conditions to be tested, it is usually easier to use the `Select Case` statement, covered next.

Select Case

The `Select Case` statement is similar to the `If...Then...Else` statement you just learned since it executes or does not execute blocks of statements based on the evaluation of an expression. Specifically, this statement evaluates a single expression, then executes one of several blocks of statements depending on the evaluation result. The syntax is

```
Select Case expression
    Case result-1
        statements-1
    Case result-2
        statements-2
    ....
    Case result-n
        statements-n
    Case Else
        statements-else
End Select
```

First, *expression* is evaluated. The result is matched against the various cases, in order from top to bottom. When a match is found, the following block of one or more statements is executed. If no match is found, the statements following the Case Else are executed. The Case Else keyword and its associated block of statements are optional but again are recommended for good coding to deal with unexpected situations. At most a single block of statements will be executed — the block following the first matching result. If there is no Case Else, it is possible that no statements in the Select Case will be executed.

Each result in a Select Case statement can contain one or more possible evaluation results, separated by commas. The following test expression, for example, would be considered a match if the test expression was 1, 2, or 99:

```
Case 1, 2, 99
```

String comparisons in a Select Case statement are case sensitive. To obtain case-insensitive matches, use the UCase function to convert the test expression to all uppercase, then code your results in uppercase as well. For example, if the test expression is a variable named fruit,

```
x = UCase(fruit)
Select Case x
    Case "APPLE"
    Case "PEACH"
...
End Select
```

Listing 7-2 shows how to use the Select Case statement in a script. This script is a variation on the one you saw in Listing 7-1, using Select Case instead of If...Then...Else.

LISTING 7–2 *Demonstrating the Select Case statement.*

```
' List0702.vbs
' Using the Select Case statement.

Option Explicit

Dim reply
Dim msg

reply = InputBox("Enter a number between 1 and 10:")

Select Case reply
    Case 1, 2
      msg = "Your number is 1 or 2."
    Case 3, 4
      msg = "Your number is 3 or 4."
    Case 4
      msg = "Your number is between 5 and 10!"
    Case Else
      msg = "Number out of range."
End Select

MsgBox msg
```

Loop Statements

VBScript's loop statements are used to execute a block of one or more statements a certain number of times. The `For...Next` and `For Each...Next` statements are used to execute a block of code a specified number of times. The `Do...Loop` statement executes statements repeatedly until a specified logical condition is met.

For . . . Next

The `For...Next` statement executes a block of statements a specified number of times. The syntax is

```
For counter = start To stop Step step
    ...
    statements
    ...
Next
```

Counter is a variable used as the loop counter. *Start* and *stop* are the starting and ending values of counter. *Step* is a numerical expression that specifies the increment for *counter*. The "`Step` *step*" part of the statement is optional; if omitted, an increment of 1 is used. Here's how the `For...Next` statement operates:

1. When execution reaches the `For` statement, *counter* is set equal to *start*.
2. *Counter* is compared to *stop*. If *counter* is less than or equal to *stop*, the statements in the loop are executed. If *counter* is greater than *stop*, execution passes to the first statement following `Next`.
3. *Counter* is incremented by the value of *step* (or by 1 if *step* is omitted).
4. Return to step 2.

For example, this simple loop sets the values of the array to 0, 10, 20, ... 1000.

```
Dim MyArray(100)
Dim i

For i = 0 To 100
    MyArray(i) = i * 10
Next
```

Code inside the loop should never change the value of the counter variable.

If you use a negative value for *step*, the `For...Next` loop will count down rather than up. When you do this, *start* must be greater than *stop*, and the loop terminates when *counter* is less than *stop*. Here's an example, which fills the elements of the array in reverse order resulting in the values 100, 99, . . . 0.

```
Dim MyArray(100)
Dim i

For i = 100 To 0 Step -1
    MyArray(i) = 100 - i
Next
```

To exit from a `For ... Next` loop before the counter variable reaches its final value, use the `Exit For` statement. You can have as many `Exit For` statements in the loop as you like. As soon as any one of them is executed, the loop terminates immediately. Here's an example, which determines if there is at least one element equal to "pizza" in a string array named Foods. Note the use of the `UBound` function to determine the array's upper boundaries.

```
Dim found
found = False
For i = 0 To UBound(Foods)
    If Foods(i) = "pizza" Then
        found = True
        Exit For
    End If
Next
```

You can nest `For...Next` loops within each other. The only requirement is that each inner loop be totally within the outer loop. Here's an example.

```
For i = 1 To 100
    For j = 10 To 20
        For k = 50 to 30 Step -1
        ....
        Next k
    Next j
Next i
```

For Each . . . Next

The `For Each...Next` loop executes a group of statements once for each element of a collection or an array. The syntax is

```
For Each item in group
    ...
    statements
    ...
Next
```

Item is the variable used to iterate through the collection. *Group* is the name of the collection or array. The statements are executed once for each element in the collection or array. Each time the loop executes, the *item* variable will refer to the next item in *group*. Here's an example that sets the `Color` property of all objects in the collection to Red:

```
Dim obj

For Each obj In MyCollection
    obj.Color = "Red"
Next
```

To exit a `For Each...Next` loop early, use the `Exit For` statement, as described above for the `For...Next` loop. Listing 7-3 demonstrates using a `For Each...Next` loop with an array.

LISTING 7-3 *Using the* `For Each . . . Next` *loop.*

```
' List0703.vbs
' Using the For Each ... Next loop.

Option Explicit

Dim va
Dim item
Dim msg

va = Array("red", "blue", "green")

msg = "The array contains:" & vbCRLF

For Each item in va
    msg = msg & item & vbCrLf
Next

MsgBox msg
```

When using `For Each...Next` with an array, the array can be a static array, a dynamic array, or a type `Variant` array.

Do . . . Loop

The `Do...Loop` statement executes a block of statements zero, one, or more times depending on a specified logical condition. There are several variants of this statement, each of which is suitable to specific programming situations. In the simplest variation, the condition is tested at the start of the loop. You can execute statements repeatedly as long as a logical condition is True using the `While` keyword:

```
Do While condition
    ...
    statements
    ...
Loop
```

You can also execute statements repeatedly as long as a condition is False; use the `Until` keyword:

```
Do Until condition
    ...
    statements
    ...
Loop
```

Here's how it works. When execution reaches the `Do` statement, *condition* is evaluated. If it is True (if using `While`) or False (if using `Until`) the statements are executed and then *condition* is evaluated again. This continues until the value of *condition* changes. Note that depending on the initial value of *condition*, this syntax creates the possibility that the statements in the loop may not be executed even once.

The other variant of the `Do...Loop` statement tests the condition at the end of the loop. Again, you have the choice between the `While` or `Until` keywords:

```
Do
    ...
    statements
    ...
Loop While condition

Do
    ...
    statements
    ...
Loop Until condition
```

With this syntax, the statements are executed once and then *condition* is evaluated. If it is True (for `While`) or False (for `Until`) the statements are executed again, and the process repeats. When the condition is tested at the end of the loop, you are guaranteed that the statements in the loop will be executed at least once.

To exit a `Do...Loop` early, use the `Exit Do` statement. Here's an example. The following loop executes until either A or B is greater than 10:

```
Do Until A > 10
    ....
    If B > 10 Then Exit Do
    ....
Loop
```

You may have realized that the same result could be obtained as follows, using the logical operator `Or`:

```
Do Until A > 10 Or B > 10
    ....
Loop
```

However, the first example using `Exit Do` provides you with the additional flexibility to exit from within the block of code in the loop, allowing prior statements to complete.

Listing 7-4 presents a script that illustrates use of the `Do...Loop` statement.

LISTING 7–4 *Demonstrating the `Do...Loop` statement.*

```
' List0704.vbs
' Using the Do...Loop statement.

Option Explicit

Dim reply

Do
    reply = InputBox("In what country is Paris located?")
Loop Until UCase(reply) = "FRANCE"

msgbox "That is correct!"
```

While . . . Wend

The `While...Wend` is a simpler but less flexible way to accomplish one of the things that the `Do...Loop` statement can do. Its syntax is

```
While condition
    ...
    statements
    ...
Wend
```

The statements in the loop are executed repeatedly as long as *condition* is True. The exact same thing can be accomplished with a `Do...Loop` statement, as follows:

```
Do While condition
    ...
    statements
    ...
Loop
```

Because of its greater flexibility and expandability, the `Do...Loop` statement should be used in preference to `While...Wend`.

Infinite Loops

When writing `Do...Loop` and `While...Wend` statements, you must always be aware of the danger of *infinite loops*, loops that will repeat forever. This will happen if, once a loop starts executing, there is nothing to change the value of the test condition. Here's an example:

```
Dim index
Dim Array(50)
index = 0
Do
    Array(index) = -22
Loop Until index = 50
```

Do you see the problem? There is no code in the loop to increment the variable index, so the loop will run forever and the program will stop responding. Here's the solution:

```
Do
    Array(index) = -22
    index = index + 1
Loop Until index = 50
```

Procedures

Procedures are an important element of script programming. Except for relatively simple scripts, you will find that a lot of your script code will be inside procedures. A procedure is a section of code that has been assigned a name. When you need to execute that code, you refer to its name in your program. This is referred to as *calling* the procedure.

Typically, procedures are used when you have a section of code that performs a discrete task, particularly when that task is something your scripts will need to do more than once. When you create a procedure to perform a task, you need write the code only once. Then you can call the procedure as many times as needed from your script. What's more, procedures can be copied from one script and used in other scripts, which can save the script programmer a lot of time. More important, maintenance can be performed in one place, preventing the problem of having to fix the same problem in many places throughout your code.

Types of Procedures

VBScript provides you with two different types of procedures:

- A sub procedure is an independent, named section of code that performs some action.
- A function procedure is identical to a sub procedure except it also returns data to the calling program (a sub procedure has no return value).

Except for returning a value, functions and subs are essentially identical. What code can you put in a procedure? Just about anything, including variable declarations. The only major exclusion is that you cannot define one procedure within another.

Defining a Procedure

The syntax for defining a procedure is quite similar for both sub and function procedures. For a sub procedure, the basic syntax is as follows:

```
Sub subname(argumentlist)
    ...
    ' Code goes here
    ...
End Sub
```

Subname is the name of the sub procedure, following the same VBScript naming rules that you learned in Chapter 6. The name must be unique within the script. The *argumentlist* specifies arguments (data) that are passed to the procedure when it is called. The details of passing arguments will be discussed soon. A procedure may have no arguments, in which case the name should be followed by an empty set of parentheses.

The syntax for defining a function procedure is almost identical:

```
Function functionname(argumentlist)
    ...
    ' Code goes here
    ...
    functionname = returnvalue
End Function
```

Functionname uniquely identifies the function and again follows the same VBScript naming rules. The *argumentlist* specifies arguments (data) that are passed to the function. The actual data that is returned by the function is specified by assigning a value to the function name within the body of the function, in this case *returnvalue*. If the return type is an object type, then you must use the `Set` statement to assign the return value:

```
Set functionname = returnobjectreference
```

If you do not explicitly assign a return value to a function, the return value will depend on the type of the function declaration. However, you should ensure that all functions have an explicitly assigned return value to avoid bugs.

Passing Arguments to Procedures

A procedure can be defined to accept as many arguments as required. Each argument represents a piece of data that is passed to the procedure when it is called. Argument syntax is identical for sub and function procedures. The *argumentlist* has the following basic syntax:

```
argname1, argname2, .....
```

Each *argname* is a unique name that follows VBScript's standard naming rules. Within the procedure, each argument is available as a regular variable. Here's an example of a function that takes one argument:

```
Function OneThirdOf(x)

     OneThirdOf = x / 3

End Function
```

To pass an array as a procedure argument, use the array name with an empty set of parentheses in the argument list. Here's a procedure that returns the sum of all elements of an array.

```
Function SumArray(array())

    Dim i
    Dim sum

    For i = 0 To UBound(array)
        sum = sum + array(i)
    Next

    SumArray = sum

End Function
```

PASSING PROCEDURE ARGUMENTS BYVAL AND BYREF

An argument to a procedure can be passed in one of two ways. *By reference* passes a reference to the original argument's location in memory, whereas *by value* creates a copy of the argument and passes the copy. The main practical difference between these two methods of passing arguments is that when an argument is passed by reference, the code in the procedure has access to the original copy of the argument and can therefore change it. When an argument is passed by value, code in the procedure cannot change the original argument. Of course, this is relevant only when a variable is passed as an argument and does not apply when a constant is passed. VBScript's default is to pass arguments by reference. To pass an argument by value, precede the argument name with the `ByVal` keyword:

```
Sub MySub(ByVal X)
    ...
End Sub
```

In general, procedure code should not change the value of arguments passed to the procedure. If you need to return data to the calling program, use a function. However, for specialized programming situations you can use by reference arguments to "return" multiple data items from a procedure.

Variables in Procedures

You can declare variables and arrays inside a procedure, without any limitations. Variables declared within a procedure are called *local* variables because they are not visible outside the procedure. Two procedures, therefore, can each have a variable named Count and they will be completely separate and independent. Variables declared outside of any procedure are referred to as *global* variables because they are visible throughout the script. It is good practice to limit the use of global variables to situations where they are really needed.

Local variables are created and initialized each time the procedure is called, and destroyed when the procedure terminates. Even if a procedure calls itself (a technique called *recursion*), each instance of the procedure is separate and has its own, independent set of local variables. Any variable declared inside a procedure is distinct from a global variable of the same name (declared outside a procedure). If, however, the procedure does not declare a variable of a given name, then inside the procedure a global variable of that name declared outside the procedure is available. The code snippets presented here will help to clarify.

```
' Declared outside any procedure.
Dim X
Dim Y

X = 1
Y = 2
' In this script, anywhere outside a procedure, X has the
' value 1 and Y has the value 2. Z is not visible.

Sub Procedure1()

' Declared inside a procedure.
Dim X
Dim Z
X = 99
Z = 5

' Inside this procedure X has the value 99,
' Y has the value 2, and Z has the value 5.

End Sub

Sub Procedure2()

' Declared inside a procedure.
Dim Y
Y = 0

' Inside this procedure X has the value 1,
' Y has the value 0, and Z is not visible.

End Sub
```

The script presented in Listing 7-5 demonstrates the relationship between local and global variables.

LISTING 7–5 *Demonstrating local and global script variables.*

```
' List0705.vbs
' Demonstrating local variables.

Option Explicit

Dim x
Dim y
Dim msg

x = "outside"
y = "outside"

msg = "Outside the procedure x = "
msg = msg & x & " and y = " & y
msgbox msg

' Call the procedure.
Sub1

Sub Sub1()

    Dim x
    Dim msg

    x = "inside"

    msg = "Inside the procedure x = "
    msg = msg & x & " and y = " & y

    Msgbox msg

End Sub
```

Calling Procedures

To execute the code in a procedure — in other words, to *call* the procedure — you use a different syntax for sub and function procedures. Because a function returns a value, it is in effect an expression, and you call it by referring to it anywhere an expression could be used. Perhaps most commonly, a function is called by referring to it on the right side of an assignment statement. If you have a function named OneThirdOf, for example, you could call it and assign the return value to X as follows:

```
x = OneThirdOf(y)
```

Or, you could call the function and display the return value in a message window:

```
Msgbox OneThirdOf(104)
```

Calling sub procedures is different. Because they do not return a value, they cannot be treated as an expression. You can use the `Call` keyword to call a sub procedure:

```
Call ProcedureName(argumentlist)
```

Or, you can omit the `Call` keyword, in which case the parentheses are omitted as well:

```
ProcedureName argumentlist
```

You can use either of these syntaxes to call a function as well as a sub. In this case the function's return value is ignored.

Overview

VBScript provides a rich set of tools for controlling script execution. The conditional statements let a script determine which code is executed based on conditions defined by the programmer. The loop statements are used to execute sections of code repeatedly, as dictated by the needs of the script. Procedures permit discrete sections of code to be called as needed and reused in multiple scripts. These VBScript capabilities are essential for writing anything but very simple scripts.

EIGHT

VBScript: Working with Text, Numbers, Dates, and Times

Most of the scripts you write will work with data of one kind or another. The data will almost always fall into one of three categories: text, numbers, and dates/times. Within each of these categories, VBScript offers you a full range of tools to work with the data.

Text Manipulation

Text data, or *strings* as they are called in VBScript, is an important part of many scripts. Many essential types of information are maintained as strings, and the ability to work with string data is an essential part of the VBScript programmer's skills. Fortunately for us, the language provides a powerful set of tools for string manipulation. Table 8-1 presents an overview of built-in VBScript string manipulation functions. Following the table, the individual functions are explained in detail (in alphabetical order).

TABLE 8-1 *Summary of VBScript's string manipulation statements, functions, and objects.*

Task	Built-in Functions
Compare two strings	StrComp
Combine or separate strings	Join, Split
Convert to lowercase or uppercase	LCase, UCase
Create string of repeating character	Space, String
Extract part of a string	Mid function, Left, Right
Find one string in another	InStr, InStrRev
Find a string in an array	Filter
Sophisticated string searches	RegExp object
Find length of a string	Len
Trim leading and/or trailing spaces	LTrim, RTrim, Trim
Work with ASCII and ANSI values	Asc, Chr

Asc

A computer uses numeric codes to represent the characters of text, such as letters and punctuation marks. These are called the ASCII codes. The `Asc` function returns an integer specifying the numeric ASCII code of its argument. The syntax is

```
Asc(string)
```

If *string* is more than one character long, the function returns the code of the first character in the string. Appendix 3 presents a list of the ASCII character codes. See the `Chr` function for converting a code into a character.

Chr

The `Chr` function returns the character represented by a specific ASCII code. It is useful for obtaining characters that are not on the keyboard, such as a right arrow (code = 26), or characters that cannot be entered directly into strings, such as the double quote (code = 34). The syntax is

```
Chr(code)
```

Code is a character code in the range 0–255. See Appendix 3 for a list of characters and their codes. Listing 8-1 shows how to use this function to include double quote characters in a string. This is not straightforward since double quotes are used to delimit strings in the code. The output of the script in Listing 8-1 is:

```
Bill said to Mary, "I love you."
```

LISTING 8-1 *Using the Chr function to include a double quote in a string.*

```
' List0801.vbs
' Using the Chr function.

Option Explicit

Dim msg

msg = "Bill said to Mary, " & Chr(34) & "I love you." & Chr(34)
Msgbox msg
```

Working with double quotes

In addition to using Chr(34), VBScript offers two other ways to include a double quote character in a string: using single quotes or using a pair of double quotes. The following two lines have the same effect as the example in Listing 8-1:

```
msg = "Bill said to Mary, " & '"' & "I love you." & '"'
msg = "Bill said to Mary, ""I love you."""
```

Filter

The `Filter` function searches a one-dimensional array of strings and returns a subset of that array based on search criteria. The syntax is

`Filter(`*`InputStrings, Value, Include, Compare`*`)`

Inputstrings is a one-dimensional array of string data. If this argument is `Null` or is not a one-dimensional array, an error occurs.

Value is the string to search for.

Include is an optional Boolean argument. If set to True (the default), the function returns those strings that contain *value*. If set to False, the function returns those strings that do not contain *value*.

Compare is an optional constant that specifies the type of comparison. Possible settings are `vbTextCompare` (value = 1), where upper- and lowercase letters match, and `vbBinaryCompare` (0), where different case letters (e.g., "A" and "a") do not match. If this argument is omitted, the search is done as a binary comparison.

The function's return value is a `Variant` array. If there is no match found, the returned array is empty. Listing 8-2 shows how to use the `Filter` function. The script performs two searches of the same array, one with the default *include* setting and the other with *include* set to False. Figure 8-1 shows the two message boxes displayed by the program.

FIGURE 8-1 *The output of Listing 8-1.*

LISTING 8-2 *Using the Filter function.*

```
' List0802.vbs
' Using the Filter function.

Option Explicit

Dim ArrayToSearch(4)
Dim Results
Dim item
Dim msg

ArrayToSearch(0) = "Smith"
ArrayToSearch(1) = "Smithfield"
ArrayToSearch(2) = "Smithson"
ArrayToSearch(3) = "Black"
ArrayToSearch(4) = "Jones"

Results = Filter(ArrayToSearch, "Smith")

msg = ""
for each item in Results
    msg = msg & item & vbCRLF
next

msgbox msg

Results = Filter(ArrayToSearch, "Smith", False)

msg = ""
for each item in Results
    msg = msg & item & vbCRLF
next

msgbox msg
```

InStr, InStrRev

To find the first occurrence of one string within another, use the `InStr` function. `InStrRev` does the same thing but starts looking at the end of the string rather than at the beginning. The syntax is

```
InStr(start, stringcheck, stringmatch, compare)
InstrRev(stringcheck, stringmatch, start, compare)
```

Stringcheck is the string being searched.

Stringmatch is the string you are looking for.

Start is an optional argument specifying the character position in *stringcheck* where the search is to begin. If omitted, `InStr` starts at the first character (position 1) and `InStrRev` starts at the last character.

Compare is an optional constant that specifies the type of comparison. Possible settings are `vbTextCompare` (1), where upper- and lowercase letters match, and `vbBinaryCompare` (0), where different case letters (e.g., "A" and "a") do not match. If this argument is omitted, the search is done as a binary comparison.

The return value of these functions is the character position at which the first match was found, or 0 if there is no match. The function returns `Null` if either *stringcheck* or *stringmatch* is `Null`. Table 8-2 shows some examples of using these functions.

TABLE 8-2 *Using InStr and InStrRev.*

Example	Return value
InStr(, "Mississippi", "ss")	3
InStrRev("Mississippi", "ss")	6
InStr(, "MISSISSIPPI", "ss")	0
InStr(, "MISSISSIPPI", "ss", vbTextCompare)	3

InStrRev

See `Instr`.

Join

The `Join` function creates a string by joining multiple substrings contained in an array. The syntax is

```
Join(list, delimiter)
```

List is a one-dimensional array containing the substrings. *Delimiter* is an optional argument specifying the character to place between the substrings. If this argument is omitted, substrings are separated by a single space. Here's an example:

```
Dim Result
Dim MyArray(2)
MyArray(0) = "Pizza"
MyArray(1) = "with"
MyArray(2) = "anchovies"
Result = Join(MyArray)
```

The variable Result contains "Pizza with anchovies". If you want no separator between the substrings, pass an empty string as the *delimiter* argument:

```
Delimiter = ""
Result = Join(MyArray, Delimiter)
```

After this code, Result contains "Pizzawithanchovies".

LCase, UCase

These functions convert a string to all uppercase (`UCase`) or all lowercase (`LCase`). The syntax is

```
LCase(string)
UCase(string)
```

The return value of the function is *string* with all letters converted to the designated case. Nonletter characters in *string* are not modified. Note that the original string is not modified. Look at this code fragment:

```
S1 = "Alaska"
S2 = UCase(S1)
```

After this code executes, S1 still contains "Alaska" while S2 contains "ALASKA".

Left, Mid, Right

The `Left`, `Mid`, and `Right` functions extract a portion of a string. `Left` extracts characters from the start of a string, `Mid` extracts them from the middle of a string, and `Right` extracts them from the end of a string. The syntax is

```
Left(string, n)
Right(string, n)
Mid(string, start, n)
```

String is the string to extract from.

N is the number of characters to extract. If *n* is greater than or equal to the length of *string*, then the entire string is returned.

Start is the character position at which to start extracting.

Table 8-3 illustrates the use of these functions.

TABLE 8-3 *Examples of the Left, Mid, and Right functions.*

Example	Return value
Left("VBScript Programming", 5)	"VBScr"
Right("VBScript Programming ", 2)	"ng"
Mid("VBScript Programming ", 2, 7)	"BScript"

Len

The `Len` function returns the number of characters in a string. The syntax is

```
Len(string)
```

If *string* contains `Null`, then `Null` is returned. Remember that spaces count as characters.

LTrim, RTrim, Trim

These functions remove leading and/or trailing spaces from a string. The syntax is

```
LTrim(string)
RTrim(string)
Trim(string)
```

The return value is *string* minus any leading spaces (`LTrim`), trailing spaces (`RTrim`), or both leading and trailing spaces (`Trim`). Here are some examples.

```
RTrim("      VBScript      ") returns "      VBScript"
LTrim("      VBScript      ") returns "VBScript      "
Trim ("      VBScript      ") returns "VBScript"
```

Mid (function)

See `Left`.

RegExp

The `RegExp` object provides support for regular expression searches in your scripts. Regular expressions are a powerful text search method that provides a great deal of flexibility and power. Rather than simply matching one string against another, regular expressions permit you to search for combinations of characters (for example, match "go" or "to"), special characters (such as tabs and line feeds), certain types of characters (for example, match any digit), and so on. The `RegExp` object has three properties and three methods, which are explained in Tables 8-4 and 8-5.

TABLE 8-4 *Properties of the RegExp object.*

Property	Description
Global	Set to True for a search to cover the entire string, or to False to detect only the first match. The default is False.
IgnoreCase	Set to True for a case-insensitive match. The default is False.
Pattern	The string being searched for. Can include regular expression characters as described in Table 8-6.

TABLE 8-5 *Methods of the RegExp object.*

Method	Description
Execute(*string*)	Executes a regular expression search against *string*. The return value is a `Matches` collection containing one `Match` object for each match that was found.
Replace(*string1*, *string2*)	Replaces each occurrence of the *pattern* property in *string1* with *string2*. The return value is a string with the replacements made.
Test(*string*)	Executes a regular expression search against *string*. The return value is True if a match was found, False if not.

TABLE 8-6 *Regular expression characters that can be used in the pattern property.*

Character(s)	Description
\	Marks the next character as either a special character or a literal. For example, "n" matches the character "n". "\n" matches a newline character. The sequence "\\" matches "\" and "\(" matches "(".
^	Matches the beginning of input.
$	Matches the end of input.
*	Matches the preceding character zero or more times. For example, "to*" matches "t" or "to" or "too".
+	Matches the preceding character one or more times. For example, "to+" matches "to" and "too" but not "t".
?	Matches the preceding character zero or one time. For example, "to?t" matches "tt" and "tot" but not "toot".
.	Matches any single character except a newline character.

TABLE 8-6 *Regular expression characters that can be used in the pattern property. (Continued)*

<table>
<tr><th>Character(s)</th><th>Description</th></tr>
<tr><td>(pattern)</td><td>Matches pattern and remembers the match. The matched substring can be retrieved from the resulting <code>Matches</code> collection, using Item [0]...[n]. To match parentheses characters ( ), use "\(" or "\)".</td></tr>
<tr><td>x|y</td><td>Matches either x or y. For example, "z|food" matches "z" or "food". "(z|f)oo" matches 'zoo" or "food".</td></tr>
<tr><td>{n}</td><td>n is an integer greater than 0. Matches exactly n times. For example, "e{2}" does not match the "e" in "Ben" but matches the e's in "beet"</td></tr>
<tr><td>{n,}</td><td>n is an integer greater than 0. Matches at least n times. For example, "e{2,}" does not match the "e" in "Ben" and matches all the e's in "beet", "beeet", etc. "e{1,}" is equivalent to "e+". "e{0,}" is equivalent to "e*".</td></tr>
<tr><td>{n,m}</td><td>m and n are integers greater than or equal to 0. Matches at least n and at most m times. For example, "e{1,3}" matches the first three e's in "peeeek." "e{0,1}" is equivalent to "e?".</td></tr>
<tr><td>[xyz]</td><td>A character set. Matches any one of the enclosed characters. For example, "[abcde]" matches the "e" in "river" as well as the "a" in "prawn".</td></tr>
<tr><td>[^xyz]</td><td>A negative character set. Matches any character except those enclosed. For example, "[^ae]" matches both occurrences of "p" as well as the "r" in "paper".</td></tr>
<tr><td>[a-z]</td><td>A range of characters. Matches any character in the specified range. For example, "[a-z]" matches any lowercase alphabetic character in the range "a" through "z".</td></tr>
<tr><td>[^n-z]</td><td>A negative range of characters. Matches any character not in the specified range. For example, "[n-z]" matches any character not in the range "n" through "z"—in other words, a through m.</td></tr>
<tr><td>\b</td><td>Matches a word boundary, that is, the position between a word and a space. For example, "ed\b" matches the "ed" in "cooked fish" but not the "ed" in "tedious job".</td></tr>
<tr><td>\B</td><td>Matches a nonword boundary. "ea*r\B" matches the "ear" in "never early".</td></tr>
<tr><td>\d</td><td>Matches a digit character. Equivalent to [0-9].</td></tr>
<tr><td>\D</td><td>Matches a nondigit character. Equivalent to [^0-9].</td></tr>
<tr><td>\f</td><td>Matches a form-feed character.</td></tr>
<tr><td>\n</td><td>Matches a newline character.</td></tr>
<tr><td>\r</td><td>Matches a carriage return character.</td></tr>
<tr><td>\s</td><td>Matches any white space including space, tab, form-feed, etc. Equivalent to " [\f\n\r\t\v]".</td></tr>
<tr><td>\S</td><td>Matches any non-white space character. Equivalent to "[^\f\n\r\t\v]".</td></tr>
<tr><td>\t</td><td>Matches a tab character.</td></tr>
<tr><td>\v</td><td>Matches a vertical tab character.</td></tr>
<tr><td>\w</td><td>Matches any word character including underscore. Equivalent to "[A-Za-z0-9_]".</td></tr>
<tr><td>\W</td><td>Matches any nonword character. Equivalent to "[^A-Za-z0-9_]".</td></tr>
<tr><td>\num</td><td>Matches num, where num is a positive integer. A reference back to remembered matches. For example, "(.)\1" matches two consecutive identical characters.</td></tr>
</table>

When you use the RegExp object, these are the steps you will normally take:

1. Create an instance of the RegExp object.
2. Construct a string containing characters and regular expressions defining the target you are searching for, and assign this string to the Pattern property of the RegExp object created in step 1.
3. If necessary, set the Global and IgnoreCase properties as desired.
4. Execute a method as appropriate:
   - To determine whether or not a match is found, execute the Test method.
   - To obtain detailed information about the individual matches that are found, execute the Execute method.
   - To replace matching text with new text, execute the Replace method.

The Test and Replace methods are straightforward, but the results of the Execute method are a bit more involved. The Execute method returns a Matches collection. This collection has one property and one method:

- The Count property returns the number of items in the collection.
- The Item(n) method returns the *n*th item from the collection. Legal values for *n* are 0 to Count-1.

The general approach, then, is to examine the Count property of the Matches collection that was returned by the Execute method. If this is greater than 0, you can use the Items method to retrieve individual matches. You can also use the For Each...Next statement to iterate through the collection.

Each Match object has three properties that provide information about the match:

- FirstIndex. The character position in the target string where the match was found
- Length. The length, in characters, of the match
- Value. The text of the match

The script in Listing 8-3 shows how to use regular expressions. The script output is shown in Figure 8-2. The desired match is any four-letter lower case word that has "ee" or "oo" as the two middle letters. Let's see how the pattern string is constructed:

1. Start with \b to match the start of a word.
2. Include [a-z] to match any single lowercase letter.
3. Include [e|o] to specify "the letter e or the letter o."
4. Add {2} to qualify the preceding to mean "exactly two occurrences of "e" or "o", in other words, "ee" or "oo".
5. Insert [a-z] to match a final single letter.
6. Finish with \b to match the end of the word.

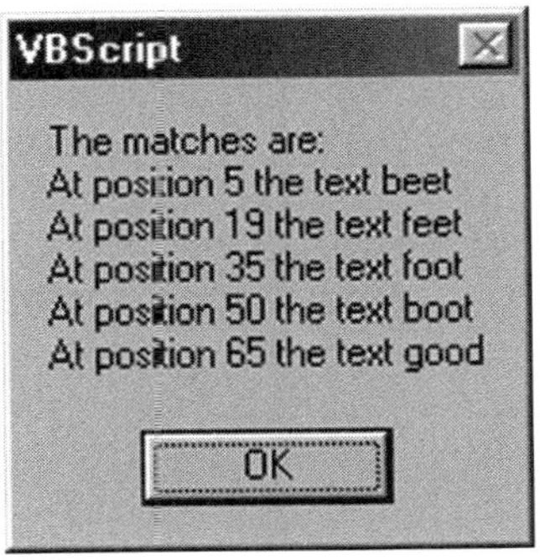

FIGURE 8–2 *The output of Listing 8.3.*

The final pattern string is "\b[a-z][e|o]{2}[a-z]\b".

LISTING 8–3 *Using the RegExp Object for complex text searches.*

```
' List0803.vbs
' Using the RegExp object.

Option Explicit

Dim RegEx
Dim Matches
Dim Match
Dim Target
Dim Msg

Target = "Each beet is three feet long. "
Target = Target & "Each foot fits in a boot, which is good."

Set RegEx = New RegExp
' Search for all four letter words where
' the middle two letters are "ee" or "oo".
RegEx.Pattern = "\b[a-z][e|o]{2}[a-z]\b"
RegEx.Global = True
Set Matches = RegEx.Execute(Target)
Msg = "The matches are: " & vbCRLF

For Each Match in Matches
    Msg = Msg & "At position " & Match.FirstIndex & _
        " the text " & Match.Value & vbCRLF
Next

msgbox msg
```

Right

See `Left`.

RTrim

See `LTrim`.

Space

The `Space` function returns a string containing a specified number of spaces. The syntax is

```
Space(n)
```

N is the number of spaces to include in the string.

Split

The `Split` function separates a string into substrings and returns a one-dimensional array containing the substrings. The syntax is

```
Split(string, delimiter, count, compare)
```

String is the string to be split into substrings.

Delimiter is an optional argument specifying the character that separates the substrings. If this argument is omitted, strings are separated at spaces.

Count is an optional argument specifying the number of substrings to return. If this argument is omitted or set to −1, all substrings are returned.

Compare is an optional constant that specifies the type of comparison. Possible settings are `vbTextCompare` (1), where upper- and lowercase letters match, and `vbBinaryCompare` (0), where different case letters (e.g., "A" and "a") do not match. If this argument is omitted, the search is done using a binary comparison.

Here's an example.

```
Dim S1, Array
S1 = "Programming!with!VBScript"
Array = Split(S1, "!")
```

After this code executes, Array(0) contains "Programming", Array(1) contains "with", and Array(2) contains "VBScript".

String

The `String` function returns a string containing a specified number of a single character. The syntax is

```
String(n, char)
```

N is the number of characters to put in the string.

Char is a string specifying the character to use. If *char* contains more than one character, the first character is used. For example, `String(6, "ABC")` returns "AAAAAA".

StrComp

The `StrComp` function compares two strings. The syntax is

`StrComp(`*`string1, string2, compare`*`)`

String1 and *string2* are the string expressions being compared.

Compare is an optional constant that specifies the type of comparison. Possible settings are `vbTextCompare` (1), where upper- and lowercase letters match, and `vbBinaryCompare` (0), where different case letters (e.g., "A" and "a") do not match. If this argument is omitted, the search is done using a binary comparison. The return value of this function is

–1 if *string1* is less than *string2*.

0 if *string1* and *string2* are equal.

1 if *string1* is greater than *string2*.

Null if either *string1* or *string2* is Null.

More string comparisons

In addition to using the `StrComp` function, you can also perform string comparisons using the comparison operators that were covered in Chapter 6 (=, >, <). Both methods produce the same results.

Trim

See `LTrim`.

UCase

See `LCase`.

Working with Numbers

Sometimes scripts need to work with numeric data. Many of the numeric manipulations you will need, such as addition and subtraction, are done with the arithmetic operators, which were covered in Chapter 6. There are other number-related functions provided in VBScript, however, and they are summarized in Table 8-7.

TABLE 8-7 *VBScript statements and functions for working with numbers.*

Function or statement	Description	Example
Abs(x)	Returns the absolute value of x.	Abs(–5) returns 5.
Atn(x)*	Returns the arctangent of x.	
Cos(x)*	Returns the cosine of x.	
Hex(x)	Returns the hexadecimal (base 16) representation of x.	Hex(123) returns 7B
Int(x)	Returns the integer part of x.	Int(9.99) returns 9
Log(x)	Returns the natural logarithm of x.	
Oct(x)	Returns the octal (base 8) representation of x.	Oct(123) returns 173
Randomize (*seed*)	Reinitializes the `Rnd` function's random number generator using the optional argument as a seed. If the argument is omitted, the current time is used as the seed.	
Rnd(x)	Returns a random number in the range 0–1. The optional argument controls how the number is generated: <0. The same number every time using x as the seed. >0 or omitted. The next random number in the sequence. 0. The most recently generated number.	Rnd(–2) returns 0.7133257
Round(x, n)	Returns x rounded to n decimal places. If n is omitted, the function returns no decimal places.	Round(9.559, 2) returns 9.56.
Sgn(x)	Returns 1 if x > 0, 0 if x = 0, and –1 if x < 0.	Sgn(–45) returns –1
Sqr(x)	Returns the square root of x. X cannot be negative.	Sqr(9) returns 3
Tan*	Returns the tangent of x.	

* In VBScript angles are expressed in radians rather than degrees. One radian equals approximately 58.63 degrees.

Using Dates and Times

Dates and times are important for many WSH applications. VBScript has a very powerful and easy-to-use set of tools for working with dates and times. The same `Variant` data type that is used for strings and numbers can also hold date/time values. The reason that dates and times are treated together is that in VBScript they are inseparably linked.

Date and Time Representation

In VBScript, dates and times are stored as floating point numbers. The integer part of the value represents the date as the number of days since December 30, 1899, with dates before then represented by negative values. The decimal part of the value represents the time as a fraction of the 24-hour day. Thus, .25 is 6 A.M., .5 is noon, and so on. Together, a single value can represent a specific time on a specific date. For example, 36860.5 represents 12:00 noon on December 1, 2000. A date value with no integer part represents a time without a date.

The advantage of representing dates and times in this manner is that they can be added and subtracted in many useful ways. For example, you can subtract two dates to determine the number of days in between. However the raw date values are not much use for displaying dates and times. As you will see, VBScript has rich capabilities for formatting dates and times as required by your scripts.

Getting the Current Date and Time

To obtain the current date and time, as set on the system clock, use the `Now`, `Date`, and `Time` functions. These functions return the current date and time, the current date, or the current time, respectively. For example,

```
Dim t
t = Time
msgbox "The current time is ", t
```

Creating Dates and Times

VScript offers you several options for creating date values. It can recognize date literals, which are simply dates written in any of the standard formats, such as 12/5/2000. To indicate that it is a date and not something else, enclose the literal in # characters. For example, in this statement the # characters make it clear that you are not performing a division:

```
Dim d As Date
d = #1/15/00#
```

You can also use the `DateValue` function, which converts a string into a date value:

```
Dim d As Date
d = DateValue("September 7, 2000")
```

If the argument contains time information, it is ignored. If, however, the time information is invalid, an error occurs. The `DateValue` function does not offer any advantage over assigning the date directly, as you saw earlier.

To assemble a date from day, month, and year information, use the `DateSerial` function. The syntax is

```
DateSerial(year, month, day)
```

The three arguments are integer expressions specifying the year (100–9999), the month (1–12), and the day (1–31). If the year argument is omitted, the current system year is used. If the *day* or *month* values are outside the given ranges, the resulting date "wraps" to the next larger unit. For example, this statement evaluates as June 6, 2000:

```
dateserial(00,5,37)
```

Under Windows 98/ME/2000, two-digit years for the *year* argument are interpreted based on user-defined settings. The default settings are that values in the range 0–29 are interpreted as the years 2000–2029, and values 30–99 are interpreted as the years 1930–1999. For all other *year* arguments, use a four-digit year. Earlier versions of Windows interpret two-digit years based on the defaults described previously. To be sure the function returns the proper value, use a four-digit year.

VBScript has similar functions for creating time values. To create a time value (`Date` data type) from a string representation of a time, use the `TimeValue` function. You can represent the time in either 12- or 24-hour style. The following two statements return the same value:

```
TimeValue("7:45PM")
TimeValue("19:45")
```

If the argument to `TimeValue` includes date information, it is ignored. If the date information is invalid, however, an error occurs.

To construct a time from hour, minute, and second information, use the `TimeSerial` function:

```
TimeSerial(hour, minute, second)
```

The three arguments are integer expressions specifying the hour, minute, and second of the time. *Hour* must be in the range 0–23. *Minute* and *second* are normally in the range 0–59 but can be outside that range and are then "wrapped" to the next larger unit. A minute value of 70, for example, is interpreted as 1 hour and 10 minutes. Likewise, a second value of 125 is interpreted as 2 minutes and 5 seconds. Thus, these two statements are equivalent:

```
TimeValue(12, 15, 0)
TimeValue(11, 75, 0)
```

Adding and Subtracting Dates and Times

To add or subtract a specified interval to or from a date, use the `DateAdd` function. It can be useful to add dates, for performing tasks such as determining what day of the week a particular future date falls on. You can add any date interval to an existing date: years, quarters, months, weeks, or days. You can also add time intervals of hours, minutes, or seconds. The syntax is

```
DateAdd(interval, number, date)
```

Interval specifies the type of interval being added. It is a string expression as shown in Table 8-8. *Number* is the number of intervals to add. Use a negative value to subtract intervals. *Date* is the date being added to or subtracted from.

TABLE 8-8 Values for the DateAdd function's *interval* argument.

Argument	Interval
yyyy	Year
q	Quarter
m	Month
y	Day of year (equivalent to "d")
d	Day
w	Weekday (equivalent to "d")
ww	Week
h	Hour
n	Minute
s	Second

Here's an example of using `DateAdd`. Suppose that, when a script is running, you want to generate a date that is one month from the present day. This code will do it:

```
Dim DateDue
DateDue = DateAdd("m", 1, Date)
```

The `DateAdd` function will never return an invalid date. If, for example, you add `1` month to January 31, the return value is February 28 if it is not a leap year, and February 29 if it is a leap year.

Getting Date and Time Information

Sometimes you need to obtain information about a date or a time, such as what day of the week a specified date falls on. VBScript has several functions for this purpose. The most flexible of them is `DatePart`. The syntax is

```
DatePart(interval, date, firstdayofweek, firstweekofyear)
```

Interval is a string specifying the interval of interest. The possible values are the same as shown in Table 8-8. *Date* is the date value you are getting information about. *Firstdayofweek* is an optional argument indicating which day is to be considered the first day of the week. Settings are shown in Table 8-9. *Firstweekofyear* is an optional argument indicating which week is to be considered the first week of the year. Settings are shown in Table 8-10.

TABLE 8-9 Settings for the *Firstdayofweek* argument.

Constant	Value	Description
vbUseSystem	0	Use the system setting.
vbSunday	1	Sunday (this is the default)
vbMonday	2	Monday
vbTuesday	3	Tuesday
vbWednesday	4	Wednesday
vbThursday	5	Thursday
vbFriday	6	Friday
vbSaturday	7	Saturday

TABLE 8-10 Settings for the *Firstweekofyear* argument.

Constant	Value	Description
vbUseSystem	0	Use the system setting.
vbFirstJan1	1	The week in which January 1 occurs (this is the default).
vbFirstFourDays	2	The first week that has at least four days in the new year.
vbFirstFullWeek	3	The first full week of the year.

The `DatePart` function returns an integer value that specifies the interval of interest. For example,

```
DatePart("q", #7/10/2000#)
```

returns the value 3 because July 10 is in the third quarter of the year. Note that the interval specifiers "w", "d", and "y" work differently in this function, as follows:

- "w" returns the day of the week, 1 for the first day (Sunday, by default), 7 for the last day (Saturday by default).
- "d" returns the day of the month.
- "y" returns the day of the year (days since January 1).

This code, for example, calculates the number of days from today until the end of the year:

```
days = DatePart("y", #12/31#) - DatePart("y", Date)
```

To calculate the number of time intervals between two dates, use the `DateDiff` function. The syntax is

```
DateDiff(interval, date1, date2, firstdayofweek, firstweekofyear)
```

Interval is a string specifying the interval of interest, as described in Table 8-8. *Date1* and *date2* are the two dates of interest. *Firstdayofweek* and *firstweekofyear* are optional arguments that work the same as was described for the `DatePart` function. The `DateDiff` function returns an integer (as a type `Variant`) specifying the number of intervals between the two dates. We can repeat the previous example, calculating the number of days to the end of the year, using this function:

```
days = DateDiff("y", Date, #12/31#)
```

Note that *date1* is subtracted from *date2*, so if *date1* is after *date2* the function will return a negative value.

Some additional VBScript functions that return specific information about date and time values are listed in Table 8-11. Each of these functions takes as its one argument any expression that represents a valid date or time. The return value is an integer value (as a type `Variant`).

TABLE 8-11 *Other date and time information functions.*

Function	Returns
Year(*date*)	A value representing the year.
Month(*date*)	A value 1–12 representing the month.
Weekday(*date, firstdayofweek*)	A value representing the day of the week (default, Sunday = 1). The *firstdayofweek* argument is optional. Possible settings are given in Table 8-9.
WeekdayName (*weekday, abbreviate, firstdayofweek*)	Returns the name of the day. *Weekday* is a numeric value 1–7 specifying the day. *Abbreviate* is an optional argument specifying whether the name should be abbreviated (True) or spelled out (False, the default). *Firstdayofweek* is an optional argument specifying which day of the week is considered the first day. See Table 8-9.
MonthName(*month, abbreviate*)	Returns the name of the month. *Month* is a value 1–12 specifying the month. *Abbreviate* is an optional argument specifying whether the name should be abbreviated (True) or spelled out (False, the default).
Day(*date*)	A value 1–31 representing the day of the month.
Hour(*date*)	A value 0–23 representing the hour of the day.
Minute(*date*)	A value 0–59 representing the minute of the hour.
Second(*date*)	A value 0–59 representing the second of the minute.

Formatting Dates and Times

When you need to display date or time values, you will often want the data formatted in a specific way. When displaying `Date` type data, VBScript is pretty good at displaying the information in an appropriate format, based on the system settings. In the United States, for example, the system settings typically result in the display of a date/time value as follows:

```
10/16/99 10:07:32 AM
```

For greater control over the display if dates and times, use the `Format` function. The syntax is

```
Format(date, format)
```

Date is the date value to format. *Format* is an optional string expression specifying how the date should be formatted. *Format* is a named date format, as described in Table 8-12. If the *format* argument is omitted, `vbGeneralDate` format is used.

TABLE 8-12 *Named formats for the FormatDateTime function.*

Constant	Value	Description
vbGeneralDate	0	Display a date and/or time. If there is a date part, display it as a short date. If there is a time part, display it as a long time. If present, both parts are displayed.
vbLongDate	1	Display a date in the long date format specified in the system's regional settings.
vbShortDate	2	Display a date in the short date format specified in the system's regional settings.
vbLongTime	3	Display a time in the time format specified in the system's regional settings.
vbShortTime	4	Display a time in 24-hour format (hh:mm).

Overview

Most scripts work with data, and that data can be divided into three categories: strings, numbers, and dates/times. VBScript offers you a full range of tools for manipulating and formatting all three kinds of data. Whether processing a text document, performing numerical calculations, or handling calendar functions, your scripts have all the tools they need.

NINE

VBScript: User Interaction, Error Handling, and Miscellaneous Topics

In this final chapter on VBScript, we cover several unrelated but important topics. We start by looking at the ways that VBScript can interact with the user while a script is running. Next, we explain error handling — an essential topic for any script programmer. The chapter closes with a few miscellaneous VBScript features.

Interacting with the User

While some scripts can run without interacting with the user, others cannot. They may need to display information to the user, get information from the user, or both. VBScript provides the `Msgbox` and `InputBox` functions for these tasks.

The MsgBox Function

To display information for the user and get simple choices from him or her, use the `MsgBox` function. The `MsgBox` function displays a dialog box containing a message and one or more standard buttons. Optionally, the dialog box can display an icon as well. The function's return value specifies which of the buttons the user clicked to close the dialog box. The syntax is

```
MsgBox(prompt, buttons, title, helpfile, context)
```

Prompt is a string expression specifying the message to display.

Buttons is an optional argument specifying what buttons and/or icons to display in the dialog box and, when there is more than one button, which one is the default. If this argument is omitted, only an OK button is displayed. Possible settings for this argument are given in Table 9-1. To combine settings, use the `Or` operator (as shown in the following example).

Title is an optional argument that specifies the title displayed in the dialog box's title bar. If this argument is omitted, the title bar will display "VBScript".

Helpfile and *context* are optional arguments that specify the help file and the context for the dialog box's context sensitive help. If you provide one of these arguments you must include the other as well.

TABLE 9-1 *Predefined constants for the MsgBox function's buttons argument.*

Constant	Value	Description
vbOKCancel	1	Display OK and Cancel buttons
vbAbortRetryIgnore	2	Display Abort, Retry, and Ignore buttons
vbYesNoCancel	3	Display Yes, No, and Cancel buttons
vbYesNo	4	Display Yes and No buttons
vbRetryCancel	5	Display Retry and Cancel buttons
vbCritical	16	Display Critical Message icon
vbQuestion	32	Display Warning Query icon
vbExclamation	48	Display Warning Message icon
vbInformation	64	Display Information Message icon
vbDefaultButton2	256	Second button is default
vbDefaultButton3	512	Third button is default

The possible return values for the `MsgBox` function are also defined by constants, which are listed in Table 9-2.

TABLE 9-2 *Constants for the MsgBox function's return value.*

Constant	Value	Button Selected
vbOK	1	OK
vbCancel	2	Cancel
vbAbort	3	Abort
vbRetry	4	Retry
vbIgnore	5	Ignore
vbYes	6	Yes
vbNo	7	No

Here's an example of using the MsgBox function. The following code displays a message asking the user whether he or she wants to delete a file, and then takes action based on whether the user selects the Yes or No button. The dialog box displays a question mark icon, and the second button ("No") is the default button.

```
reply = MsgBox("Delete file?", vbYesNo Or vbQuestion Or _
    vbDefaultButton2)
If reply = vbYes Then
    'Code to delete file goes here.
End If
```

InputBox

To permit the user to enter data into a script, use the InputBox function. This function displays a dialog box into which the user can enter text. The function's return value is the text entered by the user. The syntax is

```
InputBox(prompt, title, default, xpos, ypos, helpfile, context)
```

Prompt is the text displayed in the dialog box as a prompt to the user.

Title is an optional argument that specifies the title displayed in the dialog box's title bar. If this argument is omitted, the title bar will display "VBScript".

Default is an optional string expression that specifies the default response, if the user takes no action. If this argument is omitted the default response is an empty string.

XPos and *ypos* are optional numerical values specifying the horizontal and vertical position of the dialog box, in twips, from the left top edge of the screen (a twip is 1/1440 of an inch). If *xpos* is omitted, the dialog box is centered horizontally. If *ypos* is omitted, the dialog box is positioned about one-third of the distance from the top of the screen.

Helpfile and *context* are optional arguments that specify the helpfile and the context for the dialog box's context sensitive help. If you provide one of these arguments, you must include the other as well.

This code uses the InputBox function to get the user's country of residence, with "United States" being the default response.

```
Country = InputBox("Your country of residence?", "Country", _
    "United States")
```

Multiline prompts

If you want the prompt displayed by the MsgBox or InputBox function to be split over two or more lines, you can use the vbCrLf constant to break the text at the desired locations. Here's an example:

```
msg = "If you want to continue, Click Yes." & vbCrLf
msg = msg & "If you do not want to continue, click No."
reply = MsgBox(msg, vbYesNo)
```

Error Handling

You learned in a previous chapter that VBScript's default response to a run-time error is to halt execution of the script and display a dialog box with information about the error. Because run-time errors are usually not under the programmer's control, it is never a good idea to leave error handling to the default mechanisms. If you do, and a run-time error occurs, the script stops, and the user is left looking at a dialog box that he or she probably does not understand. It is much better to use VBScript's error handling capabilities to *trap* run-time errors. After an error is trapped, code in your script can *handle* it by taking specific action to correct the error.

Error trapping and handling involve two parts: the `On Error` statement and the `Err` object. The `On Error` statement turns error trapping on and off, and the `Err` object lets you get information about any error that occurs so that you can handle it appropriately. There are two variants of `On Error`:

- `On Error Resume Next`. Enables error trapping. When an error occurs, script execution continues with the statement immediately following the statement that caused the error.
- `On Error Goto 0`. Disables error trapping. When an error occurs, the script stops.

By including an `On Error Resume Next` statement in your code, you prevent the default VBScript response to errors. This does not, however, mean that you can simply ignore errors! When an error occurs, information about the error is stored in the `Err` object. Your code should examine the `Err` object to determine the nature of the error and take appropriate action. The `Err` object has five properties that contain information about the most recent error. These are described in Table 9-3.

TABLE 9-3 *Properties of the Err object.*

Property	Description
Description	Short text description of the error.
HelpContext	The context ID for related information in the help file (if any).
HelpFile	The help file containing information about the error (if any).
Number	The numerical code associated with the error. This is the `Err` object's default property.
Source	The name of the object or application that caused the error.

The general approach to script error handling is as follows:

1. Put the `On Error Resume Next` statement at the start of each procedure where you want error trapping enabled.
2. Examine the code in the procedure to determine which statements have the potential to cause an error.
3. After each statement or group of statements that might cause an error, test the value of the `Err.Number` property. If it is 0, no error occurred. If it is not zero, an error occurred and the value of `Err.Number` identifies the error. Appendix 4 contains a list of all VBScript error codes.
4. Based on the error that occurred, your code can take steps to remedy the situation, or alert the user that an error has occurred (using the `Err.Description` property if desired).

What can your code do to handle an error? That depends on the error. There is no "trick" to dealing with errors. Rather, you need to have a thorough understanding of what errors may happen, what the underlying causes are, and what (if anything) can be done to correct them. Some errors cannot be fixed, and all you can do is notify the user. Table 9-4 presents some typical error situations and what your code might do when the corresponding error is trapped.

TABLE 9-4 *Some typical error situations.*

Situation	Response
An error is caused by a network connection being unavailable.	Give the user the choice of trying the action again or aborting script execution.
The user enters the name of a file to be processed, but the file cannot be found.	Prompt the user to reenter the file name, then try again.
An error is caused because a diskette is not available in drive A:.	Prompt the user to insert a diskette then retry the operation.
An error occurs because an application that the script calls, such as Excel, is not available.	Notify the user and then abort the script.

Let's take a look at an example. The script in Listing 9-1 prompts the user for the name of a file and then tries to open it for reading (these file access statements will be covered in Chapter 15). If you try to open a nonexistent file for reading, an error occurs. This code tests for an error as soon as the `OpenTextFile` method is executed, and then either "processes" and closes the file if there was no error, or displays an error message if there was an error. No actual processing is done, so you do not need to worry about corrupting an existing file.

LISTING 9–1 *Error trapping in VBScript.*

```
' List0901.vbs
' Demonstration of error trapping.
Option Explicit
Dim filename
filename = InputBox("Please enter the name of the file to process.")
ProcessFile filename
sub ProcessFile(FileName)
    Dim fso
    Dim ts
    Dim msg
    On Error Resume Next
    set fso = CreateObject("Scripting.FileSystemObject")
    set ts = fso.OpentextFile(FileName, 1)
    if Err.Number = 0 then' no error
        msgbox "File proccessed successfully"
        ts.close
    else
        msgbox "Error " & Err.Number & ": " & Err.Description
    end if
end sub
```

The `Err` object has the `Clear` method, which resets all of its properties to the nonerror state. After processing an error, you should execute this method if you want to perform more error trapping in the same procedure, to make sure that `Err` does not contain "old" information from a previous error. The `Clear` method is called automatically whenever execution returns from a procedure.

Where is On Error Goto *label*?

Visual Basic provides additional error handling flexibility with the `On Error Goto label` statement, which directs execution to a specific location in code when an error occurs. Don't bother looking for this statement in VBScript, however, as it is not supported.

Other Topics

This section contains a few VBScript topics that did not fall into any of the other categories of this or the previous chapters. Specifically, I explain the VBScript statements that give you a special kind of flexibility for evaluating expressions and executing statements in your scripts.

Eval

The `Eval` function takes a string expression as its one argument. The function evaluates the string as a VBScript expression and returns the result. Here's an example:

```
a = 1
b = 2
exp = "a + b"
c = Eval(exp)
```

After this code executes, c is equal to 3. You are probably wondering what the big deal is, but `Eval` is not used like this in real-world scripts. Its usefulness comes when the expression to be evaluated is stored as a program variable. Here's an example. Suppose a retail firm awards its salespeople a bonus based on their sales, but the formula used for each person's bonus differs depending on their length of service and other factors. You could store each person's bonus formula along with their other employee information, as shown here:

```
Dim Employees(100,1)
Employees(0,0) = "John Brown"
Employees(0,1) = "(sales * 0.04) + 500"
Employees(1,0) = "Jane Smith"
Employees(1,1) = "(sales * 0.05) + 1000"
```

Then, assuming a variable named sales holds the relevant sales data, you could calculate bonuses as follows:

```
JohnBrownBonus = Eval(Employees(0,1))
JaneSmithBonus = Eval(Employees(1,1))
```

This is a fairly sophisticated technique that you will not use often, but it can be very useful in certain situations.

Execute and ExecuteGlobal

The `Execute` and `ExecuteGlobal` statements are passed a single argument that is a string containing a valid VBScript statement. `Execute` runs the statement in the current context, while `ExecuteGlobal` executes the statement in the global context. This is the only difference between the two statements.

What do I mean by *context*? It has to do with where the statement is located. If either of these statements is located inside a procedure, then *current context* means that the statement will be executed using the procedure's local variables while *global context* means that the statement will be executed using the script's global variables. Outside of procedures, the two statements are identical — both use the global context.

The reasons to use either of these statements are similar to those for using `Eval`, which you learned about in the previous section. The statements to be executed can be stored as strings in the program, or even input by the user, rather than being hard-coded into the script. Again, this is not a commonly needed capability but one that can be very powerful when your script calls for it. The script in Listing 9-2 demonstrates the use of the `Execute` statement.

LISTING 9–2 *Using the Execute statement.*

```
' List0902.vbs
' Using the Execute statement.

Option Explicit

Dim Expressions(3)
Dim a
Dim b
Dim c
Dim op
Dim msg

Expressions(0) = "a = b + c"
Expressions(1) = "a = b - c"
Expressions(2) = "a = b * c"
Expressions(3) = "a = b / c"

b = InputBox("Enter any non-zero number:")
c = InputBox("Enter another non-zero number:")
msg = "Enter 0 to add, 1 to subtract, 2 to multiply, 3 to divide:"
op = InputBox(msg)
Execute(Expressions(op))

msgbox "The answer is " & a
```

Overview

This chapter finishes our coverage of the VBScript scripting language. You learned how to display information to the user as well as to retrieve user input, important capabilities for many scripts. You also learned about error handling, which is an essential part of most scripts and should not be overlooked. Finally, you learned how to use VBScript's evaluation and execution statements for sophisticated script tasks. At this point you should have sufficient mastery of VBScript to tackle just about any scripting challenge.

T E N

JScript: Basic Syntax, Data Storage, and Operators

JScript is one of the two languages supported by the Microsoft Windows Scripting Host (the other being VBScript, which was covered in Chapters 6 through 9). In this and the following three chapters, you will learn how to use JScript to write Windows scripts. This first chapter covers the fundamental syntax of JScript, as well as its tools for data storage and manipulation.

Introduction to JScript

JScript is Microsoft's implementation of the JavaScript language. JavaScript is also a scripting language, and it was originally designed specifically for Internet scripts. The JavaScript name comes from the fact that it is loosely based on the Java language, which is a full-featured object-oriented applications programming language.

Which is better?

With two scripting languages to choose from, beginners may be wondering if one language is to be preferred over the other. VBScript and JScript are largely identical in terms of what you can do with them. JScript does come up short in a few areas, including getting input from the user. In terms of learning, however, your own experience should be the guide. If you have some background in Basic, then many aspects of VBScript will seem familiar to you. If your experience is in C, C++, or Java, then JScript is your best choice. If you are starting from scratch, then VBScript may be a little easier to learn. In the long term, however, if you plan to move beyond casual scripting, you should learn both languages.

Comparison with Java

In many ways, the relationship between JScript and Java is similar to the relationship between VBScript and Visual Basic. Again, the differences reflect the fact that JScript is a scripting language with specific needs and limitations, while Java is a full-blown development language. If you know Java, then JScript may seem like a stripped down version. In fact, JScript is only distantly related to Java and was developed from the ground up in response to a specific need. While many of the syntax elements are common between the Java and Jscript, there are differences. Some of the major differences include the following:

- JScript cannot be used to create stand-alone applications.
- JScript has essentially no file access capabilities of its own.
- JScript is an *untyped* language, meaning that the data type of variables need not be declared.
- JScript has very limited object-oriented features when compared with Java.

Just because JScript seems to lack a lot of features, do not think of it as limited. Capabilities that are missing from JScript were left out for the very good reason that they are not needed or wanted in a scripting language. For example, file access capabilities were specifically omitted from JScript because they would present a major security risk in an Internet scripting language. When using JScript for Windows scripting, file access is done through the FSO object, which is part of the Windows Scripting Host.

Syntax Fundamentals

The following are the most important general features of JScript syntax:

- There is one JScript statement per line. The end of a line is marked by a carriage return (pressing Enter). Although not required, it is good practice to mark the end of each statement with a semicolon.
- A group of two or more statements enclosed in curly braces {} is called a *block* or a *compound statement*. For every opening brace in a script there *must* be a corresponding closing brace.
- White space does not matter. You can use blank lines and indentation freely to format your code.
- The language is case sensitive.
- Execution begins with the first statement in the script file and continues in order to the last statement *unless* the order of execution is modified by statements in the script.

Most new programmers get caught by JScript's case sensitivity. When you are just getting started, you may find that many of the scripting errors you encounter are simply a result of using the wrong case for a function or an object name. You should note that this case sensitivity applies not only to elements of the JScript language, but to all aspects of a script, such as WSH object names.

Comments

A comment is part of a script file that is ignored — in other words, it does not do anything when the script is executing. Comments are used by the programmer to document their script code, to add reminders about tasks remaining to be done, and so on. JScript has two kinds of comments. A single-line comment starts with a double slash // and can be placed on a line by itself or on a line following a JScript statement. A multiline comment starts with /* and ends with */. Here are some examples:

```
// This is a single line comment.
x = 12; // This is also a single line comment.
/* This is
   a multiline
        comment. */
```

It's a good idea to get in the habit of commenting your code right from the start. Things will seem clear to you now, but if you need to come back and modify the script next month, you may have forgotten exactly how things were supposed to work. Comments can also be used as a programming tool. If you want to test how a script works with one or more statements removed, simply convert them to comments.

Data Storage

JScript offers full capabilities for using constants and variables in your scripts. It is not quite as flexible as VBScript in this regard, but with a little clever programming can do anything you need.

Constants

For data that will not change during script execution, JScript supports literal constants. A *literal* constant is simply text or a number that is typed directly into your script. In this code

```
MilesToGo = 120;
MyName = "Peter G. Aitken";
SheSaid = '"Greetings to one and all"';
```

the 120, Peter G. Aitken, and the "Greetings to one and all" are literal constants. In the last case, the double quotes are part of the literal.

Unlike VBScript, JScript does not support symbolic constants (constants with names). This is a shame, as symbolic constants can be very useful. You can get around this limitation by using variables in place of symbolic constants. One approach is to use all uppercase names for variables that are being used as constants. This indicates that they should not have their value changed in code.

JScript uses a special notation for certain characters in literal strings. Called *escape characters*, they are a holdover from JScript's roots in the C language. Each escape character consists of a letter preceded by a backslash:

\b	backspace
\f	formfeed
\n	new line
\t	tab
\r	carriage return

The most useful of these escape characters is \n, which can be used to break a long message into two or more lines for display by `WScript.Echo` or another output statement. The script in Listing 10-1 demonstrates this, and the resulting output (when the script is run using wscript) is shown in Figure 10-1. You can see that the output text is broken into two lines at the location of the newline character.

LISTING 10–1 *Using the newline character to break text.*

```
// LIST1001.js
// Using escape characters.

var message;

message = "This action is not permitted \nat this time."
WScript.echo(message);
```

FIGURE 10–1 *The output of the script in Listing 10-1.*

Because the backslash is used to denote escape characters, how do you insert the backslash character in a literal string? This is done by using two backslash characters. In a literal string, therefore, \\ means \. This is particularly important when working with file names and paths, as the backslash is used as a separator. For example, if you try the following

```
var datafolder = "c:\mydata\sales";
```

it will not work properly because JScript will try to interpret the \m and the \s as escape characters. This is true even though the literal is contained within quotes. Instead you must write the following:

```
var datafolder = "c:\\mydata\\sales";
```

Variables

A *variable* is a named location where the script can store data. The data that is stored in a variable can be changed as many times as needed by the script — hence the name *variable*. All variables in JScript are of the same type. This means that you do not need to declare the kind of data a variable will hold — for example, a number or text — when you create the variable. JScript's one variable type has the ability to store any kind of data.

NAMING VARIABLES

When you create a variable you must assign it a name. Variable names must follow these rules:

- The first character must be a letter, an underscore (_), or a dollar sign ($).
- The following characters can be any combination of letters, numbers, and the underscore and dollar sign characters.
- The name cannot be a JScript reserved word. Appendix 5 contains a list of all JScript reserved words.

While not required, it is a good idea to use meaningful names for your variables. In a script that processes files, for instance, it is quite clear what the variable numberOfFiles is for. You could have called it X or _T6 just as well. The Windows Scripting Host would not care, but the meaningful name makes the script a lot easier to read and understand.

Capitalization in Variable Names

While not required, certain conventions are commonly used in creating variable names in JScript (as well as in Java):
- The first letter of the name is lowercase.
- If the name is composed of two or more words, the first letter of the second and subsequent words is uppercase.
- All other letters are lowercase.
The following variable names meet these rules: totalSales, interestRate. yearsOfService.

DECLARING VARIABLES

Before you use a variable in a JScript script, you should declare it. This is done using the `var` statement:

```
var variablename;
```

You can declare more than one variable with a single `var` statement, separating them with commas:

```
var X1, X1, X3;
```

You can also assign a value to a variable at the same time you declare it:

```
var count = 0, name = "Joe";
```

Unfortunately, JScript does not require variable declaration, and there is no statement (like VBScript's `Option Explicit`) that you can use to make it require declaration. Still, it is good practice to declare all variables regardless. Misspelled variable names can be as much of a problem in JScript as they can be in VBScript, but your only remedy is to use care in declaring and spelling your variable names.

Data Types and Coercion

You have seen that JScript does not have strict data types, with a single variable type being used to hold all types of data: numbers, text, and object references. Even so, a particular JScript variable will have a data type based on the kind of data that has been stored there. The six data types are described in Table 10-1.

TABLE 10-1 *JScript's six data types.*

Data type	Description
Number	A numerical value (see text for more details).
String	Zero or more characters enclosed in single or double quotation marks.
Boolean	True or False. These are special values and not the –1 and 0 used for True and False in some other languages.
Object	Reference to an object.
Null	Special value meaning that the variable does not contain meaningful data.
Undefined	The variable has been created but not initialized.

Null versus Undefined

The data types Null and Undefined may sound similar but they are not the same thing. Null is a special value that is explicitly assigned to a variable to indicate that the variable does not contain valid data. In contrast, a variable is Undefined after it has been declared (with `var`) but before any value has been assigned to it.

Because JScript is a loosely typed language, the "type" of a variable depends on the data that is stored there. A variable that contains a number is different from a variable that contains string data. When you are working with JScript variables, there will be times when one type of data needs to be converted, or *coerced*, into another type. In most situations, JScript is able to do this coercion automatically. This situation most often arises when you are performing operations with variables that contain number and text data. Take a look at this code:

```
var someText = "Your age is ";
var aNumber = 29;
var result;

result = someText + aNumber;
```

After this code has executed, the variable result contains the string "Your age is 29". The value 29 has been coerced from numeric type to string type. In most situations, JScript's default is to coerce numeric data to string type. If you want to force a coercion of string data to numeric type, you can use either the `parseInt` or the `parseFloat` function, which take a string as an argument and return a corresponding numeric value. You use the `parseInt` function for integers and the `parseFloat` function for floating point values. For example,

```
var text = "10.1";
var number = 5;
var result;

result = number + parseFloat(text);
```

After this code executes, the variable result contains the value 15.1. If you did not use the `parseFloat` function, and simply tried to "add" the two variables, the outcome would be that the variable result contains the string "510.1" because the default is to coerce the numeric value to a string.

Methods versus functions

Technically, `parseFloat` and `parseInt` are methods, not functions. They belong to the `Global` object, which exists behind the scenes in JScript to provide methods. You never need to refer to `Global` in your code — its methods are called directly.

Object References

One of the data types that a JScript variable can hold is an object reference. JScript is unlike VBScript in that there is no special keyword (`Set` in VBScript) required when assigning an object reference to a variable. You simply use the assignment operator as shown here:

```
var fso;
fso = WScript.CreateObject("Scripting.FileSystemObject");
```

Arrays

An array is a technique of data storage in which multiple data items are stored under the same name and distinguished by a numerical index. JScript supports data arrays by means of the `Array` object. To create an array you use `Array` with the new keyword. You can create an empty array like this:

```
var dataArray;
dataArray = new Array();
```

To create an array with a specified number of elements, but containing no data, specify the number of elements in the parentheses:

```
var dataArray;
dataArray = new Array(20);
```

JScript arrays always start at element 0. You can also load data into the array when you create it:

```
var dataArray;
dataArray = new Array("France", "England", "China");
```

When you refer to array elements in code, you must use square brackets [] to enclose the index. For example:

```
dataArray[1] = "Canada";
myCountry = dataArray[2];
```

Because every JScript array is an object, it has properties and methods that you can use to get information about the array or to manipulate it. The one property of the `Array` object is `length`, which returns the number of elements in the array. For example, after this code:

```
var dataArray;
dataArray = new Array("France", "England", "China");
```

the expression `dataArray.length` will return 3. You can also change an array's size by setting its `length` property. For example:

```
var dataArray;
dataArray = new Array("France", "England", "China");
dataArray.length = 5;
dataArray[3] = "Nigeria";
dataArray[4] = "Tibet";
```

However, JScript's arrays are so flexible that you rarely need to change an array's `length` property. If you add new data beyond the "end" of an array, it will automatically expand as needed. This code works just as well as the preceding example:

```
var dataArray;
dataArray = new Array("France", "England", "China");
dataArray [3] = "Nigeria";
dataArray [4] = "Tibet";
```

The VBArray Function

VBScript and JScript handle arrays somewhat differently. JScript has an object called `VBArray` that is used to permit JScript code to work with VBScript arrays. You'll learn about this object in Chapter 13.

JScript Operators

An operator is a symbol (or symbols) that instructs JScript to perform some action with data. As with VBScript, the operators in JScript fall into several categories.

The Assignment Operators

The simple assignment operator, represented by the equal sign, assigns the value of an expression to a variable. For example, the statement

```
total = a + b + c;
```

adds the values in variables a, b, and c assigns the result to variable total.

JScript also has a number of compound assignment operators that let you combine a mathematical operation and assignment in one operation. These compound assignment operators consist of one of the five fundamental mathematical operators followed by an equal sign. For example, the += operator combines addition and assignment. Writing

```
a += b;
```

is the same as writing

```
a = a + b;
```

You can see that these compound operators are merely a form of shorthand. They are summarized in Table 10-2.

TABLE 10-2 *JScript's compound assignment operators.*

Operator	Example	Equivalent
+=	a += b;	a = a + b;
–=	a –= b;	a = a – b;
*=	a *= b;	a = a * b;
/=	a /= b;	a = a / b;
%=	a %= b;	a = a % b;

The Arithmetic Operators

The arithmetic operators perform mathematical operations. There are the common operations of addition, subtraction, multiplication, division, and modulus. The JScript arithmetic operators are summarized in Table 10-3.

TABLE 10-3 *The JScript arithmetic operators.*

Operator	Description	Example
+	Addition	5 + 12 evaluates to 17
–	Subtraction	17 – 7 evaluates to 10
*	Multiplication	3 * 2.5 evaluates to 7.5
/	Division	63 / 3 evaluates to 21
*	Modulus (remainder after division)	33 % 6 evaluates to 3

Unlike VBScript, JScript does not have an operator for exponentiation. Instead you use the `pow` method as follows:

```
result = pow(x, y)
```

The method returns x raised to the y power. This method belongs to JScript's `Math` object, which provides a variety of specialized mathematical capabilities. The `Math` object will be covered in Chapter 12.

The Increment and Decrement Operators

It is fairly common in programming to need to increment or decrement the value of a numeric variable by one. JScript provides the increment and decrement operators as a shorthand for doing this. Follow a variable name by ++ or `--` to either add or subtract 1 from the variable. Thus,

```
x++;
y--;
```

have exactly the same effect as

```
x = x + 1;
y = y - 1;
```

You can place the operator either before or after the variable name, which gives subtly different results when the variable is in an expression:

- If the operator precedes the variable name, the variable is incremented or decremented and then the expression is evaluated.
- If the operator follows the variable name, the expression is evaluated before the variable is incremented or decremented.

Here's an example. This code places the operators after the variable names:

```
var x = 3;
var y = 2;
var z;

z = x++ * y++;
```

After this code executes the result is that z = 6 because the multiplication was performed before x and y were incremented. Compare with this code:

```
var x = 3;
var y = 2;
var z;

z = ++x * ++y;
```

Now, z ends up with the value 12 because x and y were incremented before the multiplication. In both cases, x and y end up with the values 4 and 3, respectively.

The Comparison Operators

The comparison operators perform comparisons between expressions, with the result being either True or False depending on whether the comparison is true or not. JScript's comparison operators are listed in Table 10-4.

TABLE 10-4 *The JScript comparison operators.*

Operator	Comparison
==	Is equal to?
>	Is greater than?
<	Is less than?
>=	Is greater than or equal to?
<=	Is less than or equal to?
!=	Is not equal to?

For example, the expression

```
x == y
```

asks the question "is x equal to y?" and returns either True or False depending on the values of the two variables.

These operators can also be used to perform comparisons between strings. Strings are compared character by character, with order determined by the ASCII value for the characters. For the letters of the alphabet, this results in the standard alphabetical order we are all used to. However, because upper- and lowercase letters have different ASCII values, any uppercase letter is considered to be less than any lowercase letter. "A", for example, is less than "a", and "Z" is also less than "A". To perform a case-insensitive string comparison, use the `String` object's `toLowerCase` method to convert both strings to all lowercase. For example,

```
var s1 = "aardvark";
var s2 = "Zebra";
```

The expression

```
s1 < s2
```

will evaluate as False, but the expression

```
s1.toLowerCase() < s2.toLowerCase()
```

will evaluate as True. The `String` object will be covered in more detail in Chapter 12.

The Logical Operators

The logical operators are used manipulate logical (True/False) expressions. You had an introduction to logical expressions and operators in Chapter 6, and you can turn back to that chapter if you need more background information. The JScript logical operators are described in Table 10-5.

TABLE 10-5 *The JScript logical operators. X and Y are both assumed to be logical expressions.*

Symbol	Operation	Example	Evaluation
&&	And	X && Y	True if both X and Y are True; False otherwise.
||	Or	X || Y	True if X or Y, or both of them, are True; False only if both X and Y are False.
!	Not	!X	True if X is False, False if X is True.

The logical operators are often used in conjunction with the comparison operators. For example, the following expression evaluates as True only if x is equal to 8 and y is not equal to 3.

```
(x == 8) && (y != 3)
```

The bitwise operators

JScript has a group of bitwise operators that are used to manipulate the individual bits in integer binary data. Although they are seldom used in desktop scripts, here is a brief listing so you will recognize them should you ever see them.

& Bitwise And

| Bitwise Or

^ Bitwise Exclusive Or

<< Leftward shift

>> Rightward shift

>>> Zero-fill rightward shift

JScript also has compound operators that combine the assignment operator with one of the bitwise operator. Thus,

```
x &= y;
```

performs a bitwise And between x and y and assigns the result to x.

String Operators

There is one string operator, the + sign, which, when used with string data (or data that is coerced to string type), performs concatenation. Here's an example:

```
var s1 = "apple";
var s2 = " pie";
var s3;

s3 = s1 + s2;
```

The result is that s3 holds the string "apple pie".

Conditional Expressions

A conditional expression is not, strictly speaking, an operator but it belongs in this section because it acts like an operator in that it manipulates data. A JScript conditional expression has the following syntax:

```
(condition) ? val1 : val2
```

If `condition` is True, the expression evaluates as `val1`. If `condition` is False, the expression evaluates as `val2`. The following statement, for example, results in z having the larger of the two values x and y:

```
z = (x > y) ? x : y;
```

Operator Precedence and Parentheses

It may not be clear how some expressions that contain multiple operators are evaluated, because the result will depend on the order in which the operations are processed. Operator precedence was explained in detail in Chapter 6. Just like VBScript, the JScript operators have an assigned precedence level that determines the order in which operations are done if not modified by parentheses. Operators with the same precedence are always evaluated in left to right order, or as modified by parentheses. This order, from highest precedence to lowest, is as follows:

Logical Not (!), increment (++), decrement (--)
Multiply (*), divide (/), and modulus (%)
Addition (+), subtraction (-)
Shift (<<, >>, >>>)
Comparison (<=, <, >=, >)
Equality (==, !=)
Bitwise And (&)
Bitwise Exclusive Or (^)
Bitwise Or (^)
Logical And (&&)
Logical Or (||)
Conditional (?:)
Assignment (all of them)

If the precedence of the operators in an expression does not suit your needs, you can use parentheses to modify it. Parentheses must always be in pairs. Parts of an expression inside parentheses are evaluated first, regardless of operator precedence. Parentheses can be nested, with evaluation proceeding from the innermost set of parentheses outward. Here's an example:

```
3 + 2 * 5;          // Evaluates as 13 because the * is done first.
(3 + 2) * 5         // Evaluates as 25 because the + is performed first.
```

Overview

JScript provides the script developer with a powerful set of data storage and manipulation tools suitable for just about any circumstance. Like VBScript, JScript has only a single data type that is used to hold all kinds of data, whether numbers, text, or object references. Unlike VBScript, variable names in JScript are case sensitive, so you need to use extra care when typing in your scripts.

E L E V E N

JScript: Conditional Statements, Loops, and Functions

The code in a script normally executes in top-down order, from the first statement to the last. This is rarely sufficient. Most scripts, excepting only the simplest, require some control over the order and number of times that statements are executed. **Conditional statements** *control which statements are executed. Blocks of one of more statements may be executed or not executed based on conditions in the program.* **Loop statements** *execute blocks of code a fixed number of times, or repeatedly until a specified condition is met.* **Functions** *let you separate code into discrete, named sections that can be executed as needed. These JScript capabilities are the topic of this chapter.*

Conditional Statements

As the name suggests, a conditional statement controls program execution based on conditions in the program. JScript code is executed, or not executed, as specified in the syntax of the conditional statement. JScript has two conditional statements.

If . . . Else

The `if...else` statement executes a block of code if a condition is True, and optionally executes another block of code if the condition is False. The syntax is

```
if (condition)
{
// Executed if condition is True.
}
else
{
// Executed if condition is False.
}
```

Condition is any expression that can be evaluated as either True or False. The `else` clause and its associated block of statement are optional. If the code to be executed is only a single statement, the braces can be omitted:

```
if (condition)
    statement1;
else
    statement2;
```

Listing 11-1 shows an example of using the `if` statement. Note that this and other listings in this chapter get around JScript's lack of a keyboard input function by putting the script in a .wsf file and making use of VBScript's `InputBox` function. You'll learn the details of this technique in Chapter 14.

LISTING 11-1 *Using the `if` statement.*

```
<!--List1101.wsf. The if statement. -->
<JOB>

<SCRIPT LANGUAGE="VBScript">

function prompt(sPrompt,sTitle,sDefault)
  prompt = inputbox(sPrompt, sTitle, sDefault)
end function

</SCRIPT>

<SCRIPT LANGUAGE="JScript">

var n1;
var n2;
n1 = prompt("Enter a number: ", "", "");
n2 = prompt("Enter another number: ", "", "");
if (n1 > n2)
      WScript.Echo("The first number is larger than the second number.");
else
      WScript.Echo("The first number is larger than the second number.");
</SCRIPT>

</JOB>
```

You can nest `if` statements as needed, as long as each inner `if` is completely enclosed within the outer `if`. Here's an example:

```
if (x > 5)
{
    if (y < 12)
    {
    // Statements to be executed if both conditions are True.
    }
)
```

In many cases like this one, you can achieve the same result by using the logical operators instead of nesting `if` statements. The following code does exactly the same thing as the preceding example:

```
if (x > 5) && (y < 12)
{
// Statements to be executed if both conditions are True.
)
```

Sometimes, however, you have no choice and must nest `if` statements. Listing 11-2 shows an example. This is an extension of the script in Listing 11-1 to allow for the possibility that the two numbers are equal.

Listing 11–2 *Using nested `if` statements.*

```
<!--List1102.wsf. Nested if statements. -->
<JOB>

<SCRIPT LANGUAGE="VBScript">

function prompt(sPrompt,sTitle,sDefault)
  prompt = inputbox(sPrompt, sTitle, sDefault)
end function

</SCRIPT>

<SCRIPT LANGUAGE="JScript">

var n1;
var n2;
n1 = prompt("Enter a number: ", "", "");
n2 = prompt("Enter another number: ", "", "");
if (n1 > n2)
      WScript.Echo("The first number is larger than the second number.");
else
{
    if (n1 < n2)
      WScript.Echo("The first number is smaller than the second number.");
    else
      WScript.Echo("The first number is equal to the second number.");
}
</SCRIPT>

</JOB>
```

Switch

The switch statement directs execution to a block of statements based on the evaluation of an expression. The syntax is

```
switch (expression)
{
    case match1:
    // Code to be executed if expression == match1.
    break;
    case match2:
    // Code to be executed if expression == match2.
    break;
    ....
    default:
    // code to be executed if there is no match.
}
```

You can have as many case statements as needed. The default section is optional. If it is omitted, none of the code inside the switch statement will be executed if there is no match found.

Note the use of the break statement, which causes execution to exit the switch statement. Unlike VBScript's Select Case statement, execution in switch does not automatically exit once the block associated with a match has been executed. Without a properly placed break statement, execution will simply continue through the rest of the statements in the switch. Here's an example:

```
switch (x)
{
    case 5:
        y = 50;
    case 6:
        y = 60;
}
```

This code will set y to 60 regardless of whether x is equal to 5 or 6. If x is equal to 5 the y=50 statement is executed but then, because there is no break statement, execution continues with the y=60 statement. For the code to work properly, you would write as follows:

```
switch (x)
{
    case 5:
        y = 50;
        break;
    case 6:
        y = 60;
}
```

Sometimes you can use the fact that execution "falls through" a `switch` statement to your advantage. Here's an example that sets the variable size to either "small" or "large" depending on the name of the state.

```
switch (state)
{
    case "Rhode Island"
    case "Delaware"
    case "Vermont"
    case "New Hampshire"
        size = "small";
        break;
    case "Texas"
    case "Alaska"
    case "California"
        size = "large";
}
```

Loop Statements

JScript's loop statements execute a block of code a specified number of times. You can specify the number of iterations ahead of time, or you can specify that the code repeats until a condition is met. The `for` statement is used for the former, and the `while` and `do...while` statements are used for the latter.

For

The `for` statement has the following syntax:

```
for (initial; condition; increment)
{
statements
}
```

When execution reaches a `for` statement, here's what happens:

1. *Initial* is executed.
2. *Condition* is evaluated. If it is True, *statements* are executed. If it is False, execution leaves the `for` statement.
3. *Increment* is executed.
4. Return to step 2.

A simple example will make this a lot clearer. This code will display the numbers 1, 2, ..., 10 on the screen.

```
for (i = 1; i < 11; i++)
{
    WScript.Echo(i);
}
```

The *initial* and *increment* parts of the `for` statement can be omitted as long as the required actions are carried out elsewhere. For example, the following code is exactly equivalent to the preceding example:

```
i = 1;
for (; i < 11 ; )
{
    WScript.Echo(i);
    i++;
}
```

Note that when you omit the *initial* or the *increment* part of the `for` statement, you still must include the semicolons.

When writing `for` statements, be careful not to create an infinite loop — one that never ends. The following code is an infinite loop. Because the variable i is never incremented, the condition i < 11 will always be True and the loop will never terminate and you'll get the number 1 displayed over and over again.

```
i = 1;
for (; i < 11 ; )
{
    WScript.Echo(i);
}
```

You can terminate execution of a `for` statement by using the `break` statement. You have seen `break` used before in other types of loop and conditional statements. When execution encounters a `break` statement within a `for` statement, execution immediately leaves the `for` statement. Here's an example. Assume that data is a 100-element array of numbers. This `for` loop executes until all elements of the array have been examined, or until an element equal to 1234 is found, whichever occurs first.

```
for (i = 0; i < 100 ; i++)
{
    if (data[i] == 1234)
        break;
}
```

While

The `while` statement executes a block of JScript statements repeatedly as long as a specified condition is True. The syntax is as follows:

```
while (condition)
{
    statements
}
```

Statements will be executed repeatedly as long as *condition* is True. If there is only a single statement to execute, the braces can be omitted. Note that if *condition* is False to begin with, the block of statements will not be executed even once. Here is an example that does essentially the same thing as the final example given for the `for` statement. This code looks through the 100-element array data, stopping when it reaches the end of the array or finds an element equal to 1234.

```
i = 0;
while ((data[i] != 1234) && (i < 100))
{
    i++;
}
```

As with other loops, you can exit a `while` loop by using the `break` statement.

Do. . .While

The `do...while` statement is almost identical to the `while` statement and executes a block of JScript statements as long as a condition is True. The one difference is that the condition is tested at the end of the block, and not at the beginning. The syntax is

```
do
{
    statements
} while(condition)
```

The practical difference between `do...while` and `while` is that, with the former, you are guaranteed that the block of statements will be executed at least once. As before, you can use `break` to exit a `do...while` loop.

The Continue Statement

The `continue` statement is not itself a loop statement, but it is used with the loop statements. You can use `continue` in a `for`, a `while`, or a `do...while` loop. The purpose of this statement is to cause execution to return to the test part of the loop — the location where the condition is tested. Statements between the `continue` statement and the end of the loop are skipped. Here's an example of using the `continue` statement. This code will display the numbers 1, 2, 4, and 5 on the screen. Note how `continue` is used to skip displaying the value 3.

```
i = 0;
while (i < 5)
{
    i++;
    if i == 3
        continue;
    Wcript.Echo(i);
}
```

The With Statement

The `with` statement establishes a default object to be used for a block of statements. It is really only a programming convenience, but it can lessen the amount of typing you need to do. The syntax is

```
with (object)
{
statements
}
```

Within the block of statements, *object* will be the default object reference and need not be entered explicitly in code. Here's an example. Suppose you have an object reference myObj and you want to set several of its properties. You could write the following:

```
myObj.color = "red";
myObj.font = "Ariel";
myObj.width = 155;
myObj.height = 220;
myObj.style = "3D";
```

Using the `with` statement, you could write the following shorter code that would have the same result:

```
with (myObj) {
    color = "red";
    font = "Ariel";
    width = 155;
    height = 220;
    style = "3D"; }
```

The `with` statement applies to object methods as well as to properties.

Functions

With functions, you can create self-contained sections of code that perform specific actions. Whenever you want to execute the code in a function, you refer to its name in your script code. Functions can receive information passed by the calling program and can also return information back to the program.

Defining a Function

The basic syntax for defining a function is

```
function funcname(arguments)
{
function code
return returnvalue;
}
```

Funcname is the name of the function. Rules for naming functions are the same as for naming JScript variables, as presented in Chapter 10. The name of a function must be unique within its script.

Arguments is a list of one or more arguments that the function expects. You use arguments to pass information to the function when you call it. If a function does not take arguments, simply include an empty set of parentheses.

Function code is the code to be executed in the function. A function can contain any JScript code except for the definition of another function.

Returnvalue is the value the function will return to the calling program. If the function does not return a value, omit the `return` keyword.

Let's look at an example. The following code defines a JScript function named sum, which takes three arguments and returns their sum:

```
function sum(x, y, z)
{
    var total;
    total = x + y + z;
    return total;
}
```

The `return` statement does not have to be at the end of the function. You can have multiple `return` statements, and the first one that is executed will cause the function to terminate and return the specified value to the calling program. Here's an example, a function that returns the larger of two numbers:

```
function larger(a, b)
{
    if (a > b)
        return a;
    else
        return b;
}
```

You can place function definitions anywhere in your scripts, although it is most common to place them all at the beginning of the script. The scripting engine recognizes function definitions and does not execute them except when they are called by code in the script. You'll see an example in the next section.

Variables in Functions

You can declare variables inside a JScript function, using the `var` statement. JScript does not require variable declaration at all, but when you declare a variable inside a function (as opposed to just using the variable name) it acquires a special status — namely, it becomes *local* to the function. This means that the variable is visible only inside the function, and outside the function, even in the same script, it may as well not exist at all. This is true even if there is another variable of the same name used outside of the function. By keeping your function variables local, you lessen the chance of unwanted interactions between the code in the function and code in other parts of the script.

The code in Listing 11-3 shows this principle in action. The code has two variables, x and y, that are used outside the function. It also uses two variables, x and y, inside the function. The difference is that inside the function x is explicitly declared with `var` while y is not explicitly declared.

LISTING 11-3 *Local variables in functions.*

```
//list1103.js
// Local variables in functions.

function foo()
{
var x = 12;
y = 12;
msg = "In the function x = " + x + " and y = " + y;
WScript.Echo(msg);
}

x = 999;
y = 999;
msg = "Before the function call x = " + x + " and y = " + y;
WScript.Echo(msg);
foo();
msg = "After the function call x = " + x + " and y = " + y;
WScript.Echo(msg);
```

When you run the script, it produces the following output:

```
Before the function call x = 999 and y = 999
In the function x = 12 and y = 12
After the function call x = 999 and y = 12
```

You can see that the code in the function was able to change the value of the variable y as seen outside the function but was not able to change the value of the variable x as seen outside the function. This is because x was declared with `var` inside the function.

Here's another way to look at it. If you use a variable name inside and outside functions, then

- Declaring the variable in a function gives a new and independent copy of the variable that is used inside the function.
- Using the variable in the function without declaring it accesses the same copy that is visible outside the function.

Each function that declares a variable has its own private copy. Note, however, that local variables that are declared in functions are temporary, which means that they do not hold their value between calls to the function. Each time you call a function, its local variables are reinitialized.

Calling a Function

Functions that return a value are, in effect, expressions because they evaluate to a value. You can use such functions anywhere you would use any JScript expression, such as on the right side of an assignment statement as shown here:

```
total = sum(1, 2, 3);
```

You can also use a function as an argument to another function. Suppose you wrote a function named `halfof`:

```
function halfof(x)
{
    return x / 2;
}
```

You could then write the following to calculate half of the sum of three numbers:

```
result = halfof(sum(1, 2, 3));
```

Or you could call the functions and display the result in a single statement:

```
WScript.Echo(halfof(sum(1, 2, 3)));
```

If a function does not return a value, it cannot be treated as an expression. To call it, you simply include its name and arguments in your code. If a function does not take arguments, you must still include the empty parentheses when calling it. Listing 11-4 demonstrates a script that has two functions, one that returns a value and one that does not.

LISTING 11–4 *Using functions in a script.*

```
// List1104.js
// Demonstrating functions.

function sum(x, y, z)
{
    return x + y + z;
}

function display(message)
{
    WScript.Echo(message)
}

var answer;
answer = sum(1, 44, 99);
display(answer);
```

If you call a function and try to pass it the wrong number of arguments, WSH generates an error.

Overview

Once you get beyond simple scripts, you will need to control the path of execution in your JScript code. The language provides you with a variety of conditional and loop statements that are capable of meeting any imaginable need. You can also isolate sections of code in functions and then call the functions as needed.

TWELVE

JScript: Strings, Numbers, Math, Dates, and Times

In this chapter we cover JScript's specialized tools for dealing with data of various kinds. The `String` object provides a powerful set of capabilities for handling text data. The `Math` and `Number` objects are used for working with numerical data. Finally, the `Date` object is specialized for working with dates and times.

The String Object

Any variable that holds string data is not just a simple storage location. In JScript, string data is managed by the `String` object. The creation of `String` objects is handled automatically by JScript, so the simple act of creating a variable and assigning string data to it is all you need to do. Look at this code:

```
var name;
name = "Peter";
```

This results in name being a `String` object with all of its properties and methods available for use in the script. You can also explicitly create a `String` object, like this:

```
name = new String("Peter");
```

However, there is no advantage do doing it this way so you almost never see it.

The `String` object has a single property, `length`, that returns the length of the string (the number of characters). The script in Listing 12-1 shows how you could use this property to ensure that a password entered by the user is at least a certain length.

LISTING 12–1 *Using the `String` object's length property.*

```
<!--List1201.wsf. The String object's length property. -->
<JOB>
<SCRIPT LANGUAGE="VBScript">
function prompt(sPrompt,sTitle,sDefault)
  prompt = inputbox(sPrompt, sTitle, sDefault)
end function
</SCRIPT>
<SCRIPT LANGUAGE="JScript">
var password;
do
    password = prompt("Enter a password of at least 5 characters:", "", "");
while (password.length < 5)
Wscript.Echo("Password accepted")
</SCRIPT>
</JOB>
```

The `String` object also has a number of methods. Those methods that are relevant to WSH programming are presented in Table 12-1. The `String` object has some other properties that are relevant only to using JScript on Web pages, and they are not included here.

TABLE 12-1 *Methods of the `String` object.*

Method	Purpose	Example

charAt(*index*)	Returns the single character at position *index*. The first character has index 0.	`var s = "abcde";`
		`c = s.charAt(3);`
		`// c contains "d"`

charCodeAt (*index*)	Returns the Unicode encoding of the character at position *index*. The first character has index 0.	`var s = "abcde";`
		`c = s.charAt(1);`
		`// c contains 98`

concat (*string2*)	Returns a string consisting of the original string with *string2* concatented at the end.	`var s = "abcde";`
		`c = s.concat("!!");`
		`// c contains "abcde!!"`

indexOf (*template, start*)	Returns the location where *template* is first found in the string, starting at position *start*. If *start* is omitted, the search starts at the first character. If *template* is not found, the method returns –1.	`var s = "Mississippi";`
		`c = s.indexOf("s");`
		`// c contains 2`
		`c = s.indexOf("s", 4);`
		`// c contains 5`
		`c = s.indexOf("M", 4);`
		`// c contains -1`

TABLE 12-1 *Methods of the `String` object. (Continued)*

Method	Purpose	Example

lastIndexOf (*template, start*)	Returns the location where *template* is first found in the string, searching backwards starting at position *start*. If *start* is omitted, the search starts at the last character. If *template* is not found, the method returns –.	`var s = "Mississippi";`
		`c =`
		`s.lastIndexOf("s");`
		`// c contains 6`
		`c = s.lastIndexOf("p",`
		`4);`
		`// c contains -1`

match (*regExp*)	Returns an array containing the results of a search using the specified regular expression object.	`See text below for details.`
replace (*regExp, text*)	Returns a string with the specified text replaced as indicated by the specified regular expression object.	`See text below for details.`
search (*regExp*)	Returns the result of a search using the specified regular expression object.	`See text below for details.`

slice(*start, end*)	Returns a portion of a string starting at position *start* and ending at position *end*. If *end* is omitted, the new string extends to the end of the original string.	`var s = "abcde";`
		`c = s.slice(1, 3);`
		`// c contains "bcd"`

split (*separator*)	Returns an array of strings created by separating the original string at the indicated separator.	`See text below for details.`

substr(*start, length*)	Returns a substring from the original string beginning at position *start* and containing *length* characters. If *length* is omitted, the substring extends to the end of the original string.	`var s = "abcde";`
		`c = s.substr(1,2);`
		`// c contains "bc"`
		`c = s.substr(2);`
		`// c contains "cde"`

substring (*idxA, idxB*)	Returns a substring from the original string beginning at position *idxA* ending at the character just before position *idxB*.	`var s = "abcde";`
		`c = s.substring(1, 4);`
		`// c contains "bcd"`

toLowerCase	Returns the original string with all letters converted to lowercase.	`var s = "ABCDE99";`
		`c = s.toLowerCase()`
		`// c contains`
		`"abcde99"`

toUpperCase()	Returns the original string with all letters converted to uppercase.	`var s = "abcde99";`
		`c = s.toUpperCase()`
		`// c contains`
		`"ABCDE99"`

toString()*	Returns the string.	`var s = "abcde";`
		`c = s.toString();`
		`// c contains "abcde"`

valueOf()*	Returns the string.	`var s = "abcde";`
		`c = s.valueOf();`
		`// c contains "abcde"`

* These methods may not seem to have any purpose. They are retained for compatibility with other elements of JScript syntax.

The Split Method

The `String` object's `split` method is useful when you have a single string that contains two or more substrings, separated by a specific separator character. For example, certain text file formats utilize commas or semicolons to delineate substrings. Here's an example of a string that uses the semicolon to separate the elements of a person's address:

```
John Smith;12 Oak Street;Raleigh;NC;28818
```

The script in Listing 12-2 shows an example of using the Split method. The user is prompted to enter two or more words separated by a semicolon. The script then uses the `split` method to separate the words, which are then displayed to the user. Sample output from the script is shown in Figure 12-1.

LISTING 12-2 Using the `String` object's split method.

```
<!--List1202.wsf. The String object's split method. -->
<JOB>

<SCRIPT LANGUAGE="VBScript">

function prompt(sPrompt,sTitle,sDefault)
  prompt = inputbox(sPrompt, sTitle, sDefault)
end function

</SCRIPT>

<SCRIPT LANGUAGE="JScript">
var s;
var sa;
var msg;

s = prompt("Enter two or more words separated by a semicolon:", "", "");

sa = s.split(";");

msg = "You entered " + sa.length + " words:\n";

for (var i = 0; i < sa.length ; i++)
    msg = msg + sa[i] + "\n";

Wscript.Echo(msg)

</SCRIPT>

</JOB>
```

Working with Regular Expressions

Several of the `String` object's methods work with regular expressions that specify more sophisticated search and find options than are possible with the `indexOf` method. You use the `regExp` object to work with regular expressions. There are two different syntaxes for creating a `regExp` object:

FIGURE 12–1 *Output from the script in Listing 12.2.*

```
var re;
re = /pattern/[switch];                 //syntax 1
re = new RegExp(pattern, switch);       //syntax 2
```

Pattern is a string specifying the regular expression pattern. *Switch* is an optional argument specifying search options. Possible switches are as follows:

- i   Ignore case
- g   Global search (all occurrences, not just the first)
- gi Global search, ignore case

The first syntax for creating a `regExp` object is used when you know the regular expression pattern ahead of time. Use the second syntax when the search pattern is unknown (for example, when it is input by the user).

Details on creating search patterns and on using the `regExp` object's methods were presented in Chapter 8, and you can refer to that chapter for details (use of this object is essentially the same for VBScript and JScript). Here are only a few examples. In these methods, assume that s is a `String` object containing the string to be searched.

To find the first occurrence of "fox" with case sensitivity:

```
var result;
var re = /fox/;
result = s.search(re);
```

To find all occurrences of "cost," case insensitive:

```
var result;
var re = /cost/gi;
result = s.match(re);
```

To replace all occurrences of "hard" with "difficult," case insensitive:

```
var result;
var re = /hard/gi;
result = s.replace(re, "difficult");
```

The Number Object

When you use numerical data in JScript, the `Number` object is quietly working behind the scenes. You can, if you want, explicitly create a `Number` object using this syntax:

```
var n = new Number(value);
```

However, there is never any need to do this since any numerical variable is automatically created as a `Number` object. This object has a set of properties and methods, which are described in Tables 12-2 and 12-3. Regarding the properties of the `Number` object, it is important to note that none of them provide information about the numerical value that is stored in a particular number object. Rather, they provide information about the limitations of JScript when it comes to handling numbers.

TABLE 12-2 *Properties of the `Number` object.*

Property	Description
MAX_VALUE	Returns the largest number that can be represented in JScript. Equal to approximately 1.79E+308.
MIN_VALUE	Returns the smallest number (closest to zero) that can be represented in JScript. Equal to approximately 2.22E–308.
NaN	Not a number. A special value that indicates an arithmetic expression returned a value that is not a number.
NEGATIVE_INFINITY	Returns a value more negative than the largest negative number (–Number.MAX_VALUE) that can be represented in JScript. Mathematically this value behaves as minus infinity (-1/0).
POSITIVE_INFINITY	Returns a value more positive than the largest positive number (Number.MAX_VALUE) that can be represented in JScript. Mathematically this value behaves as positive infinity (1/0).

Note that the usage of the `NaN` property is rather obscure. The property does not return an indication of whether a specific `Number` object contains a value that is not a number. You cannot simply test the property, as shown here:

```
// Does not work!
If (val.NaN)
// val contains a value that is not a number.
else
// val contains a value that is a number.
```

To test whether a variable contains a number, you use the `isNaN` function. The syntax is

```
isNaN(expression)
```

The function returns True if the expression does not evaluate as a number, False otherwise. The `isNaN` function is most commonly used with the `parseInt` and `parseFloat` methods.

TABLE 12-3 *Methods of the `Number` object.*

Method	Description
toString(*radix*)	Returns a string representation of the number in the specified *radix* (number base). If the radix argument is omitted, base 10 is used. Use a radix argument of 2 for binary, 16 for hexadecimal, etc.
valueOf()	Returns the value stored in the object.

The script in Listing 12-3 demonstrates some of the properties and methods of the `Number` object. The user is prompted to enter a number or a string. If the entry can be interpreted as a number, it is displayed in decimal and in binary representation using the `toString` method. If the entry cannot be parsed as a number, a message is displayed to that effect.

LISTING 12–3 *Demonstrating properties and methods of the `Number` object.*

```
<!--List1203.wsf. Number object properties and methods. -->
<JOB>

<SCRIPT LANGUAGE="VBScript">

function prompt(sPrompt,sTitle,sDefault)
  prompt = inputbox(sPrompt, sTitle, sDefault)
end function

</SCRIPT>

<SCRIPT LANGUAGE="JScript">
var s;
var s1;
var msg;

s = prompt("Enter a number or a string:", "", "");
s1 = parseFloat(s);

if (isNaN(s1))
    msg = "You entered a string."
else
    msg = "You entered " + s1 + " which in binary is " +
s1.toString(2);

WScript.Echo(msg)

</SCRIPT>

</JOB>
```

The Math Object

The `Math` object has a set of properties and methods that provides constants and procedures for performing a variety of commonly needed mathematical operations. You do not need to create an instance of this object, as it is intrinsically available in JScript. For example, to set a variable equal to the mathematical constant PI you would write

```
var pi = Math.PI;
```

The properties and methods of the `Math` object are described in Tables 12-4 and 12-5. Note that the properties are used to return mathematical constants, while the methods are used to perform calculations.

TABLE 12-4 *Methods of the Math object.*

Method	Returns
abs(*n*)	The absolute value of *n*
acos(*n*)	The arc cosine of *n*
asin(*n*)	The arc sine of *n*
atan(*n*)	The arc tangent of *n*
atan2(*x, y*)	The angle from the X axis of the polar coordinate of point *x, y*
ceil(*n*)	The next larger integer greater than *n*
cos(*n*)	The cosine of *n*
exp(*n*)	e to the power of *n*
floor(*n*)	The next smaller integer less than *n*
log(*n*)	The natural logarithm of *n*
max(*n1, n2*)	The larger of the two numbers *n1* and *n2*
min(*n1, n2*)	The smaller of the two numbers *n1* and *n2*
pow(*n1, n2*)	*n1* raised to the power *n2*
random()	A pseudo-random number between 0 and 1
round(*n*)	*n* rounded to the nearest integer
sin(*n*)	The sine of *n*
sqrt(*n*)	The square root of *n*
tan(*n*)	The tangent of *n*

Universal Coordinated Time

UTC, previously known as Greenwich Mean Time or GMT, refers to the world standard time at the 0 degree meridian which passes through Greenwich, England. The abbreviation UTC is indeed correct, as opposed to UCT, as it is derived from French.

TABLE 12-5 *Properties of the `Math` object.*

Property	Returns
E	e (the base of the natural logarithms)
LN10	The natural logarithm of 10
LN2	The natural logarithm of 2
LOG10E	The base 10 logarithm of e
LOG2E	The base 2 logarithm of e
PI	pi (π)
SQRT1_2	The square root of 1/2
SQRT2	The square root of 2

Dates and Times

Many scripts need to deal with dates and times. Like VBScript, JScript provides a powerful set of tools for working with data that represent dates and/or times. These tools are encapsulated in the `Date` object. You create a new `Date` object as follows:

```
var myDate = new Date(dateinfo);
```

Dateinfo is an optional argument specifying the date and time to be stored in the new `Date` object. If this argument is omitted, the current date and time are used. You can specify *dateinfo* in several formats:

- In VT_DATE format, which is how dates are returned by some ActiveX objects.
- As a number specifying the number of milliseconds in Universal Coordinated Time (UTC) between midnight, January 1, 1970 and the date/time.
- As the year, month and day; for example, (1999, 6, 5) for June 5, 1999.
- As the year, month, and day and the hour, minute, and second. For example, (1999, 6, 5, 15, 30, 0) is 3:30:00 P.M. on the indicated date.

Dates and times are almost always treated as local dates and times, but in some cases (as we will see below) can be treated as UTC values.

The `Date` object has no properties but quite a few methods. Those dealing with dates are listed in Table 12-6, and those dealing with times in Table 12-7. You'll see that some of the methods have two variants, one that uses the locale date/time and the other that uses UTC. The latter methods are distinguished by having the letters UTC in their names. Some additional methods not dealing specifically with dates or times are presented in Table 12-8. Following the tables, Listing 12-4 shows some examples of using the `Date` object.

TABLE 12-6 *`Date` object methods that deal with dates.*

Method	Description
getDate() getUTCDate()	Returns the day of the month as an integer between 1 and 31.
getDay() getUTCDay()	Returns the day of the week as an integer between 0 (Sunday) and 6 (Saturday).
getFullYear() getUTCFullYear()	Returns a four-digit integer indicating the year.
getMonth() getUTCMonth()	Returns the month as an integer between 0 (January) and 11 (December).
getVarDate()	Returns the date in VT_DATE format.
getYear()	Returns the two-digit year as an integer.
setDate(*dayValue*) setUTCDate(*dayValue*)	Sets the day of the month. *DayValue* is an integer between 1 and 31.
setFullYear(*yearValue*) setUTCFullYear(*yearValue*)	Sets the year to the four-digit year specified by *yearValue*).
setMonth(*monthValue*) setUTCMonth(*monthValue*)	Sets the month value, where *monthValue* is a value between 0 (January) and 11 (December).

TABLE 12-7 *`Date` object methods that deal with times.*

Method	Description
getHours() getUTCHours()	Returns the hour as an integer between 0 and 23.
getMilliseconds() getUTCMilliseconds()	Returns the milliseconds as an integer between 0 and 999.

TABLE 12-7 `Date` *object methods that deal with times. (Continued)*

Method	Description
getMinutes() getUTCMinutes()	Returns the minutes as an integer between 0 and 59.
getSeconds() getUTCSeconds()	Returns the seconds as an integer between 0 and 59.
getTime()	Returns the number of milliseconds between midnight, January 1, 1970, and the current `Date` object.
getTimeZoneOffset()	Returns the number of minutes between local time and UTC.
parse(*dateString*)	Returns the number of milliseconds between midnight, January 1, 1970, and the date specified by *dateString*.
setHours(*hourValue*) setUTCHours(*hourValue*)	Sets the hour, where *hourValue* is a value between 0 and 23.
setMilliseconds(*msValue*) setUTCMilliseconds(*msValue*)	Sets the milliseconds, where *msValue* is a value between 0 and 999.
setMinutes(*minValue*) setUTCMinutes(*minValue*)	Sets the minutes, where *minValue* is a value between 0 and 59.
setSeconds(*secondsValue*) setUTCSeconds(*secondsValue*)	Sets the seconds, where *secondsValue* is a value between 0 and 59.

TABLE 12-8 *Other* `Date` *object methods.*

Method	Description
setTime(*timeValue*)	Sets the date and time, where *timeValue* is the number of milliseconds between midnight, January 1, 1970, and the date/time.
toGMTString	Same as toUTCString( ), included for backward compatibility.
toLocaleString( )	Returns the date as a string using local time.
toUTCString()	Returns the date as a string using UTC time.
UTC(*y, m, d, h, m, s*)	Returns the number of milliseconds between midnight, January 1, 1970 and the specified date.

LISTING 12–4 *Using the `Date` object.*

```
<!-- List1204.wsf. Using the Date object. -->
<JOB>

<SCRIPT LANGUAGE="VBScript">

function prompt(sPrompt,sTitle,sDefault)
  prompt = inputbox(sPrompt, sTitle, sDefault)
end function

</SCRIPT>

<SCRIPT LANGUAGE="JScript">

// Display the current date and time.
var today = new Date();
WScript.Echo("Right now it is " + today.toLocaleString());

// Get the user's graduation year.
var gradYear;
var yearsSinceGraduation;
gradYear = prompt("What year did you graduate high school (e.g., 1985)?","","");

// Calculate how many years since then.
yearsSinceGraduation = today.getFullYear() - gradYear;
WScript.Echo("You graduated " + yearsSinceGraduation + " years ago.");

</SCRIPT>

</JOB>
```

Overview

In this chapter you learned about some of JScript's specialized tools for working with data. The `String` object is automatically created whenever you store text in a variable and provides a full range of methods for working with text data. The `Number` and `Math` objects are very useful when working with numerical data. Finally, the `Date` object provides powerful tools for working with dates and times.

THIRTEEN

JScript: Built-in Objects, User Interaction, and Error Handling

This chapter completes our coverage of the JScript language. First, we take a look at those built-in JScript objects that are not covered elsewhere. Next, we explore how a JScript script can interact with the user. Finally, we examine the tools that JScript provides for dealing with run-time errors.

JScript Objects

The JScript language is heavily object-oriented, and many of its capabilities are provided in the form of objects. You have learned about some of these objects in earlier chapters, and the remaining ones are covered here. Table 13-1 summarizes all of JScript's objects and refers you to the chapter where each one is explained.

TABLE 13-1 *JScript objects.*

Object	Description	Please see
ActiveXObject	Obtains a reference to an ActiveX automation object	Chapter 15
Array	Used to create data arrays	Chapter 10
Boolean	Creates Boolean values	This chapter
Date	Works with dates and times	Chapter 12
Dictionary	Stores associative arrays	Chapter 2
Enumerator	Enumerates items in a collection	This chapter
Error	Handles run-time errors	This chapter
FileSystemObject	Works with files and folders	Chapter 15
Function	Creates a function	This chapter
Math	Mathematical operations	Chapter 12
Number	Works with numbers	Chapter 12
RegExp	Performs regular expression searches	Chapter 12
String	Works with string data	Chapter 12
VBArray	Accesses Visual Basic safe arrays	This chapter

The remainder of this section covers those JScript objects that are not covered in other chapters. The one exception is the `Error` object, which is covered later in this chapter in the section on error handling. Be aware that some of these objects are rarely if ever seen in JScript code, and, like the `Number` object, their functions are in many cases handled automatically by JScript.

The Boolean Object

The `Boolean` object serves as a wrapper for Boolean (True/False) data. You can create a new `Boolean` object as follows:

```
var variablename = new Boolean(value)
```

Value is optional. If it is omitted, False, `NaN, null, 0,` or an empty string, then the initial value of the object is False. Otherwise the initial value is True. JScript implicitly uses the `Boolean` object as needed, and you will probably never need to create it explicitly.

The Enumerator Object

The `Enumerator` object is used to access the members of a collection. The syntax is as follows:

```
var e;
e = new Enumerator(collection);
```

Collection is a reference to the collection you want to access. For example, when you use the `FileSystemObject` to work with files, you will use collections often. The `Enumerator` object has no properties. Its methods are detailed in Table 13-2.

TABLE 13-2 *Methods of the Enumerator object.*

Method	Description
atEnd()	Returns True if the Enumerator is currently at the last item in the collection. Returns False otherwise.
item()	Returns the current item in the collection. If the collection is empty or the current item is undefined, returns `undefined`.
moveFirst()	Moves to the first item in the collection.
moveLast()	Moves to the next item in the collection. If the collection is already at the last item, or the collection is empty, returns `undefined`.

Please refer to Listing 15-2 to see an example of using the `Enumerator` object.

The Function Object

The `Function` object represents functions in JScript. When you use the standard syntax for creating a function, as you learned in Chapter 11, JScript automatically encapsulates the function in a `Function` object. You can also explicitly create a `Function` object using the syntax shown here:

```
funcname = new Function(arg1, ... , argn, body);
```

Funcname is the name of the function. *Arg1* through *argn* are the function arguments, if any. *Body* is the body of the function. Here is an example of explicitly creating a function to add three numbers:

```
var sum;
sum = new Function("a", "b", "c", "return a+b+c");
```

This has exactly the same effect as the standard format shown here:

```
function sum(a, b, c)
{
    return a+b+c;
}
```

It will probably never be necessary to explicitly create a `Function` object.

The VBArray Object

The `VBArray` object is designed to permit JScript code to access the data stored in a VBscript array. Because JScript and VBScript differ in how they handle arrays, it is not possible for JScript code to work directly with certain features of VBscript arrays, such as multiple dimensions. Please refer to Chapter 6 for information on VBscript arrays.

To create a `VBArray` object, use the following syntax:

```
var vba;
vba = new VBArray(array)
```

Array is a reference to a VBscript array. This would be obtained, for example, from VBScript code. Once the `VBArray` object has been created, you use its methods as explained in Table 13-3. This object has no properties.

TABLE 13-3 *Methods of the VBArray object.*

Method	Description
dimensions()	Returns the number of dimensions in the array.
getItem(*d1, d2, ..., dn*)	Returns the specified item in the array. *d1* through *dn* specify the indexes of the item, with one index for each dimension.
lbound(*d*)*	Returns the lower bound index of the specified dimension of the array. If *d* is omitted, then 1 is assumed. If the object is empty, the method returns `undefined`. If dimension *d* does not exist or *d* is negative, an error occurs.
ubound(*d*)	Returns the upper bound index of the specified dimension of the array. If *d* is omitted, then 1 is assumed. If the object is empty, the method returns `undefined`. If dimension *d* does not exist or d is negative, an error occurs.

* Arrays created in VBScript always have a lower bound of 0. This method is required only for arrays created in Visual Basic where the lower bound may not be 0.

The basic procedure for using the `VBArray` object is as follows:

1. Obtain the VBScript array.
2. Create a `VBArray` object from the VBScript array.
3. Use the `dimensions` method to determine the number of dimensions in the array.
4. Use the `ubound` method to determine the upper bound of each dimension in the array.
5. Use the `getItem` method to retrieve individual data elements from the array.

Read-only

The `VBArray` object is a read-only object. This means that you can use it to read data from a VBScript array, but you cannot use it to create or modify a VBScript array.

Listing 13-1 shows an example of using the `VBArray` object. This script contains a VBScript function that creates an array of names. Then the JScript code creates a `VBArray` object based on that array and displays the data. The script output is shown in Figure 13-1.

LISTING 13-1 *Demonstration of the VBArray object.*

```
<!--List1301.wsf. Using the VBArray object. -->
<JOB>

<SCRIPT LANGUAGE="VBScript">

function MakeArray()
    dim array(1,2)
    array(0,0) = "Joe"
    array(0,1) = "Mary"
    array(0,2) = "Andy"
    array(1,0) = "Amy"
    array(1,1) = "Phil"
    array(1,2) = "Claudia"
    MakeArray = array
end function

</SCRIPT>

<SCRIPT LANGUAGE="JScript">
var vba;
var msg = "";

vba = new VBArray(MakeArray());

for (var i = 0; i <= vba.ubound(1); i++)
{
    for (var j = 0; j <= vba.ubound(2); j++)
    {
        msg = msg + vba.getItem(i,j) + "\n";
    }
}

WScript.Echo(msg)

</SCRIPT>

</JOB>
```

FIGURE 13-1 *The output of the script in Listing 13-1.*

User Interaction

This may surprise you, but JScript has no capabilities for user interaction, at least as implemented in the WSH. The Web version of JScript offers the `Prompt`, `Alert`, and `Confirm` methods for displaying information to, and getting information from, the user. Strictly speaking, these are methods of the `Window` object, which represents the browser window being used to display a Web page. In the WSH these are not available since a script does not have a window associated with it.

Does this mean you are left out in the cold when using JScript? Fortunately, no. You can use the `WScript.Echo` method and the `WshShell` object's `Popup` method to display information to the user (you learned about these in Chapter 2). You can also put your JScript in a WSF file and make use of VBScript's rich set of user interactivity tools. You saw an example of this in Chapter 4, where the VBScript `InputBox` function was encapsulated in a procedure so it could be called from JScript code. The bottom line, then, is that while JScript itself does not provide user interactivity tools, such tools are still available to the JScript programmer writing WSH scripts.

The tools mentioned in the previous paragraph let a JScript script display information and get text input from the user. There is one more thing that will be useful — getting a Yes/No answer from the user. The script in Listing 13-2 shows a function that uses the VBScript `MsgBox` procedure to do just this. This function is named "confirm" since it is a replacement for the Web-based JScript function of the same name. Figure 13-2 shows an example of this function in action.

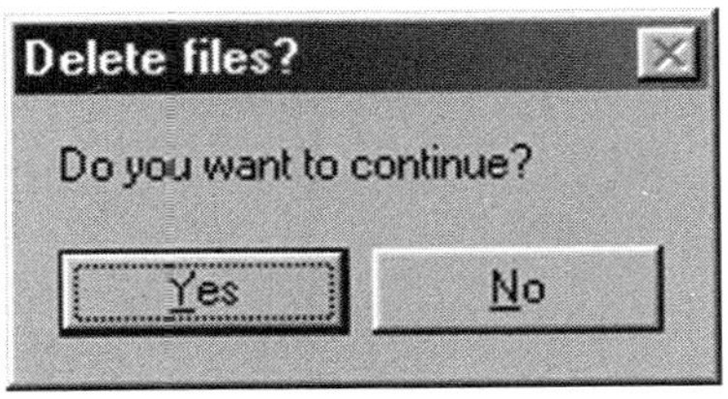

FIGURE 13–2 *The confirm dialog box displayed by the script in Listing 13-2.*

LISTING 13–2 *Getting a Yes/No answer from the user.*

```
<!--List1301.wsf. A function to return a Yes/No answer to JScript. -->
<JOB>

<SCRIPT LANGUAGE="VBScript">

function confirm(sPrompt, sTitle)
    dim reply
    reply = msgbox(sPrompt, vbYesNo, sTitle)
    if reply = vbYes then
        confirm = -1
      else
          confirm = 0
      end if
end function

</SCRIPT>

<SCRIPT LANGUAGE='JScript">
var answer;
var msg;

answer = confirm('Do you want to continue?", "Delete files?");

if (answer == -1)
    msg = "You answered YES."
else
    msg = "You answered NO.";

WScript.Echo(msg)

</SCRIPT>

</JOB>
```

Error Handling

JScript has a mechanism for handling run-time errors that is similar to, but not the same as, the VBScript mechanism. A run-time error is an error that occurs as the script is running, as distinguished from a syntax error that will be caught by the scripting engine. Causes of run-time errors vary, and range from running out of memory to calling a nonexistent function or trying to read from a diskette that has not been inserted. JScript's mechanism for dealing with run-time errors is based on the `Error` object and the `try...catch` statement. Run-time errors in JScript are sometimes called *exceptions*.

The Error Object

Whenever a run-time error occurs, JScript creates an instance of the `Error` object. This instance contains information describing the error, and your script can use this information to correct the error, display information to the user, and so on. The `Error` object has no methods and only two properties:

- `Number`. Contains the numerical code associated with the error. This is the default property of the object.
- `Description`. Contains a brief text description of the error.

You'll find a complete listing of JScript error codes and descriptions in Appendix 6. The `number` property is a bit more complicated than it might seem. This is a 32-bit value, and the information it returns consists of two parts. The lower 16 bits contain the actual error code, and the upper 16 bits contain the facility code. The latter value is rarely of any interest to WSH programmers, but you need to be able to extract the lower 16 bits in order to get the true value of the error code. This can be done using a bitwise `And` operation with the hexadecimal value 0xFFFF, as shown here (assuming `e` is an instance of the `Error` object):

```
actualErrorCode = e.number & 0xFFFF;
```

To make use of the capabilities of the Error object, you must also understand the `try...catch statement.`

Try. . .Catch

The `try...catch` statement lets your script handle, or *catch*, run-time errors. The syntax is as follows:

```
try
    trystatement
catch(exception)
    catchstatement
```

Trystatement is a statement or a block of statements where an error might occur. *Exception* is the name of a variable. *Catchstatement* is a statement or block of statements that will be executed if an error occurs in *trystatement*.

Similarities with VBScript error handling

You can see that JScript's method for handling run-time errors has some similarities to the methods used by VBScript. `Try` has a similar function to `On Error`, the `Error` object is similar to the `Err` object, and `Catch` is similar to an error handler.

Here is how this works. If a run-time error occurs in a `try` block, JScript creates an instance of the `Error` object containing information about the error. A reference to this `Error` object is passed to the *exception* variable, and then the code in the `catch` block is executed. This code can access the `Error` object to help it determine what action to take. If the code in the `catch` block cannot handle the error, it can *rethrow* the error using the `throw` statement, which passes the error up the chain to the system. Here's an example of a `try...catch` block that is set up to handle error number 5 and rethrow all other errors.

```
try
{
    // Code that might cause an error goes here.
}
catch(e)
{
    if (e == 5)
        WScript.Echo(e.description);
    else
        throw(e);
}
```

What happens if an error occurs outside of a `try` block? Then it is handled by the system, typically with an error message and termination of the script. It is possible to nest `try...catch` statements, which is done by placing the inner `try...catch` statement inside the `try` block of the outer `try...catch` statement:

```
try
{
    //Try block 1
    try
    {
        //Try block 2
    }
    catch(e)
    {
        //Catch block 2
    }
}
catch(e)
{
    //Catch block 1
}
```

In this example, errors in Try Block 1 are handled by Catch Block 1, and errors in Try Block 2 are handled by Catch Block 2. Note that if Catch Block 2 rethrows an exception, it will be passed up to Catch Block 1 for handling. Only if Catch Block 1 rethrows an error will it be passed up to the system.

The Throw Statement

In addition to rethrowing exceptions, as was described in the previous section, the `throw` statement can be used to create your own errors. These are not errors in the same sense as a run-time error but are errors from the point of view of your script. To throw your own error, create an `Error` object, set its properties as desired, and then call the `throw` statement:

```
var er = new Error;
er.number = -1;
er.description = "Naughty naughty!";
throw(er);
```

Of course, for your custom error to be handled this code must be inside a `try` block. The script in Listing 13-3 shows how to create and throw your own error in response to program conditions or user input. In this case, the error is thrown if the user enters a string outside the specified length limits.

LISTING 13–3 *Using throw to create a custom exception.*

```
<!--List1303.wsf. Throwing a custom exception. -->
<JOB>

<SCRIPT LANGUAGE="VBScript">

function prompt(sPrompt,sTitle,sDefault)
  prompt = inputbox(sPrompt, sTitle, sDefault)
end function

</SCRIPT>

<SCRIPT LANGUAGE="JScript">

function getUserName()
{
var username;
```

```
try
{
    username = prompt("Enter a user name 4 to 8 characters long:", "", "");
    if (username.length < 4 || username.length > 8)
    {
        var e = new Error;
        e.number = -1;
        e.description = "Username incorrect length.";
        throw(e);
    }
    else
        return username;
}
catch(e)
{
    WScript.Echo(e.description);
    return 0;
}

} // End of getUserName function.

// Script execution starts here.
if (getUserName() == 0)
    WScript.Echo("User name not accepted.");
else
    WScript.Echo("User name OK.");

</SCRIPT>

</JOB>
```

Overview

This chapter has concluded our coverage of the JScript language. You saw how some of the language's built-in objects can be used in your scripts. You also saw that while JScript lacks its own user interaction capabilities, there are several ways around this shortcoming. Finally, we covered the important topic of run-time error handling. With this foundation, you should be prepared for the more advanced topics covered in the remainder of the book.

FOURTEEN

WSH 2.0 and WSF Files

Most of what has already been covered in this book was already a part of WSH version 1, the first release of the scripting host. Many of your scripts will not need to go beyond these capabilities. Not too long ago, however, Microsoft released version 2.0 of WSH, and it adds some powerful and potentially useful enhancements. These additions to WSH 2.0 are the topic of this chapter.

Using WSF Files

Perhaps the most obvious enhancement of WSH 2.0 is support for WSF files. This script file format, identified by the .wsf extension, opens a variety of new possibilities. One of these possibilities is using both VBScript and JScript in the same script. Why would you want to do this? I can think of two reasons:

- Combine the capabilities of the two languages. JScript, for example, is notably lacking in user interaction features, while VBScript has some excellent ones. If you prefer to program in JScript, you can write the bulk of your scripts in that language and then call VBScript procedures for user interaction as needed.
- Reuse existing code. If you are writing a script in VBScript but already have JScript code to perform some needed tasks, you can avoid the hassle of rewriting it in VBScript.

WSF files have some additional capabilities beyond using two languages. We'll look at those in due time.

XML and WSF Files

WSF files are actually XML, or Extensible Markup Language, files. This may seem confusing — what does the XML language have to do with Windows scripting? The parts of XML that are used in WSF files are actually quite limited and represent a very small subset of the entire XML language. The function of these XML elements is primarily one of organization and reference:

- XML elements organize a WSF file into functional sections.
- XML elements reference items that are external to the WSF file and make them available for use by the scripting code.

Within a WSF file, the work is still performed by your JScript and VBScript code. However, with the added features of WSF files and the organization and references provided by the XML elements, your scripts can be a lot more powerful and flexible.

The elements of XML are commonly referred to as *tags*. Every HTML tag is enclosed in angle brackets, like this:

```
<job>
```

Some tags stand on their own, while other tags operate in pairs to mark the beginning and end of a section of the file. Those tags that come in pairs always use the convention that the closing tag is the same as the opening tag with the addition of a slash. For example, `<job>` marks the beginning of an XML job, and `</job>` marks the end of a job. There are only a few XML tags used in WSF files. Let's look at these in turn.

The <script> Tag

The `<script>` tag is used to mark off blocks of VBScript or JScript code and to identify the language in use. A given `<script>` block can contain only one language. Script tags look like this:

```
<script language="VBScript">
...
</script>

<script language="JScript">
...
</script>
```

In a WSF file, all script blocks must be part of a job.

The <job> and <package>Tags

Perhaps the most fundamental XML element that you will use in your WSF files is the `<job>` tag. This tag is used to mark the beginning and end of jobs. A job contains script code (inside `<script>` tags) and other elements to perform a specific task. A WSF file may contain only a single job, in which case the `<job>` tag is the root (highest-level) XML element in the file. When you run a WSF file that has only a single job, then that job is executed. A very simple WSF file with one job would look like this:

```
<job>
<script language="VBScript">
WScript.Echo "Hello, world."
</script>
</job>
```

A WSF file can contain more than one job, which in effect combines two or more scripts (jobs) into one file. To use multiple jobs you must do two things. First, all jobs must be enclosed within `<package>` tags. Second, each job must be identified by a unique name. Here's an example:

```
<package id="package1">

<job id="job1">
<script language="VBScript">
...
</script>
</job>

<job id="job2">
<script language="JScript">
...
</script>
</job>

</package>
```

An XML package must contain at least one job, and a WSF file can contain at most one package. When you execute a WSF file that contains multiple jobs, you specify the job to run with a switch on the command line. For example, to run job2 in MyScript.wsf you would use this command:

```
Wscript MyScript.wsf //job:job2
```

If you omit the //job option on the command line, the first job in the WSF file will be executed. If you specify a job that does not exist, an error occurs.

There is no limit to the number of `<script>` blocks in a job. When a job is run, execution starts with the first script block in the job and moves sequentially to the end of the job. Of course, the order of execution may be modified by statements in the script code. Also, code inside functions and procedures is not executed unless specifically called by other statements in the script.

The <object> Tag

The `<object>` tag is used to create instances of objects. You may wonder why we need an XML tag to create objects when both the JScript and VBScript languages provide statements for this purpose, as does the `WScript` object's `CreateObject` method. The main reason is that objects created with the `<object>` tag are global to the entire job and can be accessed by all the JScript and VBScript code in the job.

In order to create an object using `<object>`, you must know either the object's programmatic identifier (ProgID) or its class identifier (CLSID). The syntax is as follows:

```
<object id=name progid=progid />
<object id=name classid=classid />
```

The *name* identifier is the name that the object will be referred to in the job and must be unique in the job. Here is the `<object>` tag to create an instance of the Shell.Application object using its ProgID:

```
<object id="myshell" progid="Shell.Application" />
```

This tag does the same thing but uses the CLSID instead of the ProgID:

```
<object id="myshell" classid="clsid:13709620-C279-11CE-A49E-444553540000" />
```

`<object>` tags are placed inside a job, typically at the beginning before any script blocks. They cannot be inside script blocks.

ProgIDs and CLSIDs

Where do you get the ProgID or CLSID information required to create a specific type of object? In this book, I will provide the ProgID of the objects you will be learning about. For other objects, the ProgID should be provided with the documentation. Note that using ProgIDs rather than CLSIDs is preferred for obvious reasons. However, you may occasionally run into an object that has no ProgID, so you will have to use its CLSID.

ProgIDs and CLSIDs are two different ways of doing the same thing — uniquely identifying a specific automation class. ProgIDs are clearly easier to use since they identify the class and the application that exposes it in plain English. However, some automation classes are not exposed by a specific application, and as a result have no ProgID but only a CLSID.

The <reference> Tag

The `<reference>` tag is used to create a reference to a type library. This can be very useful when working with objects, be9cause the type library for an object contains defined constants that are designed for use with the object's properties and methods. These constants can make your programming easier and your script code easier to understand, because they are descriptive of their action. For example, suppose you want to create an `ADODB.Recordset` object with a static cursor (don't worry about the details of this object, which you will learn about in a later chapter). You could write this and it will work just fine:

```
Set rs = CreateObject("ADODB.Recordset")
rs.CursorType = 3
```

However, the following code that uses a defined constant is a lot better:

```
Set rs = CreateObject("ADODB.Recordset")
rs.CursorType = adOpenStatic
```

The constant `adOpenStatic` is defined in the type library of the `adodb.Recordset` object as having the value 3. The resulting code is easier to write and to understand. However, for the constant to be available in your script you must insert a reference to the type library. You do this using the `<reference>` tag in one of two ways: by referring to the object itself by its ProgID or by referring to the type library by its CLSID. The syntax is

```
<reference object=ProgID version=version />
<reference guid=CLSID version=version />
```

In my opinion referencing the object's ProgID is the easier approach, as you will probably already have this information. The *version* argument is optional and refers to the version number of the type library. The default is version 1.0. If you need to specify a particular version it should be mentioned in the documentation for the related object.

Here's a real example. This tag inserts a reference to the type library for the `ADODB.RecordSet` object, version 1.0:

```
<reference object="ADODB.Recordset" />
```

You place `<reference>` tags inside a job, before any script code. If the WSF file contains multiple jobs, then the reference is available only within the one job where the tag is located.

Importing Files

The purpose of importing files is to make the contents of one script file available in another script file. You could, for example, write a group of utility functions that perform commonly needed scripting tasks and then import that utility script into all the other script files you create to make its functionality available. Unfortunately, WSH does not at this time provide a really flexible importing mechanism. You cannot import one WSF file into another but are limited to importing VBScript and JScript files. Even so, this capability provides significant flexibility.

To import a file, you use the <script> tag. The syntax is

```
<script language=language src=filename>
</script>
```

For example, to import a VBScript file you might write the following:

```
<script language="VBScript" src="VBSUtils.vbs">
</script>
```

The language in the script file must match the language specified in the <script> tag. The end result is the same as if the <script> tag contained the code in the specified file. When you import a file in this manner, you must be alert to the possibility that there will be conflict between the names of functions and procedures in the two files (source and destination). To avoid this problem, it is a good idea to use a special prefix for procedure names in any script file that is intended for import.

XML Compliance

When you run WSF files, the first thing that happens is that the XML tags are parsed. The module that performs the parsing looks for an XML declaration at the start of the file. This declaration, which is optional, tells the parser what set of rules to follow when parsing the code — in other words, which version of XML to utilize. You do this as follows:

```
<?xml version="1.0"?>
```

If present, this tag must be the very first thing in your WSF file. Note that at present there is only the one version of XML, version 1.0. Your choice therefore is not which version to specify but whether to specify a version at all. If you omit this tag the parser uses a looser set of rules that is, strictly speaking, not XML at all but more akin to standard HTML.

Why should you care about this? For writing WSH scripts it really does not make any difference that I can tell. In the future, however, as scripting becomes more sophisticated and more use is made of XML elements, it may in fact make a difference.

If you do opt for XML compliance, writing scripts gets a little more complicated. This is because certain elements of script code are also recognized as XML elements. For example, the & (ampersand) character, used to concatenate strings in VBScript, is also an XML element. When the XML parser comes across this character in VBScript code it applies XML rules to it, and you end up with an error message. Similar errors will occur with certain other VBScript characters, such as <.

To avoid these problems you must enclose your script code in character data delimiters. The syntax is as follows:

```
<![CDATA[
your script code goes here
]]>
```

This special tag tells the XML parser to ignore whatever is enclosed, so the types of errors that I described will not occur. The character data delimiter must be placed inside the `<script> tags`:

```
<script language="VBScript">
<![CDATA[
...
]]>
</script>
```

XML Errors and Debugging

The XML specification lets you specify options for error handling and debugging. You can turn either on or off by using the `<?job>` tag in your WSF file. The syntax is

```
<?job error=flag debug=flag?>
```

In both cases, *flag* can be either "true" or "false." Setting the error flag to true causes the scripting engine to display error messages for syntax and run-time errors. Setting the debug flag to true enables debugging, which permits you to run the script debugger (which was covered in Chapter 5). You place the `<?job>` tag at the start of the WSF file, outside of any `<job>...</job>` tags but after the XML version tag, if you are using one. For example,

```
<?xml version="1.0"?>
<?job error="true" debug="true"?>

<job>
...
</job>
```

My practice is to have the error flag set to true at all times, except in special circumstances when you do not want any error messages displayed to the user. Debug should be set to true while you are developing and testing the script, and then set to false for distribution.

Overview

Support for XML elements in WSF files is a major advance in scripting capabilities, opening up a number of new possibilities. Most exciting is the ability to use more than one scripting language in the same script. This lets you use the strong features of each language, avoiding their weak areas, and also makes code reuse a lot more practical. Support for global objects, using the `<object>` tag, is another significant improvement, as is the ability to reference type libraries with their handy defined constants. You may still use "pure" VBScript and JScript files for your simpler scripting needs, but for more advanced tasks WSF files are certainly the way to go. You'll see plenty of examples of .wsf files in subsequent chapters.

FIFTEEN

File Access and Management

Of all the types of tasks that WSH is used for, working with files is certainly one of the most common. There are so many different operations that involve files, and automating these operations with scripts can be very helpful in terms of saving time and reducing errors. Whether it be moving and copying files, creating folders, reading and writing data, or making backups, you'll find that WSH provides the capabilities you need.

Strictly speaking, all of the file-related capabilities available to a script programmer are not part of WSH, nor are they part of the VBScript or JScript languages. Rather, Microsoft has encapsulated the file-related tools in the scripting run-time library, or SRL. Since the SRL is freely accessible from VBScript and JScript, this is a technical distinction that does not have any real practical consequences. In this chapter we cover the capabilities of the SRL, both those related to file management (moving, copying, deleting, and creating files and folders) and file access (reading and writing file data).

The Scripting Run-time Library

The scripting run-time library consists of a group of objects that provide the file management and access capabilities available to your scripts. There are five objects and three collections in the library. At the top of the SRL hierarchy is the `FileSystemObject` object, which you will often see abbreviated as FSO. Your first step before performing any file-related activities is always to create an instance of the FSO object. This is done using the object creation methods that you have learned previously in this book. To review briefly, here is the syntax for creating an instance in VBScript:

```
Dim fso
Set fso = CreateObject("Scripting.FileSystemObject")
```

In JScript the code looks like this:

```
var fso;
fso = new ActiveXObject("Scripting.FileSystemObject");
```

The ActiveXObject object

The `ActiveXObject` object is provided to permit compatibility between JScript and automation objects that are exposed by other applications, such as Microsoft Word and Excel. The syntax is

```
newObj = new ActiveXObject(servername.typename, location)
```

***Servername* is the name of the server, and *typename* is the name of the class or object. *Location* is an optional argument specifying the name of the network server where the object is to be created, if you do not want it created locally. This code creates locally an instance of the `Excel.Sheet` object:**

```
myXLSheet = new ActiveXObject("Excel.Sheet");
```

This code creates the same object on the indicated server:

```
myXLSheet = new ActiveXObject("Excel.Sheet", "Server1");
```

The server name can also be specified using an IP (Internet Protocol) address or its DNS (Domain Name Server) name. Note that remote object creation is possible only if Internet security is turned off.

If you are using a WSF file and want to use XML to create a global instance of the `FileSystemObject`, here is the required tag:

```
<object id="fso" progid="Scripting.FileSystemObject" />
```

The `FileSystemObject` is your entry point into all of the SRL's file manipulation and access capabilities. You never need more than one instance of this object. Table 15-1 lists the objects and collections in the SRL, with a brief description of what each one does. The remainder of the chapter covers the use of these objects and collections in detail, with file management and file access in separate sections.

TABLE 15.1 *Objects and collections of the Scripting Runtime Library.*

Object or collection	Description
FileSystemObject (object)	The top object in the SRL hierarchy.
Drives (collection)	Available as the `Drives` property of the `FileSystemObject` object. Contains one `Drive` object for each available drive.
Drive (object)	Represents a single drive. Use this object's properties to get information about the drive, and its methods to manipulate the drive. The `Drive` object's `RootFolder` property returns a reference to a `Folder` object representing the drive's root folder.
Folders (collection)	Available as the `SubFolders` property of the `Folder` object. Contains one `Folder` object for each subfolder in the folder.
Folder (object)	Represents a single folder. Use this object's properties to get information about the folder, and its methods to manipulate the folder.
Files (collection)	Available as the `Files` property of a `Folder` object. Contains one `File` object for each file in the folder.
File (object)	Represents a single file. Use this object's properties to get information about the file, and its methods to manipulate the file.
TextStream	Represents an open text file. Used to write to and read from the file.

Many operations start with the `Folder` object obtained through the `Drive` object's `RootFolders` property. Starting here, you can "drill down" through the drive's folder structure to find the file or folder you need to work with.

File Management

The term *file management* refers to the types of tasks that you would perform with the Windows Explorer: moving, copying, and deleting files, and creating, deleting, and moving folders. By utilizing the capabilities of the `FileSystemObject` object, your scripts can perform just about any file management task you could imagine. In the remainder of this chapter, you should assume that the variable name fso refers to an instance of the `FileSystemObject` object that has been created previously in code.

Copying and Moving Files

Copying and moving files are very similar operations, the one difference being that when you move a file the original copy is deleted, while a copy operation leaves the original intact. There is an additional difference that is part of the SRL: You can overwrite existing files with a copy operation, but not with a move operation.

To copy a file, use the `CopyFile` method. The syntax is

```
fso.CopyFile source, destination, overwrite
```

The *source* argument is the name of the file to copy. You can use wildcards to specify multiple files. *Destination* is either a file name or a folder name, as follows:

- If *destination* ends with a backslash it is considered to be a folder. The source file is copied to that folder under its original name. Note that the destination folder must already exist.
- If *destination* does not end with a backslash it is considered to be a file name. The source file is copied using the specified destination name.

Let's look at two examples. This statement copies the file data.txt under its original name to the folder c:\project1:

```
fso.CopyFile "c:\documents\data.txt", "c:\project1\"
```

In contrast, this statement copies the file data.txt to a file named project1 in the root folder on drive c:

```
fso.CopyFile "c:\documents\data.txt", "c:\project1"
```

The *overwrite* argument is optional. If True (the default) existing files are overwritten by the `CopyFile` method. If set to False, trying to copy over an existing file will generate a run-time error. This is not a particularly useful feature, and while such run-time errors can be trapped, it is easier, when you do not want to overwrite existing files, to see if the file exists before trying to copy over it. See the section "Seeing If a Drive, Folder, or File Exists" later in this chapter for information on how to do this. You cannot overwrite files whose read-only attribute is set.

To move a file, use the `MoveFile` method. It's syntax is identical to `CopyFile` except that there is no *overwrite* argument:

```
fso.MoveFile source, destination
```

The *source* and *destination* arguments are the same as described for `CopyFile`. If you try to overwrite an existing file with this method, a run-time error occurs. You should therefore always trap these errors in code that uses `MoveFile`, or verify that the file does not exist before calling the method. As with `CopyFile`, `MoveFile` requires that the destination folder exists.

Relative and absolute paths

In most situations you will be specifying folder and file names using an absolute path that fully specifies the drive and path to the file or folder. For example,

```
c:\mydata\reports\January.doc
```

is a full, absolute path that leaves no room for misinterpretation. However, you can also use relative paths, which are based on the fact that there will be a default drive and folder based on the location of the script file that is executing. Thus,

```
\mydata\reports\January.doc
```

is a relative path that will refer to the specified folder and file on whatever drive the script is executing from. Likewise,

```
January.doc
```

is a relative file name that will be interpreted as being located in the same folder as the script. Finally, the notation .. can be used to refer to the parent folder of the default folder. For example, if the script is executing in the folder c:\documents\scripts, then the relative notation

```
..\data\sales.doc
```

refers to the file c:\documents\data\sales.doc.

Copying and Moving Folders

Copying and moving folders is similar is some respects to copying and moving files. When you copy or move a folder, its entire contents comes along too. The `CopyFolder` and `MoveFolder` methods have the following syntax:

```
fso.CopyFolder source, destination, overwrite
fso.MoveFolder source, destination
```

Source and *destination* specify the folder to copy or move and the destination for the operation. The *overwrite* option is True by default and has the same effect as for the `CopyFile` method that was described previously. When you use either of these methods, the destination tree must exist (excepting the final folder) or an error will occur. For example, look at this code:

```
fso.CopyFolder "c:\reports", "d:\backup\reports"
```

If the folder d:\backup does not exist, a Path Not Found error will occur. You need to implement appropriate error trapping or use the techniques presented later in this chapter to ensure that the path does exist before calling the `CopyFolder` or `MoveFolder` method.

Creating Folders

To create a folder, use the `CreateFolder` method. The syntax is

```
fso.CreateFolder foldername
```

Foldername is the full path of the folder to create. For example,

```
fso.CreateFolder "c:\mydata\spreadsheets"
```

will create a folder named spreadsheets in the folder c:\mydata. Note that CreateFolder cannot create an entire tree of folders but can only add a new folder to the end of an existing tree. In the preceding example, the folder c:\mydata must already exist or an error will occur.

Deleting Files and Folders

To delete a file or a folder, use the `DeleteFile` or `DeleteFolder` method. The syntax is

```
fso.DeleteFile filename, force
fso.DeleteFolder foldername, force
```

Filename and *foldername* identify the file or folder to delete. The optional *force* argument specifies whether read-only files will be deleted. The default is True. The *filespec* argument can contain wildcards to delete multiple files with one call to the `DeleteFile` method. For both of these methods, an error occurs if a matching file or folder is not found.

Be aware that files and folders deleted with these methods are not placed in the Windows recycle bin — they are deleted permanently.

Seeing if a Drive, Folder, or File Exists

There are situations where you will need to see if a drive, a folder, or a file exists before performing some operation. To verify the existence of a drive, use the `DriveExists` method:

```
fso.DriveExists drivename
```

Drivename is the name of the drive, either a drive letter by itself or a letter followed by a colon. The method returns True if the drive exists, False if not. This method works with network drives, but only if they have been mapped to a drive letter. The method tells you that the drive exists, but not that it is ready. This means that a removable media drive will return True regardless of whether there is media inserted.

To determine whether a file or a folder exists, use these methods:

```
fso.FileExists filename
fso.FolderExists folderspec
```

You can use relative or absolute paths with both methods.

Obtaining Object References

The file management operations you have learned so far all rely on methods of the `FileSystemObject` object. These methods permit you to perform certain operations without obtaining a reference to a file or folder. For example, you can delete a file using the `DeleteFile` method without creating a `File` object that refers to the file in question. At times, however, you will need to obtain a reference to a drive, a folder, or a file in order to get information about the object. The `FileSystemObject` object has methods to do this:

```
fso.GetDrive drivespec
fso.GetFolder folderspec
fso.GetFile filename
```

Each of these methods returns a reference to the relevant kind of object: `Drive`, `Folder`, or `File`. You then can use the object as needed. For example, this VBScript code displays the amount of free space available on drive c:

```
Dim d
Set d = fso.GetDrive("c")
WScript.Echo "There are " & d.FreeSpace & " bytes free on C:."
```

In JScript, the equivalent code would be as follows:

```
var d;
d = fso.GetDrive("c");
WScript.Echo("There are " + d.FreeSpace + " bytes free on C:.");
```

The next several sections explain the methods and properties of the `Drive`, `Folder`, and `File` objects, and how to use them.

Working with the Drives Collection and Drive Object

The `FileSystemObject` has only a single property, `Drives`, which is a reference to the `Drives` collection. This collection contains a `Drive` object for each drive on the system. This includes all local drives as well as shared network drives. The `Drives` collection is a standard collection and uses the same collection syntax that you learned previously. The `Drive` object has properties that provides information about the physical drive. These properties are listed in Table 15-2. These properties are all read-only except where noted. The `Drive` object has no methods.

TABLE 15.2 *Properties of the Drive object.*

Property	Description
AvailableSpace	Returns the number of bytes of free space available for the current user (see text below for details).
DriveLetter	Returns the drive letter.
DriveType	Returns a value indicating the type of drive: 0 = unknown, 1 = removable media, 2 = local fixed, 3 = network, 4 = cd-rom, 5 = RAM disk.
FileSystem	Returns a string indicating the type of file system: FAT, FAT32, NTFS, or CDFS.
FreeSpace	Returns the number of free bytes on the drive.
IsReady	Returns True or False, indicating whether the drive is ready.
Path	Returns the path of the drive, consisting of the drive letter followed by a colon (e.g., C:)
RootFolder	Returns the root folder of the drive, consisting of the drive letter followed by a colon and a backslash (e.g., C:\)
SerialNumber	Returns the drive's decimal serial number.
ShareName	Returns the share name of network drives, an empty string for nonnetwork drives.
TotalSize	Returns the size of the disk for the current user in bytes.
VolumeName*	Specifies the volume name of the drive.

* This is the only property that is not read-only.

There are two concerns relating to getting the amount of free space on a drive. In most situations the `AvailableSpace` and `FreeSpace` properties return the same value, the total free space on the drive. In Windows 2000, however, it is possible for the administrator to assign each user a quota of space on a disk. On a 30-GB disk, for example, user MarySmith might be allotted only 4-GB. In this case the `AvailableSpace` method returns the amount of free space the current user has in his or her quota, and not the total free space on the drive (which is obtained with `FreeSpace`).

The second concern has to do with the values returned. The two properties that return free space may appear to give inaccurate results for large drives because the numeric storage for integers in both VBScript and JScript is limited to a maximum value of approximately 2 billion, which is the same as 2 GB. With today's huge drive capacities it is not uncommon to have more than 2 GB free, and when this is the case these properties will return a value of 2 GB (specifically, 2,147,155,968 bytes). There is no easy way around this, but in reality it is not much of a problem. The most common usage for the `AvailableSpace` and `FreeSpace` properties is to see whether a disk has sufficient space to copy files or folders to it. If either of these properties returns a value of 2 GB, then you know that at least this amount of space is available, which should be more than adequate for most purposes.

It is important to note that the `Drives` collection will contain an entry for a network drive only if the drive has been mapped (that is, assigned a drive letter). Note also that CD-ROM and DVD drives will report 0 bytes free, as they are read-only devices. Rewritable CD-ROM drives will return a valid free space value as reported by the driver software.

Listings 15-1 and 15-2 illustrate the use of the `Drives` collection and `Drive` object to obtain information about the drives on a system. The script output is shown in Figure 15-1.

LISTING 15–1 *Demonstrating the Drives collection and Drive object (VBScript).*

```
' List1501.vbs
' Demonstrating the Drive object and Drives collection.
' Displays free space on ready drives, or "not ready"
' if the drive is not ready.

Option Explicit

Dim fso
Dim d
Dim msg

msg = ""
Set fso = CreateObject("Scripting.FileSystemObject")
for each d in fso.Drives
    if d.IsReady then
        msg = msg & "Drive " & d.Path & " has " & _
            d.AvailableSpace & " bytes free." & vbCrLf
    else
        msg = msg & "Drive " & d.Path & " is not ready." & vbCrLf
    end if
next

WScript.Echo msg
```

FIGURE 15–1 *The output of the script in Listing 15-1.*

LISTING 15–2 *Demonstrating the Drives collection and Drive object (JScript).*

```
// List 1502.js
// Demonstrating the Drives collection and the Drive object.
// Displays free space on ready drives, or "not ready"
// if the drive is not ready.

var fso;
var e;
var msg;
var d;

fso = new ActiveXObject("Scripting.FileSystemObject");
e = new Enumerator(fso.Drives);

msg = "";
for ( ; !e.atEnd(); e.moveNext())
{
    d = e.item();
    if (d.IsReady)
        msg = msg + "Drive " + d.Path + " has " + d.AvailableSpace +
            " bytes free.\n";
    else
        msg = msg + "Drive " + d.Path + " is not ready.\n";
}

WScript.Echo(msg);
```

Working with the Folders Collection and Folder Object

Every folder on a drive is represented by a `Folder` object. The entry point into the tree of folders is the `RootFolder` property of the `Drive` object, which references a `Folder` object representing the drive's root folder. Each `Folder` object has the `SubFolders` property, which returns a `Folders` collection. This collection contains one `Folder` object for each subfolder in the folder. You can start at the root folder and drill down through the folder hierarchy to locate any folder on a given drive. You can also obtain a reference to a specific folder using the `FileSystemObject` object's `GetFolder` method, as was covered earlier in this chapter.

The `Folder` object has a set of properties and methods, detailed in Tables 15-3 and 15-4. Listings 15-3 and 15-4 demonstrate use of the `Folders` collection and the `Folder` object. These scripts use a process called *recursion*, where a procedure calls itself in order to perform a repetitive task. The scripts count the total number of folders on drive C:, and also count those folders that are empty (contain no files or subfolders). The script output is shown in Figure 15-2.

FIGURE 15-2 Output of the script in Listing 15-3.

TABLE 15.3 Properties of the Folder object.

Property	Description
Attributes*	Specifies the folder attributes (see text below for details).
DateCreated	Returns the date the folder was created. Not available for the root, \Windows, and \Windows\System folders.
DateLastAccessed	Returns the date the folder was last accessed. Not available on Windows 9x, in which this property returns the same value as `DateCreated`. Not available for the root folder.
DateLastModified	Returns the date the folder was last modified. Not available on Windows 9x, in which this property returns the same value as `DateCreated`. Not available for the root folder.
Drive	Returns the drive letter where the folder is located, consisting of a letter followed by a colon.
Files	Returns a `Files` collection containing all the files in the folder.
IsRootFolder	Returns True if the folder is the root folder, False if not.
Name*	Specifies the folder name, without path. For example, for c:\data\reports\ this property returns "reports." Set this property to rename a folder.
ParentFolder	Returns a `Folder` object representing the folder's parent folder.
Path	Returns the full absolute path to the folder.
ShortName	Returns the folder name in the old 8.3 format. For example, for the folder c:\my documents\performance reports\ this property would return perfor~1.
ShortPath	Returns the full absolute path to the folder in 8.3 format.
Size	Returns the total size of the folder and its contents (files and subfolders).
SubFolders	Returns a `Folders` collection containing the folder's subfolders.
Type	Returns a string describing the type of folder. Most folders are type FileFolder.

* Read/write property

TABLE 15.4 *Methods of the Folder object.*

Method	Description
Copy *destination*, *overwrite*	Copies the folder and its contents to the specified destination. The optional *overwrite* argument is a Boolean value specifying whether existing files and folders will be overwritten. The default is True.
Move *destination*	Moves the folder and its contents to the specified destination.
Delete *force*	Deletes the folder and its contents. *Force* is an optional Boolean value specifying whether files or folders with the read-only attribute are to be deleted. The default setting is False.

LISTING 15-3 *Demonstrating the Folders collection and Folder object (VBScript).*

```
' List1503.vbs
' Demonstrating the Folders collection and Folder object.
' Counts all folders and empty folders on drive C:.

Option Explicit

Dim fso
Dim f
Dim total
Dim total1
Dim msg
Dim d

'******************
Sub ProcessFolder(fld)
Dim f
For Each f in fld.SubFolders
    if f.Files.Count = 0 And f.SubFolders.Count = 0 then
        total1 = total1 + 1
    end if
    total = total + 1
    ProcessFolder f
Next

End Sub
'******************

Set fso = CreateObject("Scripting.FileSystemObject")
Set d = fso.GetDrive("C")
ProcessFolder d.RootFolder

msg = "Drive C has a total of " & total & " folders." & vbCrLf
msg = msg & total1 & _
    " of those folders contain no files or subfolders."
WScript.Echo msg
```

LISTING 15–4 *Demonstrating the Folders collection and Folder object (JScript).*

```
// List1504.js
//Demonstrating the Folders collection and Folder object.
//Counts all folders and empty folders on drive C:.

var fso;
var total;
var total1;
var msg;
var d;

//******************
function ProcessFolder(fld)
{
var f;
var e;

e = new Enumerator(fld.SubFolders);
for ( ; !e.atEnd(); e.moveNext())
{
    f = e.item();
    if (f.Files.Count == 0 && f.SubFolders.Count == 0)
        total1++;
    total++;
    ProcessFolder(f);
}
}
//******************

fso = new ActiveXObject("Scripting.FileSystemObject");
d = fso.GetDrive("C");
total = 0;
total1 = 0;
ProcessFolder(d.RootFolder);

msg = "Drive C has a total of " + total + " folders.\n";
msg = msg + total1 + " of those folders contain no files or subfolders.";
WScript.Echo(msg);
```

Recursion as a programming tool

The scripts in Listings 15-3 and 15-4 make use of a programming technique called *recursion*. This can be a very powerful tool when circumstances require it. Recursion means that a procedure or function calls itself repeatedly as needed by the situation. In these scripts the function ProcessFolder is recursive. It performs two tasks: One is to determine how many files the folder contains and update the relevant total as needed. Then for each subfolder within the folder it calls itself. Each subfolder is processed in the same way and the recursion repeats until the code drills down to a folder that does not contain any subfolders. If you are doubtful that recursion can be a useful technique, I suggest that you try writing these scripts without using it!

Working with the Files Collection and File Object

The Folder object has a Files property, which returns the Files collection. This collection contains one File object for each file in the folder. You can obtain a reference to a specific file from the Files collection, or you can use the FileSystemObject object's GetFile method that was explained earlier in this chapter. Once you have a reference to a specific file, you can use the File object's methods and properties to get information about the file and to manipulate it. The properties of this object are listed in Table 15-5, and the methods in Table 15-6.

TABLE 15.5 *Properties of the File object.*

Property	Description
Attributes	Returns a value summarizing the file's attributes (see text below for details).
DateCreated	Returns the date and time the file was created.
DateLastAccessed	Returns the date and time the file was last accessed.
DateLastModified	Returns the date and time the file was last modified.
Drive	Returns the drive letter of the drive where the file resides.
Name	Sets or returns the name of the file.
ParentFolder	Returns a Folder object representing the file's parent folder.
Path	Returns the full path of the file, including drive letter.
ShortName	Returns the short file name used by programs that require the old 8.3 naming convention.
ShortPath	Returns the short path used by programs that require the old 8.3 naming convention.
Size	Returns the size of the file, in bytes.
Type	Returns a string containing information about the type of the file. For example, for files with the .DOC extension this property returns "Microsoft Word Document."

TABLE 15.6 *Methods of the File object.*

Method	Description
Copy *dest, overwrite*	Copies the file to *dest*. An existing file is overwritten only if the optional *overwrite* argument is True (the default).
Move *dest*	Moves the file to *dest*.
Delete *force*	Deletes the files. Read-only files are deleted only if the optional *force* argument is True. The default is False.

The Attributes property of the File object provides information about the file's attributes, such as whether it is read-only or a system file. Some file attributes can be changed in code, as well. This property returns a single numerical value, which is a logical combination of the individual attribute values. The individual attributes, and whether they are read-only or read/write, are described in Table 15-7.

TABLE 15.7 *Individual file attributes.*

Attribute	Value	Description
Normal	0	Normal file with no attributes set.
ReadOnly	1	The file is read-only. Read/write.
Hidden	2	The file is hidden. Read/write.
System	4	The file is a system file. Read/write.
Volume	8	The file is a disk drive volume label. Read-only.
Directory	16	The file is a folder. Read-only.
Archive	32	The file has changed since the last backup. Read/write.
Alias	64	The file is a link or shortcut. Read-only.
Compressed	128	The file is compressed. Read-only

To extract individual attributes from the value of the `Attributes` property, you use your scripting language's logical operators. To determine if a specific attribute is set, use `And`. If f is a `File` object, then the following VBScript code determines if the file's Hidden attribute is set:

```
If f.Attributes And 2 Then
    ' Hidden attribute is set.
Else
    ' Hidden attribute is not set.
End If
```

In JScript the code would be as follows:

```
if (f.Attributes && 2)
    // Hidden attribute is set.
Else
    // Hidden attribute is not set.
```

This VBScript code checks to see if the file's ReadOnly attribute is set and, if it is, clears it:

```
If f.Attributes And 1 Then
    f.Attributes = f.Attributes - 1
End If
```

Here's the same code in JScript:

```
if (f.Attributes && 1)
    f.Attributes = f.Attributes - 1;
```

The scripts in Listing 15-5 and 15-6 show how to use the `Files` collection and `File` object. The script contains a procedures called CopyFiles. This procedure takes two `Folder` objects as arguments. It copies all files from one folder to the other folder. If a file already exists in the destination folder, the file is copied only if the source file is newer (has been modified more recently). As the script is written, the source and destination folders are hard-coded into the script, but it would be a simple matter to pass them as arguments.

This procedure only copies files in the source folder — it does not copy files in subfolders within the source folder. It would be a good exercise for you to modify the procedure so it copies subfolders as well.

LISTING 15–5 *Demonstrating the Files collection and File object (VBScript).*

```
' List1505.vbs
' Demonstrating the Files collection and File object.
' Copies all files from one folder to another.
' Overwrites existing files only if the source file is newer.

Option Explicit

' *************************
Sub CopyFiles(src, dest)
' Copies all files from the src folder to the dest folder.
' Existing files are overwritten only if the source file is newer.
' Assumes the destination folder exists.

Dim fs
Dim fd
Dim dName

' If no files to copy, exit.
if src.Files.Count = 0 then exit sub

' Loop for each file in the source folder.
For Each fs in src.Files
    ' Create the destination path.
    dName = dest.path & "\" & fs.Name
    ' See if it already exists.
        if fso.FileExists(dName) then
        ' Destination file exists - copy only if src is newer.
        Set fd = fso.GetFile(dName)
        if fs.DateLastModified > fd.DateLastModified then
            fs.Copy dName, True
        end if
    else
        ' Destination file does not exist.
        fs.Copy dName
    end if
Next

End Sub
' *************************

Dim fso

Set fso = CreateObject("Scripting.FileSystemObject")
CopyFiles fso.GetFolder("c:\test"), fso.GetFolder("d:\test")
```

LISTING 15–6 *Demonstrating the Files collection and File object (JScript).*

```
// List1506.js
// Demonstrating the Files collection and File object.
// Copies all files from one folder to another.
// Overwrites existing files only if the source file is newer.
// ************************
function CopyFiles(src, dest)
{
// Copies all files from the src folder to the dest folder.
// Existing files are overwritten only if the source file is newer.
// Assumes the destination folder exists.
var fs;
var fd;
var dName;
var e;
// If no files to copy, exit.
if (src.Files.Count == 0)
    return;
e = new Enumerator(src.Files);
// Loop for each file in the source folder.
for (; !e.atEnd(); e.moveNext())
{
    // Create the destination path.
    fs = e.item();
    dName = dest.Path + "\\" + fs.Name;
    // See if it already exists.
    if (fso.FileExists(dName))
    {
      // Destination file exists - copy only if src is newer.
      fd = fso.GetFile(dName);
      if (fs.DateLastModified > fd.DateLastModified)
        fs.Copy(dName);
    }
    else
      // Destination file does not exist.
      fs.Copy(dName);
}
}
// ************************
var fso;
fso = new ActiveXObject("Scripting.FileSystemObject");
CopyFiles(fso.GetFolder("c:\\test"), fso.GetFolder("d:\\test"));
```

Other FileSystemObject Methods

The `FileSystemObject` object has several methods that have not been covered yet. Most of them have to do with manipulating path and folder names. They are described in Table 15-8.

TABLE 15.8 *Additional methods of the FileSystemObject object.*

Method	Description	Example
BuildPath(*path, name*)	Returns a new path consisting of *path* with *name* appended.	BuildPath("c:\windows", "system") returns c:\windows\system.
GetAbsolutePathName(*path*)	Returns a complete and unambiguous path specification corresponding to the relative *path*. Understands . and .. as referring to the current and parent folder, respectively.	If the current folder is c:\windows\system, then GetAbsolutePathName("..\temp") returns c:\windows\temp.
GetBaseName(*path*)	Returns the base name of the specified file or folder.	GetBaseName("c:\windows") returns windows. GetBaseName("c:\docs\report.xls") returns report.
GetExtensionName(*path*)	Returns the extension of the specified path.	GetExtensionName("c:\sales.xls") returns xls. GetExtensionName("c:\documents") returns an empty string.
GetFileName(*pathspec*)	Returns the file name portion of the specified path, or an empty string if *pathspec* does not contain a file name.	GetFileName("c:\docs\report.txt") returns report.txt.
GetParentFolderName(*path*)	Returns the name of the parent folder of the last item in the specified path.	GetParentFolderName("c:\documents \data.txt") returns c:\documents. GetParentFolderName("c:\windows\t emp") returns c:\windows.
GetSpecialFolder(*folderspec*)	Returns a `Folder` object corresponding to the specified special folder: 0 for the Windows folder, 1 for the Windows system folder, or 2 for the temporary folder.	On most systems, GetSpecialFolder(2) returns a reference to c:\windows\temp.
GetTempName()	Returns a string containing a temporary folder or file name that is guaranteed no to already be in use.	

File Access

The term *file access* refers to reading data from files and writing data to files. The object-oriented file system represented by the `FileSystemObject` object provides the tools required to read and write files, with one limitation: You can work only with text files and not with binary files. What does this mean?

A text file is any file that contains nothing but text — letters, numbers, punctuation marks, and so on. The script files you create are an example. Binary files contain at least some of their data in nontext format. Microsoft Excel files, executable program files, and PhotoShop graphics files are some examples of binary files. If you are not sure whether an existing file is text, try to open it using the Windows Notepad program. If the file can be read in Notepad, it is a text file.

It may seem like a serious limitation to be unable to read binary files, and this capability has been promised for a future upgrade of WSH. For the present, we have no choice but to put up with the limitation. Actually, it is not as much of a problem as you might fear, as many of the file access tasks that scripts typically need to perform involve text files. Also, for many binary files, it is more appropriate to use the parent application to read them.

The TextStream Object

To work with a text file, you must create an instance of the `TextStream` object associated with the file. The `FileSystemObject` object has two methods for creating a `TextStream` object:

- `CreateTextFile` creates a new text file. If a file of the specified name exists, it is overwritten.
- `OpenTextFile` opens a text file for reading and/or writing. If the file already exists, new data is appended to existing data.

The syntax for the `CreateTextFile` method is (assuming that fso is an instance of the `FileSystemObject` object)

```
fso.CreateTextFile(filename, overwrite, unicode)
```

Filename is a string expression specifying the name of the file, including a path if necessary. *Overwrite* is an optional Boolean value specifying whether an existing file of the same name will be overwritten. If this argument is omitted the default is False. If *overwrite* is False and *filename* already exists, an error occurs. You can trap this error to permit the user to verify file overwrites. *Unicode* is a Boolean value. Pass True to create a Unicode file, False (the default) for an ASCII file.

ASCII and Unicode

Computers use numbers to represent the characters and punctuation marks in a text file. There are two systems for this: ACSII (also called ANSI) and Unicode. ASCII uses one byte for each character, which permits only 256 different symbols to be represented. This is adequate for English but not for many other languages. Unicode uses 2 bytes per character, allowing for over 65,000 different symbols. Which text file format you use will depend on the specific requirements of your project.

The syntax for the `OpenTextFile` method is as follows:

```
fso.OpenTextFile(filename, iomode, create, format)
```

Filename specifies the file and path. *IOMode* is an optional argument. Possible values are `ForReading` (value = 1) to open the file in read-only mode, `ForAppending` (8) to write new data to the end of the file, and `ForWriting` (2) to write data without appending. The default is `ForWriting`.

Create is an optional True/False value specifying whether a new file will be created if *filename* does not exist. The default is False.

Format is a tristate argument (one that can have three values) that determines the format of the file. `TriStateTrue` (–1) opens the file as Unicode, `TriStateFalse` (0, the default) opens the file as ASCII, and `TristateUseDefault` (–2) uses the system default format setting.

Using constants

The constants mentioned in the text are defined in the type library that is associated with the FileSystemObject object. To have these values available in your script you must use a .wsf file and use the <reference> tag to import the type library into the script:

```
<reference object="Scripting.FileSystemObject" />
```

Otherwise you must use the associated numerical values directly, as follows:

```
ForReading = 1
ForWriting = 2
ForAppending = 8
TriStateTrue = -1
TriStateFalse = 0
TriStateUseDefault = -2
```

There is another way to obtain a `TextStream` object. First, create a `File` object that is associated with the desired file, and then call the `File` object's `OpenAsTextStream` method. This method's syntax is:

```
f.OpenAsTextStream(iomode, format)
```

The *iomode* and *format* arguments are the same as for the `OpenTextFile` method described previously. You can use this technique only to create a `TextStream` object for an existing file and not for creating a new file. This VBScript code, for example, creates a `TextStream` object associated with the existing file c:\comments.txt:

```
Dim ts
Dim f

Set f = fso.GetFile("c:\comments.txt")
Set ts = f.OpenAsTextStream
```

In JScript the code is as follows:

```
var ts;
var f;

f = fso.GetFile("c:\\comments.txt");
ts = f.OpenAsTextStream;
```

Once you have created a `TextStream` object that is associated with the text file (new or existing), then you can start working with the file. The `TextStream` object has properties and methods that you use to work with the file. The properties are described in Table 15-9, and the methods in Table 15-10. All of the `TextStream` object's properties are read-only.

Certain methods are applicable only when the file has been opened for reading or for writing. An error will occur if you try to use a method that is inappropriate for the file's mode. To switch from writing to reading, or *vice versa*, you must close then re-open the file in the new mode.

You'll see that every `TextStream` object has a *current character position*, or *file pointer*, that indicates where the next read or write operation will take place. The first character in a file is at position 1. There does not seem to be a way to move the file pointer backward in a `TextStream` object. You must close and then reopen the file, which resets the file pointer to the start of the file.

TABLE 15.9 *Properties of the TextStream object.*

Property	Description
AtEndOfLine	True if the file pointer is at the end of a line; False otherwise. `AtEndOfLine` applies only to files that are open for reading; otherwise an error occurs.
AtEndOfStream	True if the file pointer is at the end of the file; False otherwise. `AtEndOfStream` applies only to files that are open for reading; otherwise an error occurs
Column	Returns the column number of the file pointer. The first character on a line is at column 1.
Line	Returns the current line number of the file pointer.

TABLE 15.10 *Methods of the TextStream object.*

Method	Description
Close	Closes the file associated with the `TextStream` object. A file should always be closed when you are finished working with it.
Read(*n*)	Reads the next *n* characters from the file and returns the resulting string.
ReadAll	Reads the entire file and returns the resulting string.
ReadLine	Reads an entire line (up to, but not including, the newline character at the end of the line) from the file and returns the resulting string.
Skip(*n*)	Moves the file pointer forward by *n* characters.
SkipLine	Moves the file pointer to the beginning of the next line.
Write(*s*)	Writes the string *s* to the file without adding any extra or newline characters.
WriteBlankLines(*n*)	Writes *n* blank lines to the file.
WriteLine(*s*)	Writes the string *s* to the file followed by a newline character.

A TextStream Demonstration

Text file access with the `TextFile` access is quite easy to accomplish. The methods and properties of this object are well designed for the tasks that your scripts may need. The scripts in Listings 15-7 and 15-8 demonstrate how to use the `TextStream` object to write and read text files.

LISTING 15-7 *Demonstrating text file writing and reading (VBScript).*

```
<!-- List1507.wsf
Demonstrates text file access in VBScript. -->

<job>
<reference object="Scripting.FileSystemObject" />
<script language="VBScript">
<![CDATA[
Option Explicit

Dim fso
Dim ts
Dim temp

Set fso = CreateObject("Scripting.FileSystemObject")
Set ts = fso.CreateTextFile("fso_demo.txt", True)

Do
    temp = InputBox("Enter text, a blank when done:")
    If temp = "" Then Exit Do
    ts.WriteLine temp
Loop While True
ts.Close
```

```
Set ts = fso.OpenTextFile("fso_demo.txt", ForReading)
Do Until ts.AtEndOfStream
    WScript.Echo ts.ReadLine
Loop
ts.Close
]]>
</script>
</job>
```

LISTING 15–8 *Demonstrating text file writing and reading (JScript).*

```
<!-- List1508.wsf
Demonstrates text file access. -->

<job>
<reference object="Scripting.FileSystemObject" />

<SCRIPT LANGUAGE="VBScript">
function prompt(sPrompt,sTitle,sDefault)
    prompt = inputbox(sPrompt, sTitle, sDefault)
end function
</SCRIPT>

<script language="JScript">
var fso;
var ts;
var s;

fso = new ActiveXObject("Scripting.FileSystemObject");
ts = fso.CreateTextFile("fso_demo.txt", -1);

do
{
    s = prompt("Enter text, a blank when done:", "Enter Text", "");
    if (s == "")
        break;
    ts.WriteLine(s);
} while(-1);
ts.close();

ts = fso.OpenTextFile("fso_demo.txt", ForReading);
while (!ts.AtEndOfStream)
    WScript.Echo(ts.readLine());
ts.close();

</script>
</job>
```

Overview

After reading this chapter, I think you will agree that your scripts have a full set of file management and file access capabilities available to them. By means of the `FileSystemObject` object, scripts written in either VBScript or JScript can perform all types of file management, including working with folders. File access is currently limited to text files, but since binary file access is rarely needed in a script this does not pose much of a problem.

SIXTEEN

Creating Windows Script Components

Throughout this book you have seen many instances of the power of classes, or objects, in WSH scripts. Until now, however, the classes you had available to you were only those classes that are part of the WSH environment, such as the `FileScriptingObject` *and the* `WScript.Shell` *classes. As powerful as these "built-in" classes are, you can obtain even greater power and flexibility by defining your own classes. This is the topic of this chapter.*

The material in this chapter is necessarily limited to VBScript as the keywords required to create your own classes are not found in the JScript language. You can use VBScript to define classes and then use those classes in a JScript script, using the techniques for WSF files that were presented in Chapter 14.

Defining a Class

To define a class, you use the `Class` and `End Class` statements, as shown here:

```
Class classname
...
End Class
```

This code defines a class named *classname*. Between the two statement you put the VBScript code that defines the behavior of the class — in other words, its properties and methods. A class property, you may recall, serves to store data, while a class method carries out some action.

Classes and objects

The terms *class* and *object* are often used interchangeably, but you should remember that strictly speaking they have different meanings. A class is a plan or blueprint for an object, whereas an object is an actual functional code component created from a class. Multiple objects can be created from one class, just like you can build many tables from the same blueprint.

Creating Class Instances

Once a class is defined, you create instances of it (objects) using the New keyword. Assuming you have defined a class named MyClass, this code will create three instances of the class:

```
Dim obj1
Dim obj2
Dim obj3
Set obj1 = New MyClass
Set obj2 = New MyClass
Set obj3 = New MyClass
```

When you are finished with an object, you can destroy it by setting it equal to the special Nothing keyword. Doing this does not destroy the variable, but only the object it refers to. You can then use the variable for other purposes, if desired.

Defining Class Properties

One way to create a class property is to declare a variable within the class. This is done using the Public keyword. You use Public rather than Dim to make the variable, or property, visible outside the class. Here's an example that creates a class named Person with three properties:

```
Class Person
    Public FirstName
    Public LastName
    Public SSNumber
End Class
```

When you instantiate a class, and before you assign data to its properties, the properties will have the initial value of Empty. You access a property, either reading or setting it, using the ObjectName.PropertyName syntax that you have seen before:

```
Dim Someone
Dim SomeoneElse
Set Someone = New Person
Set SomeoneElse = New Person
Someone.LastName = "Smith"
Someone.FirstName = "Alex"
SomeoneElse.LastName = "Gomez"
SomeoneElse.FirstName = "Juan"
WScript.Echo "The name is " & Someone.FirstName & " " _
    & Someone.LastName
```

You can also assign directly between objects that are from the same class, which results in all property values from one object being assigned to the corresponding properties in the other object:

```
Someone = SomeoneElse
```

In addition to simple variables, a class can contain an array as a property. Here is the definition of a class named MonthlyIncome that uses an array:

```
Class MonthlyIncome
    Public Data(12)
End Class
```

You then access the property using this syntax:

```
Dim Year1999
Set Year1999 As New MonthlyIncome
Year1999.Data(1) = 1234.50
Year1999.Data(2) = 2222.00
...
```

There is another way to create class properties, called *procedural properties*, that will be covered later in this chapter.

Defining Class Methods

A class method is nothing more than a procedure defined inside a class. The syntax for defining methods is the same as for regular VBScript procedures, which was covered in Chapter 7, with the addition of the `Public` keyword. You can define both sub methods, which do not return a value, and function methods, which do. Here is the syntax:

```
Class classname

Public Sub MySubMethod(arguments)
' Sub statements here.
End Sub

Public Function MyFunctionMethod(arguments)
' Function statements here.
MyFunctionMethod = ReturnValue
End Function

End Class
```

The use of argument lists and function return values is the same as for regular procedures, and you can refer back to Chapter 7 if you need some review. Code in a method can access the class's properties directly, without the need to use the object name. You'll see this demonstrated soon.

The syntax for calling class methods is the same as for properties: object name followed by a period and the method name and, if required, the argument list. Let's take a look at a complete script, shown in Listing 16-1, that defines and uses a class. This class contains two properties and one method. Note how the code in the method can access the property Balance directly, simply by referring to it by name, while code outside the class must use the object name qualifier. The script's output is shown in Figure 16-1.

LISTING 16-1 *Defining and using a class.*

```
' List 1601.vbs
' Defining and using a class.

Option Explicit

Class BankAccount

    Public Balance
    Public OwnerName

    Public Function CalculateInterest(rate)
        CalculateInterest = Balance * rate
    End Function

End Class

Dim Account1
Dim msg

Set Account1 = New BankAccount
Account1.OwnerName = "Alice B. Toklas"
Account1.Balance = 1500

msg = Account1.OwnerName & " has a balance of "
msg = msg & FormatCurrency(Account1.Balance) & vbCrLf
msg = msg & " and has earned "
msg = msg &
FormatCurrency(Account1.CalculateInterest(0.05))
msg = msg & " in interest."
WScript.Echo msg
```

FIGURE 16–1 The output of the script in Listing 16-1.

Defining Private Class Information

So far, the class variables you have seen have all been public, which means they are accessible from outside the class. Generally this is what you want, but you can also define procedures and variables that are private and are accessible only within the class. You cannot refer to such private variables and procedures as properties and methods, since by definition properties and methods are visible outside the class. To create a private variable or procedure, simply use the `Private` keyword in place of `Public`:

```
Private Total

Private MySub()
...
End Sub
```

Private variables and procedures are accessible only to code that is within the class.

Procedural Class Properties

You have already seen one way to create a class property by defining a public variable to hold data. Another approach to class properties is to create a special type of procedure, called a *property procedure*, associated with each property (hence the name *procedural properties*). You use a procedural property when you need to execute some code whenever the property value is set or read. There are three types of property procedures, although you will use only one or two of them for any given procedural property:

- A `Property Get` procedure is use to read the value of a property.
- A `Property Let` procedure is used to set the value of a property when the property is simple text or numerical data.
- A `Property Set` procedure is used to set the value of a property when the property is an object reference.

Let's see how this would work, creating a property that is regular data and not an object reference. The first step is to create a `Property Get` and a `Property Let` procedure. They must both have the same name, which is the name of the property. Here is the syntax for the empty property procedures (we'll add the code soon):

```
Public Property Get PropName()
...
End Property

Public Property Let PropName(value)
...
End Property
```

As we will see, the `Property Get` procedure is actually a function as it returns a value. The next step is to create a private storage location for the property. This is done, as you learned in the previous section, by declaring a variable with the `Private` keyword. You can use any name you like for this variable, as long as you follow VBScript's naming rules, but I think it is a good idea to assign a name that identifies it as a variable where a property value is stored. My method is to use the property name prefixed by p, for property. Thus

```
Private pPropName
```

The final step is to add code to the property procedures to transfer the data to and from the property variable:

```
Public Property Get PropName()
    PropName = pPropName
End Property

Public Property Let PropName(value)
    pPropName = value
End Property
```

Here's how it works. When code in the script (outside of the object) sets the value of the property by using the property name on the left side of an assignment statement, the `Property Let` procedure is called with the new value passed in its argument. Code in that procedure assigns the passed value to the object's private internal storage location. When code in the script retrieves the value of the property, by using its name on the right side of an assignment statement (or in any other expression) the `Property Get` procedure is called. Code in that procedure retrieves the property value from the object's private internal storage location and returns it as the property procedure's return value.

Listing 16-2 demonstrates a simple class with one procedural property.

LISTING 16–2 *Creating a procedural property.*

```
' List1602.vbs
' Demonstrating a procedural class property.

Option Explicit

Class Person

Private pName

Public Property Get Name()
    Name = pName
End Property

Public Property Let Name(value)
    pName = value
End Property

End Class

Dim Someone
Set Someone = New Person
Someone.Name = "Alexandra"
WScript.Echo "The name is " & Someone.Name
```

So far this seems fairly simple, but you may be wondering why bother? As implemented in this example, a procedural property seems to offer no advantages over a regular property implemented as a public class variable. The advantages of procedural properties become apparent in two situations:

- When you want the property to be read-only
- When you want some code executed whenever the property is set or read

To make a property read-only, all that is necessary is to omit the `Property Let` (or `Property Set`) procedure. In the unusual situation where you want a property to be write-only, omit the `Property Get` procedure.

To execute code, simply place the code in the corresponding property procedure. You can put any VBScript code in a property procedure, and it will be executed whenever the property is set or read. There are many uses for code in property procedures. In a `Property Let` procedure, for example, you can include code that performs range checking to ensure that the property is not outside the allowable range. Here's a `Property Let` procedure for a property named InterestRate that will not permit the property to be set below .01 or above .20:

```
Public Property let InterestRate(value)

    If value < .01 or value > .20 then
        WScript.Echo "Sorry, that value is out of range."
    Else
        pInterestRate = value
    End If

End Property
```

You can also use a procedural property when the value of the property is calculated on the fly rather than being stored statically in the class. Suppose, for example, you have created a class named Rectangle that stores the dimensions — height and width — of a rectangle. You could create a read-only property named Area that is calculated as needed. Listing 16-3 shows the code for such a class.

LISTING 16–3 *Using a Property Get procedure.*

```
' List1603.vbs
' Using a Property Get procedure.

Option Explicit

Class Rectangle

    Public Height
    Public Width

    Public Property Get Area()
        Area = Height * Width
    End Property

End Class

Dim r
Set r = New Rectangle
r.Height = 20
r.Width = 15

WScript.Echo "The area is " & r.Area
```

Defining a Default Class Property

A class defined with VBScript can have a single default property. By designating a property as default, you can access it in code using only the object name without the property name qualifier. Suppose you have defined a class named MyClass with the property Count as the default property. Then look at this script code:

```
Dim obj
Dim x
Dim y
Set obj = New MyClass
obj.Count = 100
x = obj
y = obj.Count
```

The result is that both variables x and y have the value 100 because referring to the object name alone is the same as referring specifically to the property. To create a default property, use the Default keyword in the `Property Get` procedure definition:

```
Public Default Property Get()
...
End Property
```

The `Default` keyword is applicable only to `Property Get` procedures and cannot be used with either `Property Let` or `Property Set` procedures. A given class definition can include only a single default property.

While default properties may seem like a good idea, I suggest that you avoid using them. The reason is clarity — when you explicitly refer to a property name using `Object.Property` syntax, it is always clear that you are referring to a property. In contrast, when you access a default property using the object name alone, it may not be as clear that you are dealing with a property. In my opinion, the small amount of typing that you save is not worth the potential for confusion.

Using a Class in Multiple Scripts

The techniques presented so far in this chapter will give you a class that can be used only in the script where it is located. If you have devised a general-purpose class, you will probably want to use it in many of the scripts you create. Other than cutting and pasting the source code, which can be bothersome, is there a way to share a class between scripts?

Yes, there is, and you already learned about it in Chapter 14. The way to reuse a class is to save the class source code in its own file and then import it into any script that needs it. In order to do this, your script must be in a WSF file. Please turn to Chapter 14 if you need general review on how to create and use WSF files.

To import a file into a WSF file, you use the `<script>` tag. The syntax is

```
<script language=language src=filename>
</script>
```

For example, suppose you had saved one or more class definitions in a file named ClassLibrary.vbs. Then, this tag in your WSF file would make the classes in ClassLibrary.vbs available to the scripts in the WSF file:

```
<script language="VBScript" src="ClassLibrary.vbs">
</script>
```

My procedure has been to keep all of the classes that I think may be reused together in a single file, and then import the file as needed using this technique. It may be slightly less efficient than keeping each class definition in its own separate file, but it makes it easier to keep track of things.

A Class Example

I end this chapter with a demonstration of a class that pulls together many of the topics that have been covered. The code in Listing 16-4 defines a class called SuperString, intended for use with string data. The class provides a way to store text and also to obtain information about it — in this case, its length and also whether it contains a substring. In some ways, the SuperString class is similar to JScript's String class, although it is a lot simpler. I am sure you can think of many more capabilities that could be added to this class in order to make it a really useful programming tool.

LISTING 16–4 *Defining a class for storage of string data.*

```
' List1604.vbs
' A class demonstration.

Option Explicit

Class SuperString

Private pValue

Public Default Property Get Value()
    value = pValue
End Property
```

```
Public Property Let Value(s)
    pValue = s
End Property

Public Property Get Length()
    Length = len(pValue)
End Property

Public Function Contains(template)
    Dim p

    If len(template) = 0 or len(pValue) = 0 then
        Contains = False
        Exit Function
    End If

    p = instr(1, pValue, template, 1)
    If p = 0 Then
        Contains = False
    Else
        Contains = True
    End If

    End Function

End Class
'****************

Dim s1
Dim s2

Set s1 = New SuperString
Set s2 = New SuperString

s1.Value = "Mississippi"
s2.Value = "is"

WScript.Echo "The first string is " & s1.Length & "characters long."
If s1.Contains(s2) then
    WScript.Echo "The first string contains '" & s2 & "'"
else
    WScript.Echo "The first string does not contain '" & s2 & "'"
end if
```

Overview

The ability to define your own classes can be an extremely useful tool for the script programmer. Simpler classes can serve only for data storage, in effect defining new "data types" that are matched to the needs of the script. More complex classes can provide data validation and methods for carrying out actions. While classes can be created only in VBScript, you can use them in a JScript script by utilizing the import features of WSF files. As you develop a collection of useful general-purpose classes, they can also be made available to all of your scripts in this way.

S E V E N T E E N

Database Access with Scripting

Some of the most useful things that you can do with scripting involve access to databases. A database is a way to store persistent information—that is, information that is retained between sessions. There are other ways a script can store persistent information, such as the file access techniques that you learned about in Chapter 15. However, database technology offers many advantages over other methods of storing information. For example, the database tools available to your scripts provide highly sophisticated ways for you to add, retrieve, and organize information.

We start this chapter with a review of basic database terminology and technology. Then, we look at some of the details of Active Data Objects, which is the database technology that Microsoft has made available for use by Windows Script Host. Finally, we see some examples of how scripting and database technology can be integrated to solve real-world problems.

You'll note that all examples in this chapter are presented in VBScript. While JScript can certainly be used for database access, various aspects of VBScript make it the better choice.

Database Fundamentals

At the heart of database technology is a method for storing information that is based on records and fields. In a given database table, each record holds the information related to a specific object or thing — this could be an individual person, an item in a company's inventory, a book on a library shelf, or a compact disk in someone's music collection. Each field in the table holds a specific detail about an object. In a books database table, for example, each record would contain fields for the book's title, its author, its publication date, and so on. The most common example of databases, one that almost everyone is familiar with, is an address book. Each person in your address book constitutes a record, and each record has fields for name, address, phone number, and so on.

In a given database table, all records contain the same fields. The table is often visualized in a row and column format, with each row corresponding to a record and each column corresponding to a field. This is illustrated in Figure 17-1.

A database that contains only a single table is referred to as a flat-file database. An address book is an example of this kind of database. Many databases, however, contain two or more tables that are related to each other by having one or more fields in common. These are called relational databases. Let's look at an example.

Consider a database used by an automobile parts store to keep track of its inventory. For each individual part, the database will contain information such as part number, price, and quantity on hand. It is also desired to store information about the suppliers from which the various parts are obtained. For each supplier, the name, address, telephone number, and contact person's name need to be kept. Each part is obtained from only a single supplier; however, a given supplier may provide multiple different parts. If all of his information were to be combined in a single table, it might look like the table illustrated in Figure 17-2.

If you look at the structure of the table in Figure 17-2, perhaps you'll notice that it is rather inefficient. All of the information about a given supplier

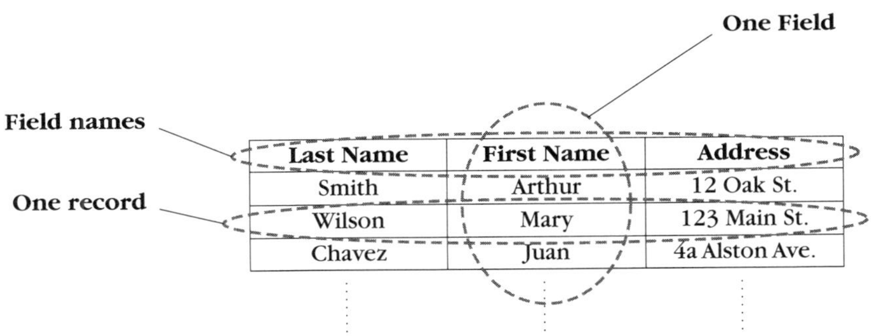

FIGURE 17–1 *A database table contains records and fields.*

Part No.	Description	Price	Supplier	Supplier Address	Supplier Telephone
10427	Screw puller	47.00	Acme Mfg.	104 Court St.	123-456-7890
11249	Bold cutter	19.00	Acme Mfg.	104 Court St.	123-456-7890
10120	Wrench	11.50	ABC Products	22 West Ave.	555-555-1212
9115	Stripper	14.45	Acme Mfg.	104 Court St.	123-456-7890

FIGURE 17–2 *A flat-file database for auto parts inventory.*

must be entered for every single part that is obtained from that supplier. Not only is this structure very wasteful of storage space, it also requires a lot of extra work should the information about a given supplier change. Relational databases were developed for just this sort of situation. Rather than keep the part and supplier information together in a single table, information about these two elements is kept in separate tables that are related by virtue of having one field in common. This structure is illustrated in Figure 17-3.

Table 1: Parts

Part No.	Description	Price	Supplier
10427	Screw puller	47.00	Acme Mfg.
11249	Bold cutter	19.00	Acme Mfg.
10120	Wrench	11.50	ABC Products
9115	Stripper	14.45	Acme Mfg.

Relational Link

Table 2: Suppliers

Supplier	Supplier Address	Supplier Telephone
Acme Mfg.	104 Court St.	123-456-7890
ABC Products	22 West Ave.	555-555-1212

FIGURE 17–3 *A relational database for auto parts inventory.*

The field that these two tables have in common is Supplier. Based on the relation between these two tables, database software will permit you to do things such as determine the telephone number of the supplier for a given part, or list all of the parts that are obtained from a particular supplier. There is no storage space wasted, updating information is greatly simplified, and flexibility for data retrieval and analysis is enhanced. This is a very simple example of a relational database, and much more complicated situations involving multiple data tables are possible. For the present purposes, however, this fundamental understanding will be perfectly sufficient.

Every database table will (or at least should) have a *primary key*. This is a field whose data is guaranteed to identify each record uniquely. In other words, the field data is never duplicated between records. In some cases, the data itself will provide a primary key, with Social Security number and e-mail address being two examples of field data that can safely be assumed to be unique. When the data cannot provide a primary key, one will be generated. Typically this is a sequential number that is generated incrementally as records are added to the table. The data in this sort of generated primary key is meaningless but serves the important purpose of uniquely identifying each record.

Database Technologies

While the fundamental underlying principles are the same for all relational databases, many different technologies have been developed to implement them. Each software vendor has its own standard, and even within a given software vendor, technology advances and improves over time. Microsoft, recognizing the central importance of database technology, has built many of the necessary tools into the Windows operating system. It is these database tools that you, the Windows script host programmer, can make use of. It is important to note that these database tools are independent of Microsoft's database application program, Access. Regardless of whether Access is installed, your scripts will have a full range of database tools available to them.

Over the years, a variety of database access technologies have been made available in Windows. These include Structured Query Language (SQL), Open Database Connectivity (ODBC), Data Access Objects (DAO), and Remote Data Objects (RDO). These technologies are still supported, but from the perspective of the programmer have been largely if not completely superseded by Active Data Objects, or ADO, Microsoft's latest data access technology. ADO is more powerful and easier to use than its predecessors and provides access to the full range of providers. Except for supporting legacy applications with certain specialized needs, I can think of no reason to use anything else.

Active Data Objects

As with many other things you have encountered, ADO has an object model that defines the relationships between the various components of which it is comprised. Compared with other database technologies, the ADO object model is a wonder of simplicity. It is diagrammed, in slightly simplified form, in Figure 17-4.

The `Connection` object represents the connection between your script and the data source (the file where the actual data is located). When you create a `Connection` object you must specify the details that are required to open the data source, such as the provider (which identifies the type of data source), the username and password if required, and so on. A `Connection` object also permits changes to be made to the data source, by means of transactions. In some situations you will explicitly create a `Connection` object for use in your script. At other times a connection will be created implicitly, behind the scenes. Each `Connection` object has an `Errors` collection that contains one `Error` object for each error (if any) that has occurred for this connection.

The `Command` object is used to request that some action be carried out. You can do a lot of things with ADO without ever using the `Command` object, but there are times when it is necessary. A `Command` object can represent an

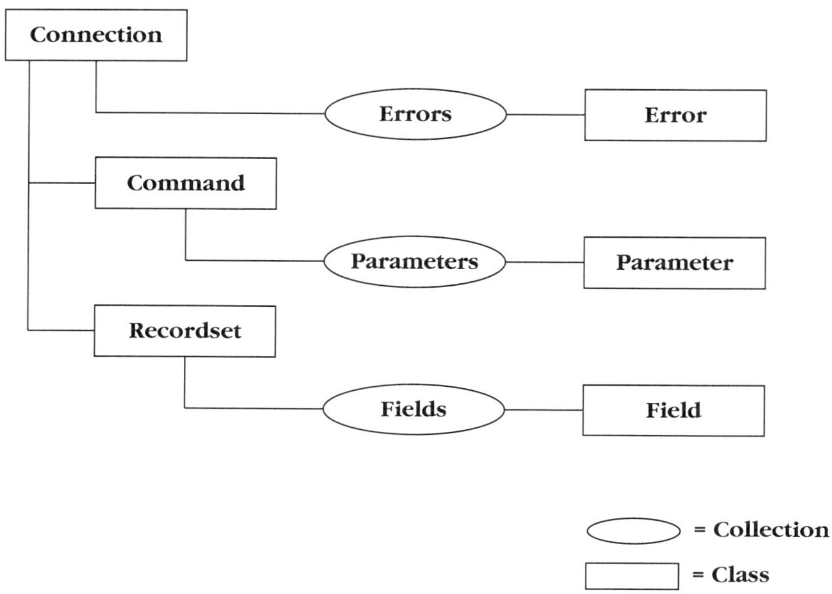

FIGURE 17–4 *The ADO object model.*

SQL statement, a stored procedure, or a query. A `Command` object has a `Parameters` collection that contains one Parameter object for each of the command's parameters.

The `RecordSet` object is the object you will work with most often. As the name implies, a `RecordSet` object contains a set of the data records from the data source. A recordset, sometimes called a result set, can contain records from a single table in the data source or, when working with a relational database, it can contain records that are composed of fields from two or more tables in the data source. A recordset can contain all the records from the data source, or selected records based on criteria you specify. Each `RecordSet` object contains a `Fields` collection that contains one `Field` object for each field in the recordset.

Each of the four main classes in the object model (`Connection`, `Command`, `Recordset`, and `Field`) also has a `Properties` collection (not shown in Figure 17-4) that contains the object's properties.

SQL

Structured Query Language has become the de facto standard for accessing and manipulating databases. It can be rather complex, but the fundamentals are reasonably easy to understand. SQL is unlike VBScript and JScript in that it is a nonprocedural language — it contains no statements to control the execution and sequence of specific steps. Instead, SQL lets you specify the desired end result, and the database engine takes care of the details of how to accomplish it. Let's look at an example. Suppose you have a table named Contacts that contains fields for name, address, city, state, phone number, e-mail address, and so on. You want to obtain a list of the names and e-mail addresses of all the contacts who live in California, in order by name. Here is the SQL statement that is needed:

```
Select Name, Email From Contacts Where State = 'CA' Order By Name
```

If a field name contains a space, it must be enclosed in single quotes:

```
Select 'First Name', 'Last Name' From Contacts Where State = 'CA'
```

Many of the most commonly used SQL statements have this same fundamental structure:

```
Select Fields From Table Where Condition Order By OrderField
```

SQL statements can be a lot more complicated, particularly when working with relational databases. You can learn more about SQL by referring to one of the books published on the subject, or almost any book that specializes in database programming.

Creating a Connection

The first step in accessing a database from your script is to create a connection. In general, this requires three steps:

1. Create an instance of the ADO `Connection object.`
2. Set its properties to define the desired connection.
3. Execute its `Open method.`

Before I present an example of creating an ADO connection, you need to know about the properties and methods of the `Connection` object. Tables 17-1 and 17-2 present the most commonly needed properties and methods. Since this is an introductory treatment, I have for clarity's sake omitted some more advanced properties and methods that you will rarely need to change from their default values. Note that `Connection` object properties are read/write-only when there is no connection open. If a connection is open they are read-only.

TABLE 17.1 *Properties of the `Connection` object.*

Property	Description
CommandTimeout	The time, in seconds, that the `Connection` object will try to execute a command before canceling the command and returning an error. The default value is 30.
ConnectionString	A string specifying the details of the database connection. See text below for more information.
ConnectionTimeout	The time, in seconds, that the `Connection` object will try to establish a connection before canceling the attempt and returning an error. The default value is 15.
Mode	Specifies read, write, and share permissions. See Table 17-3 for permitted settings.
State	Returns the state of the `Connection` object, either `adStateClosed` (value = 0) or `adStateOpen` (1).

TABLE 17.2 ***Methods of the `Connection object.`***

Method	Description
BeginTrans()	Begins a new transaction. See text below for details.
Close()	Closes the current database connection.
CommitTrans()	Commits the current transaction.
Execute(*command*)	Executes the specified SQL command. With certain commands, this method returns a reference to the results recordset.
Open(*ConnectString, User, password*)	Opens a connection to a data source. You can specify the connection information in the `ConnectionString` property, in which case the `Open` method is called without arguments.
OpenSchema(*QueryType, Criteria, SchemaID*)	Returns information about the organization of the data source. See the section "Obtaining Data Source Information" later in this chapter for more information.
RollbackTrans()	Ends the current transaction and cancels any changes to the data source.

TABLE 17.3 Settings for the Connection object's Mode property.

Constant	Value	Description
adModeUnknown	0	The default. Permissions have not been set and/or are unknown.
adModeRead	1	Read-only access.
adModeWrite	2	Write-only access.
adModeReadWrite	3	Read/write access.
adModeShareDenyRead	4	Prevents others from opening a read-mode connection.
adModeShareDenyWrite	8	Prevents others from opening a write-mode connection.
adModeShareExclusive	12	Prevents others from opening any type of connection.
adModeShareDenyNone	16	Prevents others from opening a new connection with permissions.

Creating a Connection String

A connection string can take two forms. One is a Data Source Name, or DSN. You can use this type of connection string only if a DSN has been set up for the database that you want to access. If you cannot do this yourself, your system administrator should be able to help you.

The second form for a connection string is a string with embedded parameters that specify the details of the connection. The parameters, which are separated by semicolons, are as follows:

- Provider: The name of the OLE DB provider.
- Data Source: The name of the data source.
- ID: The user's ID (if required).
- Password: The password (if required).
- File Name: The name of a provider-specific file that contains connection information.
- Remote Provider: When using Remote Data Service, the name of the remote provider.
- Remote Server: When using Remote Data Service, the name of the remote server.
- Other parameters: There may be provider-specific parameters supported as well.

Any given connections string will require only some of these parameters. It is impossible to give examples of all the possible types of connection strings, but here are a couple of samples. This connection string opens a connection to a Microsoft Jet OLE DB version 4 database file named Sales2001.mdb (this is the database format used by the Microsoft Access database program):

```
Provider=Microsoft.Jet.OLEDB.4.0;Data Source=Sales2001.mdb;
```

This connection string opens a connection to an SQL Server database named Employees located on the server named HDQTR1, with the user name "peter" and the password "grapes."

```
driver={SQL Server};server=HDQTR1;database=employees;uid=peter;pwd=grapes
```

The details of creating a proper connection string can seem daunting at first. If you are working with a data source that you created, you should be able to find information about connection string details in the program documentation. If it is a shared data source on a company network, the network administrator should be able to help you.

The Northwind Database

The examples in this chapter all make use of Northwind.mdb. This is a sample database that is installed along with the Microsoft Access database application, and many readers will already have it on their system or will have access to it. If you do not, you can substitute any other OLE DB compatible data source by making the necessary changes to the connection strings in the example code.

Listing 17-1 presents an example of creating and opening an ADODB `Connection` object. This script does not actually do anything with the data source but shows you the basic steps required to open a connection, check for errors, and close the connection. The importance of checking for errors cannot be overemphasized. There are so many possibilities for errors, particularly when your script is working with information entered by the user, where there is always the chance of a typo or other mistake. This script shows the general approach that is advised for ADO error handling: execute `On Error Resume Next` and then, after any ADO operation that has the potential to cause an error, check the `Err` object and respond appropriately if an error has occurred. Please refer to Chapter 9 for more details on VBScript error handling.

LISTING 17–1 *Opening an ADODB connection.*

```
'List1701.vbs
'Opening an ADO data connection.

Option Explicit

Dim adoCon
Dim conString
Dim msg

On Error Resume Next
```

```
' Set up the connection string.
conString = "Provider=Microsoft.Jet.OLEDB.4.0;"
conString = conString & "Data Source="
conString = conString & "c:\data\northwind.mdb;"

' Create the Connection object.
Set adoCon = WScript.CreateObject("ADODB.Connection")
adoCon.ConnectionString = conString

' Open the connection.
adoCon.Open

'Test for error and display appropriate message.
If Err = 0 Then
    WScript.Echo "Connected to Northwinds database."
else
    msg = "An error occurred trying to connect to the
Northwinds database:" & vbCrLf
    msg = msg & "Error number: " & Err & vbCrLf
    msg = msg & "Description: " & Err.Description
    WScript.Echo msg
end if

' Code to work with the data source would go here.

' Close the connection.
adoCon.Close
```

Recordsets

Much of what you do with databases will involve recordsets. As you learned earlier in this chapter, a recordset is represented by the ADODB `Recordset` object. In essence, a recordset lets you extract a subset of the data in a database table. A simple example would be a recordset that extracts from an address list table all those records where the STATE field is "California." The rules that determine which records are extracted to a recordset are called the *criteria*. With few exceptions, criteria are specified using SQL. Before getting to the details of recordsets, let's look at the basics of SQL.

SQL FUNDAMENTALS

Following is the SQL statement that would define the recordset just described (assuming the data table is named ADDRESSES):

```
SELECT * FROM ADDRESSES WHERE STATE="California"
```

Criteria can be essentially as complex as you need. You can combine individual criteria to create a complex selection. For example, from an inventory database you could create a recordset containing records for those items where QOH (Quantity on Hand) is less than 5 and SUPPLIER equals "Acme Machine Parts." The SQL statement for this is as follows:

```
SELECT * FROM INVENTORY WHERE QOH<5 AND SUPPLIER="Acme Machine Parts"
```

There are two operators for combining individual criteria into a complex criterion (there are actually more, but these are the ones you'll use most). AND requires that both individual criteria be true, as in the preceding example. OR requires that either one, or both, of the individual criteria be true. For example, this SQL statement selects those parts for which SUPPLIER is either Acme Machine Parts or Wilson Electronics:

```
SELECT * FROM INVENTORY WHERE SUPPLIER="Acme Machine Parts" OR
    SUPPLIER="Wilson Electronics"
```

Table 17-4 describes the most commonly used SQL comparison operators.

TABLE 17.5 *Commonly needed SQL comparison statements.*

Operator	Comparison
=	Equal to
<>	Not equal to
>=	Greater than or equal to
<=	Less than or equal to
<	Less than
>	Greater than
BETWEEN *Value1* AND *Value2*	Is between Value 1 and Value 2, inclusive.
IN (*list*)	Is in the list of values, *List* is a comma-delimited list of data values, e.g. (2, 4, 8).
IS NULL	The data value is NULL.

The NOT SQL operator

When designing an SQL statement for creating a recordset, sometimes it is easier to specify what you *don't* want in the recordset rather than defining what you *do* want. This is done using the NOT operator. By placing NOT before a criterion, the result is selection of those records that do not meet the criterion. For example, this SQL statement selects all records where STATE does not equal "California:"

```
SELECT * FROM ADDRESSES WHERE NOT STATE="California"
```

You can use NOT before any SQL criteria.

You do not need to specify criteria in an SQL statement. If you omit criteria the result is that all the records in the table are extracted to the recordset.

For example this SQL statement would create a recordset that contains all records and all fields from the specified table:

```
SELECT * FROM ADDRESSES
```

An SQL statement also lets you specify which fields from the data table will be included in the recordset. In the SQL examples given previously, the first part of the statement

```
SELECT *
```

specifies that all fields from the data table will be included in the recordset. At times you may not need all fields, and you can use the `SELECT` keyword to specify those fields to include in the recordset. For example, this SQL statement defines a recordset that contains only the FIRSTNAME, LASTNAME, and PHONE fields for those records where STATE = "New York:"

```
SELECT FIRSTNAME, LASTNAME, PHONE FROM ADDRESSES WHERE STATE="New York"
```

You will note from this example that the field or fields used for the selection criteria need not be part of the resulting recordset.

The final aspect of SQL statements that we cover is those dealing with sorting the recordset. If your SQL statement does not specify a sort order, the recordset will be sorted in whatever order the extracted records exist in the data table. If you want the recordset sorted on a specific table, you can specify this using the `ORDER BY` clause in the SQL statement. This clause comes at the end of the SQL statement and specifies the field to sort on. This field may or may not be a field that is included in the recordset. Here's an SQL statement that results in a recordset sorted by LASTNAME:

```
SELECT * FROM ADDRESSES WHERE STATE="Ohio" ORDER BY LASTNAME
```

The default is to sort in ascending order. If you want a reverse order sort, include the `DESCEND keyword after the field name:`

```
SELECT * FROM ADDRESSES WHERE STATE="Ohio" ORDER BY LASTNAME DESCEND
```

Creating a Recordset

In order to create a recordset, you must first establish a connection with the data source, as described earlier in this chapter. Then there are two ways to create the `Recordset` object.

The first method for creating a recordset is to first create an (empty) instance of the `Recordset` object, then call its `Open` method with arguments that specify the details of the data. The simplified syntax is:

```
recordset.Open Source, ActiveConnection, CursorType, LockType, Options
```

Source is an SQL statement that defines the recordset.

ActiveConnection is a reference to a `Connection` object that is connected to the data source.

CursorType is an optional argument specifying the type of cursor to use when opening the recordset.

LockType is an optional argument that specifies the type of locking, or concurrency, to use when opening the recordset.

Options is an optional argument that specifies how the *source* argument should be interpreted.

The last three of these arguments need some more explaining. The term *cursor* refers to the nature of the link between the recordset and the underlying data source, particularly as regards changes to the data made by other users (applicable only in a shared environment, obviously). The possibilities for this argument are presented in Table 17-6.

TABLE 17.6 **Values for the CursorType argument.**

Constant	Value	Description
adOpenForwardOnly	0	The default. Only forward movement through the recordset is permitted.
adOpenStatic	3	Forward and backward movement is permitted, but changes made by other uses to the underlying data source are not reflected in the recordset.
adOpenKeyset	1	Same as `adOpenStatic`, but edits made by other users to the underlying data are reflected in the recordset (but added and deleted records are not).
adOpenDynamic	2	Same as `adOpenKeyset`, but records added and deleted by other users in the underlying data are reflected in the recordset.

Why four different cursor types? Cursors with greater capabilities place greater demands on the system, requiring memory space and processor time. By selecting the simplest cursor that meets your needs, your script will operate at maximum efficiency. If you need only to go through the records and extract data, use the default `adOpenForwardOnly` cursor. If you will need to move forward and backward in the recordset, use the `adOpenStatic` cursor. The other two cursor types are applicable only when you are working with a multiuser database.

The *Locktype* argument is related to how the data in the recordset is updateable — in other words, can the data be changed. This argument also controls record locking, which affects the ability of other users to modify the record. A locked record cannot be modified by another user. Possible settings for this argument are listed in Table 17-7.

TABLE 17.7 *Values for the LockType argument.*

Constant	Value	Description
adLockReadOnly	1	The default. The recordset is read-only and no changes can be made.
adLockPessimistic	2	The record is locked as soon as editing begins.
adLockOptimistic	3	The record is locked when the `Update` method is called.
adLockBatchOptimistic	4	The record is locked when a batch update is performed.

The locking settings `adLockOptimistic` and `adLockBatchOptimistic` are used mostly in more complex multiuser database situations. For scripting purposes, it is almost always appropriate to use `adLockReadOnly` if you do not need to change the data, or `adLockPessimistic` if you do.

The *options* argument specifies how the information in the source argument should be interpreted. I have said that *source* is an SQL statement, which is more than adequate for our purposes. *Source* can also be various other things, such as a `Command` object, but these details are beyond the scope of the book. This is, however, why the `Open` method requires the options argument. When passing an SQL statement as the *source* argument, use `adCmdText` (value = 1) as the *options* argument. You can also omit this argument, in which case the database provider will examine the *source* argument and determine what type it is. This does degrade performance slightly, however.

Listing 17-2 shows you how to create a recordset using the `Open` method.

LISTING 17–2 *Creating a recordset using the Open method.*

```
' List1702.vbs
' Creating a recordset using the Open method.

Option Explicit

Dim adoCon
Dim conString
Dim sqlStr
Dim msg
Dim rs

On Error Resume Next

' Set up the connection string.
conString = "Provider=Microsoft.Jet.OLEDB.4.0;"
conString = conString & "Data Source="
conString = conString & "c:\data\northwind.mdb;"
```

```
' Create the Connection object.
Set adoCon = WScript.CreateObject("ADODB.Connection")
adoCon.ConnectionString = conString

' Open the connection.
adoCon.Open

'Test for error and display appropriate message.
If Err <>0 Then
    msg = "An error occurred trying to connect to the Northwinds
database:" & vbCrLf
    msg = msg & "Error number: " & Err & vbCrLf
    msg = msg & "Description: " & Err.Description
    WScript.Echo msg
end if

Err.Clear

' Create an empty recordset.
Set rs = CreateObject("ADODB.RecordSet")

' Create the SQL statement.
sqlStr = "Select * From Customers Where Country='Mexico'"

' Open the recordset
rs.Open sqlStr, adoCOn
'Test for error and display appropriate message.
If Err <>0 Then
    msg = "An error occurred trying to create the recordset:" & vbCrLf
    msg = msg & "Error number: " & Err & vbCrLf
    msg = msg & "Description: " & Err.Description
    WScript.Echo msg
Else
    WScript.Echo "Recordset created successfully."
end if
```

In this example, note that the criterion Mexico is enclosed in single quotes. SQL can work with either single or double quotes, but because you use double quotes to delimit strings in VBScript, single quotes are typically used to set off text criteria in SQL statements.

The second method to create a recordset is to call the `Connection` object's `Execute` method, passing an SQL command as an argument. This method creates the recordset defined by the SQL statement and returns a reference to it. You store this reference in a script variable and then use that reference to access the contents of the recordset. The limitation of this technique is that the recordset created is always read-only with a forward-only cursor. If you want a recordset with other options, you must use the `Recordset` object's `Open` method discussed earlier in this section.

Here's an example of creating a recordset using the `Execute` method. This code assumes that adoCon refers to a `Connection` object associated with the Northwinds database:

```
Dim rs
Dim conString

conString = "Select * From Customers Where Country='Mexico'"
Set rs = adoCon.Execute(conString)
```

After this code executes, rs refers to a recordset that contains all records from the Customers table where Country equals Mexico. You can then use the Recordset object to access and manipulate the data as needed. Listing 17-3 later in this chapter shows how to create a recordset using this method.

Working with Recordsets

Once you have created a recordset that contains the data you need, you use the properties and methods of the `Recordset` object to work with the data. The structure of the data inside a recordset is the same as in a data table, being organized into rows (records) and columns (fields). Of course, the recordset contains only those records and fields that were specified by the SQL statement when the recordset was created.

Accessing Field Data

At almost any time, a recordset will have a current, or active, record. When you initially create a recordset, its first record (as defined by the sort order) will be current. You access the data in the current record on a field-by-field basis using the `Recordset` object's `Fields` collection. This collection has the `Count` property, which returns the number of fields in the recordset. It also has the `Item` method, which returns the contents of a specific field. You can specify a field either by its name or by its ordinal position. For example, assuming that rs refers to a recordset,

```
rs.Fields.Item(n)
```

This code returns the data in the *n*th field of the current record in rs. *n* can range from 0 (the first field) to Count −1. Because `Item` is the default method of the Fields collection, you do not have to specify it. These two lines of code are exactly equivalent:

```
rs.Fields.Item(2)
rs.Fields(2)
```

To retrieve data based on the field name, pass the name as the argument to the `Item` method, as shown here. This code again makes use of the fact that `Item` is the default method.

```
rs.Fields("FirstName")
```

No bangs

In Visual Basic, ADO recordsets support the so-called bang operator (!) to retrieve data from a specified field. Thus, this code retrieves the contents of the field LastName from the recordset's current record:

```
rs!LastName
```

However, the bang operator is not supported in VBScript. You must use the `Fields` collection to access recordset data.

Moving through a Recordset

At any moment, a recordset will have a current position. Usually this position points to a record in the recordset, called the *current record*. The current position can also be set to before the first record or after the last record, referred to BOF (Beginning of File) and EOF (End of File), respectively. If the position is at BOF or EOF, no data record is active.

Many data manipulation operations require that you move through a recordset, changing the current record. The `Recordset` object has several methods that are used for this purpose. These methods are described in Table 17.8.

TABLE 17.8 *Movement methods of the Recordset object.*

Method	Description
Move *n*	Moves the current record forward (if n is positive) or backward (if n is negative) in the recordset. If the operation would move the current position past the beginning or end of the recordset, the position is set to BOF or EOF. If an attempt is made to move forward when already at EOF, or backward when already at BOF, an error occurs.
MoveFirst	Moves to the first record in the recordset.
MoveLast	Moves to the last record in the recordset.
MoveNext	Moves to the next record in the recordset. If MoveNext is called while the last record is current, the position is set to EOF.
MovePrevious	Moves to the previous record in the recordset. If MovePrevious is called while the first record is current, the position is set to BOF.

The `Recordset` object has a number of properties that are useful when moving through the recordset. They are described in Table 17.9.

TABLE 17.9 *Movement-related properties of the Recordset object.*

Property	Description
AbsolutePosition	Returns a number indicating the position of the current record, ranging from 1 to `Recordset.RecordCount`. Returns `adPosBOF` (value = –2) or `asPosEOF` (–3) if the position is at BOF or EOF. Returns `adPosUnknown` (–1) if the recordset is empty or the current position is unknown.
BOF	Returns True if the current position is at BOF.
EOF	Returns True if the current position is at EOF.

Detecting an empty recordset

It is possible that a recordset you create will be empty, and this is something your script should check for before trying to work with the data in the recordset. There are two ways to detect an empty recordset: the `RecordCount` property will return 0 and the `BOF` and `EOF` properties will both return True.

Listing 17-3 shows how to use the `MoveNext` methods and the `EOF` property to loop through all the records in a recordset and display the data in two of the fields. Figure 17-5 shows the script output.

LISTING 17–3 *Looping through all records in a recordset.*

```
' List1703.vbs
' Looping through all records in a recordset.

Option Explicit

Dim adoCon
Dim conString
Dim msg
Dim rs

On Error Resume Next

' Set up the connection string.
conString = "Provider=Microsoft.Jet.OLEDB.4.0;"
conString = conString & "Data Source="
conString = conString & "c:\data\northwind.mdb;"

' Create the Connection object.
Set adoCon = WScript.CreateObject("ADODB.Connection")
adoCon.ConnectionString = conString
```

```
' Open the connection.
adoCon.Open

'Test for error and display appropriate message.
If Err <>0 Then
    msg = "An error occurred trying to connect to the Northwinds
database:" & vbCrLf
    msg = msg & "Error number: " & Err & vbCrLf
    msg = msg & "Description: " & Err.Description
    WScript.Echo msg
end if

Err.Clear

' Create the recordset.
Set rs = adoCon.Execute _
    ("Select * From Customers Where Country='Mexico'")
' If error, display message then quit.
If Err <> 0 then
    msg = "An error occurred trying to create the recordset:" & vbCrLf
    msg = msg & "Error number: " & Err & vbCrLf
    msg = msg & "Description: " & Err.Description
    WScript.Echo msg
    adoCon.Close
    WScript.Quit
End If

' Make sure the recordset is not empty.
If rs.EOF and rs.BOF then
    WScript.Echo "No matching records found."
    adoCon.Close
    WScript.Quit
End If

' Loop through the recordset, getting the ContactName
' and ContactTitle data for all records.
msg = ""
Do While Not rs.EOF
    msg = msg & rs.Fields("ContactName") & ", " &
rs.Fields("ContactTitle") & vbCrLf
    rs.MoveNext
Loop

' Display the list.
WScript.Echo msg

' Close the connection.
adoCon.Close
```

FIGURE 17–5 *The output of the script in Listing 17-3.*

Modifying Recordset Data

There are three types of modifications that can be made to a recordset:

- Modifying data in an existing record.
- Adding a new record.
- Deleting an existing record.

In order to modify a recordset, the recordset must have been opened in an updatable mode. This is controlled using the *LockType* argument to the `Open` method, as discussed earlier in this chapter. If you try to modify a read-only recordset, an error will occur.

To modify an existing record, the first step is to make that record current. You could do this by creating a recordset (based on the SQL statement) that contains only the single record of interest. Or, you could create a multi-record recordset and then look through the records until you find the right one. Once the desired record is current, the modifications are a simple matter of placing the new data in the appropriate field(s) and then calling the `Update` method to save the changes.

The script in Listing 17-4 demonstrates how to open a recordset containing a single record and modify the data in that record. You should be aware that this script does not check to verify that there is only a single record for the specified SQL criteria. This is something that a real-world script should do. Note how this script is in a WSF file, permitting a reference to the `ADODB.Recordset` object and its defined constants to be made.

LISTING 17–4 *Modifying an existing record in a recordset.*

```
<!-- List1704.wsf
 Modifying recordset data. -->

<job>
<reference object="ADODB.Recordset" />
<script language="VBScript">

Option Explicit

Dim adoCon
Dim conString
Dim sqlStr
Dim msg
Dim rs

On Error Resume Next

' Set up the connection string.
conString = "Provider=Microsoft.Jet.OLEDB.4.0;"
conString = conString & "Data Source="
conString = conString & "c:\data\northwind.mdb;"

' Create the Connection object.
Set adoCon = WScript.CreateObject("ADODB.Connection")
adoCon.ConnectionString = conString

' Open the connection.
adoCon.Open

'Test for error and display appropriate message.
If Err <>0 Then
    msg = "An error occurred trying to connect to the Northwinds
database:" & vbCrLf
    msg = msg & "Error number: " & Err & vbCrLf
    msg = msg & "Description: " & Err.Description
    WScript.Echo msg
    WScript.Quit
end if

Err.Clear

' Create an empty recordset.
Set rs = CreateObject("ADODB.RecordSet")

' Create the SQL statement to select the desired record.
sqlStr = "Select * From Employees Where LastName='Peacock' And
FirstName='Margaret'"
```

```
' Open the recordset
rs.Open sqlStr, adoCon, adOpenStatic, adLockPessimistic, adCmdText
'Test for error and display appropriate message.
If Err <>0 Then
    msg = "An error occurred trying to create the recordset:" & vbCrLf
    msg = msg & "Error number: " & Err & vbCrLf
    msg = msg & "Description: " & Err.Description
    WScript.Echo msg
    WScript.Quit
end if

' Update the data.
rs.Fields("Title") = "Sales Manager"
rs.Update
If Err <>0 Then
    msg = "An error occurred trying to update the recordset:" & vbCrLf
    msg = msg & "Error number: " & Err & vbCrLf
    msg = msg & "Description: " & Err.Description
    WScript.Echo msg
    WScript.Quit
else
    WScript.Echo "Table updated successfully."
end if

</script>
</jcb>
```

To add a new record to a recordset, call the `AddNew` method. Assuming rs is a reference to the recordset, the syntax is

```
rs.AddNew
```

This method adds a new, empty record to the recordset and makes it the current record. You then add data to the individual fields in the record and finally call the `Update` method to save the new record. Here's an example.

```
rs.AddNew
rs.Fields("FirstName") = "Joan"
rs.Fields("LastName") = "Sutherland"
rs.Fields("PhoneNumber") = "123-456-7890"
rs.Update
```

To delete one or more records, call the `RecordSet` object's `Delete` method. The syntax is:

```
rs.Delete AffectRecords
```

The *AffectRecords* argument can be set to `adAffectCurrent` (value = 1) to delete the current record, or to `adAffectAll` (3) to delete all records in the recordset.

Overview

The database tools provided by Active Data Objects are powerful and flexible. Your scripts can make use of this power to access existing information in database tables, to modify or delete information, and to add new data. Because so many computer-related activities make use of databases in one way or another, this can be a very important capability for the script programmer.

EIGHTEEN

Scripting Microsoft Office Components

Much of the flexibility of the WSH comes from its ability to manipulate other applications. Many of the capabilities that you have already seen in this book fall into this category. For example, file management and access using the `FileSystemObject` *object is not a capability of WSH itself, but rather the result of the ability of your scripts to manipulate the file system components that are exposed elsewhere. On a typical Windows system, many of the most powerful and useful things you can do involve scripting the Microsoft Office suite. This set of office application programs is in widespread use and is installed on a significant majority of Windows computers. With WSH, you can access almost all of the capabilities of Office, and those are some significant capabilities indeed.*

The Office Object Model

You have seen that much of what you can do with WSH involves objects. Things are no different when working with Microsoft Office. Each of the applications in Office exposes a set of objects. These objects along with their properties and methods are called the application's *object model*. In broad outline, then, the procedure for scripting Office applications is to obtain a reference to the object or objects whose functionality you need, and then manipulate those objects' properties and methods to achieve the desired results. In principle, this sounds simple, but in practice it can be rather complicated because of the unavoidable fact that the Office object model is quite complex. It is impossible to do more than scratch the surface of this topic in this chapter, and I limit coverage to Word and Excel, which are specialized for word processing and spreadsheet calculations, respectively. You'll learn about scripting Outlook in Chapter 19 when we cover messaging with WSH.

Learning More about Office

Microsoft Office has its own built-in programming language, Visual Basic for Applications, which is similar in many respects to VBScript. There's a lot to learn about Office programming, much of which is applicable to scripting as well. You might want to check out another of my books, *Developing Solutions with Office 2000 Components and VBA*, published by Prentice Hall in 2000.

All Office applications have certain things in common. At the top of each program's object model is the `Application` object. This is not the same thing in each case, it just has the same name. Thus, at the top of the Word object model is the `Word.Application` object, at the top of the Excel object model is the `Excel.Application` object, and so on. Then, below the `Application` object, you'll find the entire hierarchy of objects that provide the specific application's functionality. Generally, these objects correspond to the actual things you work with in the application. In the Word object model, you'll find objects that correspond to documents, paragraphs, words, and so on. Likewise, the Excel object model has objects that represent worksheets, cells, formulas, and charts.

Because the Office object models are hierarchical, you will usually need to start at the top and "burrow down" to obtain a reference to a specific object. The first step is to create an instance of the specific Office application that you want to use. This is done using the `WScript` object's `CreateObject` method. Here's an example:

```
Set myWordApp = WScript.CreateObject("Word.Application")
```

For Excel and Outlook the class names are `Excel.Application` and `Outlook.Application`. Creating an instance of an Office application in this way does not cause the application to become visible on screen (although you can make it visible if desired). The instance of the application exists behind the scenes, ready to respond to your scripting commands.

Asynchronous Operation

When a script sends commands to an Office application, the commands are carried out asynchronously. This means that the script does not wait around for the Office application to finish, but rather will continue executing subsequent commands in the script. In practical terms this can result in the script finishing execution before the Office application has completed its tasks.

The Word Object Model

Word is a word processing program, with sophisticated capabilities for creating and formatting documents. At the top of the Word object model is, of course, the `Application` object. Just below that is the `Documents` collection, which contains a `Document` object for every open document. You can create a `Document` object corresponding to either an existing document or to a new, empty document. The `Document` object is central to almost everything Word can do, and most of the other Word components you will work with are subsidiary to the `Document` object. In broad outline, the Word object model is as follows:

- The `Application` object has a `Documents` collection that contains one `Document` object for each open document.
- Each document contains a number of stories representing different parts of the document. The `wdMainTextStory` story represents the main document text. There are also stories for footnotes, headers, endnotes, and other document components.
- Each document has a `Paragraphs` collection that contains one `Paragraph` object for each paragraph in the document. Paragraphs are separated from each other by the user pressing Enter.
- Each document and each paragraph has a `Sentences` collection that contains one `Sentence` object for each sentence in the document or paragraph.
- Each document, paragraph, and sentence has a `Words` collection that contains one `Word` object for each word in the document, paragraph, or sentence.
- The `Range` object represents part of a document, anything from a single character to the entire document text. The `Range` object has `Paragraphs`, `Sentences`, and `Words` collections.

The Document Object

Each open Word document is represented by a `Document` object. There are two ways to get a `Document` object: Create a new one or open an existing one. Once you are done working with the document, the object must be saved (at least if you want to use it again) and then closed. Let's look at these tasks first; then we examine some of the tools available for manipulating document content.

To create a new document, use the `Documents` collection's `Add` method. The VBScript syntax is (assuming wdApp is an instance of the `Word.Application` object)

```
Set MyDoc = wdApp.Documents.Add(Template, NewTemplate)
```

In JScript the syntax is

```
MyDoc = wdApp.Documents.Add(Template, NewTemplate);
```

The *Template* argument specifies the name of the template that the new document is to be based on. The *NewTemplate* argument specifies whether the new document is a document template (*NewTemplate* = True) or a regular document (*NewTemplate* = False). The two arguments to this method are optional. If omitted the defaults are to create a new regular document based on the Normal template.

To open an existing document from disk, use the `Open` method. In VBScript the syntax is

```
Set MyDoc = wdApp.Documents.Open(FileName)
```

and, in JScript,

```
MyDoc = wdApp.Documents.Open(FileName);
```

The *`FileName`* argument specifies the path and name of the document file to open. If the specified file does not exist or is not a valid Word document, an error occurs.

To close a document, use the `Document` object's `Close` method. The syntax is

```
MyDoc.Close(SaveChanges, OriginalFormat, RouteDocument)
```

The *`SaveChanges`* argument specifies whether the document should be saved. Possible values are `wdDoNotSaveChanges` (value = 0), `wdPromptToSaveChanges` (value = –2, the default), and `wdSaveChanges` (value = –1).

Using defined constants

Remember that in order to have access to the values of defined constants in your script you must use a .WSF file and include a reference to the relevant type library. This technique was explained in Chapter 14 and will be used in some of this chapter's sample scripts. If you do not reference the relevant type library in your script, then you cannot use the constants but must use the explicit numerical values.

The *`OriginalFormat`* argument specifies the format the document is to be saved in. Your choices are `wdOriginalDocumentFormat` (value = 1), `wdPromptUser` (value = 2), and `wdWordDocument` (value = 0, the default).

The `RouteDocument` argument is a True or False (the default) value indicating whether the document should be sent to the next recipient in a routing list. A value of True has no effect unless the document has a routing slip attached to it.

You can close all open documents by calling the `Documents` collection's `Close` method. The arguments are the same as described previously for the `Document` object's `Close` method.

Manipulating Document Content

Once you have a reference to a document, you can manipulate the document contents in just about any way you can imagine. You can add, edit, delete, and move text, change formatting, add footnotes, images, and headers, and more. Almost everything you do with a document's contents is done with objects that are subsidiary to the `Document` object. For most document manipulation tasks, you must specify the document location where you want the actions to take effect. The `Selection` and `Range` objects are used for this purpose. The `Selection` object represents highlighted text in a document (for example. text the user selected with the mouse). There can be only one selection in a document at a time. A `Range` object represents a section of a document. It is defined by the starting and ending characters and can have any size ranging from being empty to including the entire document. A document can have multiple ranges defined at the same time. The `Range` and `Selection` objects are similar in many other respects, and because the `Range` object is more flexible I limit discussion to it.

THE RANGE OBJECT

To work with a range in a document you must first create a `Range` object that refers to the desired section of the document. One way to do this is by using the `Document` object's `Range` method. The syntax in VBScript is

```
Set MyRange = MyDoc.Range(Start, End)
```

In JScript the syntax is

```
MyRange = MyDoc.Range(Start, End);
```

The optional arguments *Start* and *End* give the character positions of the start and end of the range (the first character in the document has position 0). If these arguments are omitted, the returned range contains the entire document. This VBScript code creates a `Range` object that refers to the first 20 characters in the active document:

```
Dim Range1
Set Range1 = MyDoc.Range(0, 19)
```

In JScript the code is as follows:

```
var Range1;
Range1 = MyDoc.Range(0, 19);
```

You can also obtain a range reference using the `Range` property of various objects. In each case the returned range contains the part of the document — a paragraph, for example — corresponding to the object whose `Range` property was obtained. For example, this VBScript code gets a range corresponding to the second paragraph in the document Report.doc:

```
Dim Range1
Set Range1 = Documents("report.doc").Paragraphs(2).Range
```

In JScript the code is as follows:

```
var Range1;
Range1 = Documents("report.doc").Paragraphs(2).Range;
```

Tables 18-1 and 18-2 describe those properties and methods of the Range object that you will probably use most often.

TABLE 18.1 *Important properties of the Range object.*

Property	Description
Bold	Returns True or False indicating whether text in the range is formatted as bold. Returns `wdUndefined` (value = 9999999) if part of the text is formatted as bold. Set to True or False to change the range's formatting, or to `wdToggle` (9999998) to toggle between bold and unbold.
Case	Returns or sets the case of text in the range. Possible values include `wdLowerCase` (0), `wdUpperCase` (1), `wdTitleSentence` (4) (first letter of sentences uppercase), `wdTitleWord` (2) (first letter of words uppercase), and `wdToggleCase` (5) to invert case.
Characters	Returns a `Characters` collection representing the characters in the range.
End, Start	Returns or sets the character position of the end and the start of the range.
Font	Returns or sets a `Font` object representing the character formatting of the range.
Italic	Returns True or False indicating whether text in the range is formatted in italics. Returns `wdUndefined` (9999999) if part of the text is in italics. Set to True or False to change the range's formatting, or to `wdToggle` (9999998) to toggle between italics and normal.
ParagraphFormat	Returns or sets a `ParagraphFormat` object that represents the paragraph settings for the range.
Paragraphs	Returns a `Paragraphs` collection that contains one `Paragraph` object for each paragraph in the range. If the range contains less than one paragraph, this collection will be empty.
Sentences	Returns a `Sentences` collection that contains one `Sentence` object for each sentence in the range. If the range contains less than one sentence, this collection will be empty.
StoryLength	Returns the length, in characters, of the story containing the range.
StoryType	Returns the story type of the text where the range is located. Possible return values are descriptive defined constants, including `wdMainTextStory` (value = 1, main document text), `wdFootnotesStory` (2, a footnote), `wdEndNotesStory` (3, an endnote), and `wdCommentsStory` (4, a comment).
Text	Returns or sets the text in the range. Setting this property replaces the original text in the range with the new text.
Underline	Returns or sets the type of underlining for the range. Possible settings are descriptive `wdUnderlinexxxx` constants, including `wdUnderLineNone` (0), `wdUnderLineSingle` (1), `wdUnderLineDotDash` (9), and `wdUnderlineWords` (2).
Words	Returns a `Words` collection representing all the words in the range. If the range contains less than one word, this collection will be empty.

TABLE 18.2 *Important methods of the Range object.*

Method	Description
Copy, Cut	Copies or cuts the range to the clipboard.
Delete	Deletes the range.
InsertAfter(*Text*) InsertBefore(*Text*)	Inserts the specified text either before or after the range. The range expands to include the new text.
InsertParagraphAfter InsertParagraphBefore	Inserts a new paragraph before or after the range.
Paste	Inserts the contents of the clipboard at the range. The range will be replaced by the clipboard contents.
SetRange(*Start*, *End*)	Sets the starting and ending character positions for the range. Has the same effect as setting the `Start` and `End` properties.

Let's take a look at some specific script code that works with the `Range` object to manipulate document content. The scripts in Listings 18-1 and 18-2 open the specified document and format the first sentence of each paragraph in italics. The specified document (c:\test1.doc) must exist or an error occurs.

LISTING 18–1 *Formatting text in an existing document (VBScript).*

```
<?xml version="1.0"?>
<?job error="true" debug="true"?>
<!-- List1801.wsf
Demonstrates using the Word Document and Range objects. -->

<job>
<script language="VBScript">
<![CDATA[
Option Explicit

Dim wdApp
Dim doc
Dim p
Dim r

' Create the Word application.
Set wdApp = WScript.CreateObject("Word.Application")
' Open the document.
Set doc = wdApp.Documents.Open("c:\test1.doc")
' Loop for each paragraph in the document.
For Each p in doc.paragraphs
    ' If the paragraph contains at least one sentence,
    ' format it in italics.
    If p.Range.Sentences.Count > 0 then
        Set r = p.Range.Sentences(1)
        r.Italic = True
    end if
next
```

```
' Close the document, saving changes.
doc.Close -1
]]>
</script>
</job>
```

LISTING 18–2 *Formatting text in an existing document (JScript).*

```
<?xml version="1.0"?>
<?job error="true" debug="true"?>
<!-- List1802.wsf
Demonstrates using the Word Document and Range objects. -->

<job>
<script language="JScript">
<![CDATA[

var wdApp;
var doc;
var p;
var r;
var e;

// Create the Word application.
wdApp = WScript.CreateObject("Word.Application");
// Open the document.
doc = wdApp.Documents.Open("c:\\test1.doc");
// Loop for each paragraph in the document.
e = new Enumerator(doc.Paragraphs);
for ( ; !e.atEnd() ; e.moveNext())
{
    // If the paragraph contains at least one sentence,
    // format it in italics.
    p = e.item();
    if (p.Range.Sentences.Count > 0)
    {
        r = p.Range.Sentences(1);
        r.Italic = -1;
    }
}

// Close the document, saving changes.
doc.Close(-1);
]]>
</script>
</job>
```

FINDING AND REPLACING TEXT

The ability to find text in a document and optionally replace it is an important part of many things you might want to do with Word scripting. In a script you use the `Find` object for find and replace tasks. The `Range` object has a `Find` property that provides a reference to a `Find` object that you can use with that range. The general procedure is as follows:

1. Define a range that includes the part of the document you want to search. This may be the entire document.
2. Set the `Find` object's properties to specify the search details, such as what text to find.
3. Call the `Find` object's `Execute` method to perform the search.

The important properties of the `Find` object are described in Table 18-3.

TABLE 18.3 *The important properties of the Find object.*

Property	Description
Forward	Specifies whether the search goes forward through the document (True, the default) or backward (False).
Found	True if the previous search found a match.
MatchCase	Specifies whether the search operation is case sensitive (True) or case insensitive (False).
MatchWholeWord	Specifies whether the search operation matches whole words only (True) or matches partial words (False).
Replacement	Sets or returns a `Replacement` object with the replace criteria for a find and replace operation. See text for details.
Text	Returns or sets the text to find.

The `Replacement` object is used when doing a search and replace. It has a `Text` property that specifies the replacement text. You'll see how this works in the examples.

The `Find` object has two methods you need to know about. The `ClearAllFormatting` method removes all `Find` object options that may have been set previously, making sure that the next find operation will use only those options you set and not any left-over options from before. You should call this method every time you use the `Find` object to ensure that any previous settings are cleared. The `Execute` method performs the search and replace operation according to the options set.

When you perform a successful search operation, the `Range` object being used changes so that it includes only the results — in other words, the found text. Here's an example, which assumes that Range1 refers to some text in the document.

```
Range1.Find.ClearAllFormatting
Range1.Find.Text = "bananas"
Range1.Find.Execute
```

If the text "bananas" is found within the range, then after this code executes Range1 refers to the first instance of the text "bananas." If the text is not found, the range will continue to refer to the original text. If you need to restore the original range after your search and replace operations are done, you can save it as a separate `Range` object.

Now let's look at an example. The scripts in Listings 18-3 and 18-4 replace all instances of "San Francisco" in the document with "New Orleans." Please note that in the JScript example, Listing 18-4, it is necessary to put the call to the `Find` object's `Execute` method in a VBScript procedure, which is then called from JScript. This is required because JScript does not support optional arguments, which are marked by commas in the call.

> **References in Office**
>
> **You learned in Chapter 14 how, in a WSF file, you can use the `<reference>` tag to add a reference to a type library to a script, enabling you to use the mnemonic constant names for arguments and property values. In Office, however, the organization of the type libraries seems to be incompatible with the `<reference>` tag, at least in some instances. Efforts to add a reference to either the `Word.Application` or `Word.Document` objects, for example, do not work. This is why in some listings in this chapter you will see literal constants used for properties and arguments of Word objects and methods.**

LISTING 18-3 *Finding and replacing text in a document (VBScript).*

```
<?xml version="1.0"?>
<?job error="true" debug="true"?>
<!-- List1803.wsf
Demonstrates using find and replace in a Word Document. -->

<job>
<script language="VBScript">
<![CDATA[

Option Explicit

Dim wdApp
Dim doc
Dim r

' Create the Word application.
Set wdApp = WScript.CreateObject("Word.Application")
' Open the document.
Set doc = wdApp.Documents.Open("c:\test1.doc")
```

```
Set r = doc.Content
With r.Find
    .ClearFormatting
    .Wrap = 1
    .Text = "San Francisco"
    With .Replacement
        .ClearFormatting
        .Text = "New Orleans"
    End With
    .Execute ,,,,,,,,,,2
End With

' Close the document, saving changes.
doc.Close -1
]]>
</script>
</job>
```

LISTING 18-4 *Finding and replacing text in a document (JScript).*

```
<?xml version="1.0"?>
<?job error="true" debug="true"?>
<!-- List1804.wsf
Demonstrates using find and replace in a Word Document. -->

<job>
<script language="VBScript">
<![CDATA[
sub Execute(findobj)
    findobj.Execute ,,,,,,,,,,2
end sub
]]>
</script>

<script language="JScript">
<![CDATA[

var wdApp;
var doc;
var r;

// Create the Word application.
wdApp = WScript.CreateObject("Word.Application");
// Open the document.
doc = wdApp.Documents.Open("c:\\test1.doc");

r = doc.Content;
r.Find.ClearFormatting();
r.Find.Wrap = 1;
r.Find.Text = "San Francisco";
r.Find.Replacement.ClearFormatting();
r.Find.Replacement.Text = "New Orleans";
Execute(r.Find);
```

```
// Close the document, saving changes.
doc.Close(-1);
]]>
</script>
</job>
```

Other Document Properties and Methods

In this section I describe some other properties and methods of the Document object that are used for sending faxes, printing a document, and sending a document as an e-mail message.

SENDING FAXES

If the system is set up to send faxes, you can use script code to fax a document using the SendFax method. The syntax is (assuming MyDoc is a reference to a Document object)

```
MyDoc.SendFax(Address, Subject)
```

Address is a required argument specifying the recipient's fax number. *Subject* is optional and specifies the subject of the fax. When this method is executed the document is faxed without any further user interaction.

The Application object also has a SendFax method, which takes no arguments and starts the Fax Wizard, which the user then completes.

PRINTING

To print a document use the PrintOut method. This method can be applied to the Application or Document object to print all open documents or the specified document, respectively. This method takes many arguments that correspond to the settings in Word's Print dialog box. All arguments are optional, and if omitted the current Print dialog box settings will be used. The more commonly used arguments are described in Table 18-4.

TABLE 18.4 *Arguments to the PrintOut method.*

Argument	Description
Range	The range of pages to print. Can be one of the following defined constants: wdPrintAllDocument (0), wdPrintCurrentPage (2), wdPrintFromTo (3), wdPrintRangeOfPages (4), or wdPrintSelection (1).
From, To	The starting and ending page numbers when Range is wdPrintFromTo (3).
PageType	Specifies which pages to print: wdPrintAllPages (0), wdPrintEvenPagesOnly (2), or wdPrintOddPagesOnly (1).
Collate	True to collate documents when printing multiple copies, False otherwise.
Pages	The page numbers and ranges to be printed. For example, "2, 5–9" prints page 2 and pages 5 to 9.

SENDING E-MAIL

To send a document using e-mail, use the `SendMail` method. This method takes no arguments and applies only to the `Document` object. When the method executes, a message window open in which the user must enter the To address and other information. If the `Options.SendMailAttach` property is True, the document is sent as an attachment to the message. If this property is False, the document is sent as text within the message body. For this method to work, the system must be configured for sending e-mail.

To send a Word document automatically, without user interaction, you must work with some of the objects exposed by Outlook. These will be covered in Chapter 19.

The Excel Object Model

Excel is a spreadsheet program that is designed for working with numerical data (although Excel can work with text data as well). With Excel, you can perform calculations with the data and create charts based on the data. Excel has many specialized functions for commonly needed financial, statistical, and scientific calculations.

An Excel file can be thought of as a ledger book containing many pages, with each page ruled into rows and columns. On each page, columns are identified by letters; the first 26 are A–Z, the second 26 are AA–AZ, and the last one is IV. Rows are identified by numbers starting at 1. Worksheets, or pages, are identified by name. At the intersection of each row and column is a cell. A cell can contain a number, text, or a formula. Much of what you will do with scripts and Excel involves locating specific worksheet cells and either putting data or a formula into the cell or reading the data from the cell.

A single Excel file is represented by a `Workbook` object. Each `Workbook` object has a `Worksheets` collection, which contains one `Worksheet` object for each worksheet, or page, in the file. Because the Excel application can have more than one workbook open at a time, there is also a `Workbooks` collection that contains one `Workbook` object for each open file. As with all Office applications, the `Application` object is at the top of the object hierarchy.

The `Range` object is central to many things you will do in Excel. The name is the same, but this is a completely different object than the `Range` object that is part of the Word object model. It has essentially the same function, however, to indicate a section of the worksheet to operate on. A range can be a single cell or a two-dimension block of cells in a worksheet.

The Workbook Object

Each Workbook object represents an open .XLS or .XLA file. When you open Excel as a normal application (not from VBScript) it automatically creates a new, blank workbook. When you start Excel from VBScript, however, it does not contain any workbooks. In the following sections, assume that XLApp refers to an instance of the Excel.Application object created previously with WScript.CreateObject.

OPENING AND CREATING WORKBOOKS

To create a new workbook, use the Workbooks collection's Add method:

```
Workbooks.Add(Template)
```

The *Template* argument specifies the name of the .XLS file to use as the template for the new workbook. If the *Template* argument is omitted, a new default workbook is created containing three worksheets. The Add method returns a reference to the new workbook. This VBScript code creates a new workbook and stores a reference to it in the variable MyWorkbook:

```
Dim MyWorkbook
Set MyWorkbook = XLApp.Workbooks.Add()
```

In JScript the code would be:

```
var MyWorkbook;
MyWorkbook = XLApp.Workbooks.Add();
```

To open an existing workbook from disk, use the Open method. The simplified syntax is

```
XLApp.Workbooks.Open(FileName)
```

FileName is a required argument specifying the path and name of the file to open.

SAVING AND CLOSING WORKBOOKS

To save a workbook that already has been assigned a name, use the Workbook object's Save method. This method takes no arguments. To save a newly created workbook for the first time, assigning it a file name, or to save a named workbook under a different file name, use the SaveAs method. The simplified syntax for this method is

```
MyWorkbook.SaveAs(FileName)
```

The *FileName* argument specifies the name of the file, including path if required.

To close a workbook use the Close method. The simplified syntax is

```
MyWorkbook.Close(SaveChanges, FileName)
```

All three arguments are optional. *SaveChanges* specifies what to do if the workbook contains unsaved changes. Possible values are True to save changes, False to discard changes. If this argument is omitted, the user is prompted to save changes.

FileName is the name for the workbook file. If this argument is omitted, the current name is used. If there is no current name, the user is prompted to supply a name.

PRINTING WORKBOOK DATA

When scripting Excel you have full control of printing workbooks. You use the `PrintOut` method to print; this method is available with the following objects and collections:

Range

Sheets

Workbook

Worksheet

Worksheets

Thus, to print a specified worksheet range you would first define a `Range` object that references the range and then call the `Range` object's `PrintOut` method. Likewise, to print all the worksheets in a workbook you would call the `Worksheets` collection's `PrintOut` method. The syntax for this method is shown here. Note that the relevance of the various arguments will depend on the object you use when calling this method.

```
object.PrintOut(From, To, Copies, Preview, ActivePrinter, _
    PrintToFile, Collate, PrToFileName)
```

All of the arguments are optional. If `PrintOut` is called with no arguments, it prints one copy of the entire contents of the specified object to the default printer.

From and *To* specify the starting and ending page numbers to print. Default values are the beginning and end of the data.

Copies specifies the number of copies to print. The default is 1.

Preview is a True/False value specifying whether the print preview window will be opened before printing. The default is False.

ActivePrinter specifies the name of the printer to use. If omitted, the default Windows printer will be used.

PrintToFile is a True/False value specifying whether output should go to a file instead of the printer. The default is False.

Collate is a True/False value specifying whether multiple copy output should be collated.

PrToFileName specifies the name of the file where output is to be placed when *PrintToFile* = True. If omitted, Excel prompts the user for a file name.

E-MAILING A WORKBOOK

To email a workbook as an attachment to one or more recipients, use the `Workbook` object's `SendMail` method. The syntax is

```
SomeWorkbook.SendMail(Recipients, Subject, ReturnReceipt)
```

Recipients is a required argument specifying the name or address of the recipient. If there are multiple recipients, then *Recipients* is an array of text strings. *Subject* is an optional string specifying the subject line of the message. *ReturnReceipt* is an optional True/False value specifying whether a return receipt is requested, with the default being False. This code sends the active workbook to the individual identified as "Joe Smith" in your address book:

```
SomeWorkbook.SendMail "Joe Smith"
```

This code sends the specified workbook to two recipients with the subject "Sales figures" and a return receipt requested:

```
Dim r
r = Array("joe@company.com", "mary@industry.com ")
SomeWorkbook.SendMail r, "Sales figures", True
```

The Worksheet Object

Much of your programming in Excel will deal directly with worksheets, as represented by the `Worksheet` object. In this section I will cover the important aspects of manipulating worksheets and worksheet data.

ADDING AND DELETING WORKSHEETS

You use the `Add` method to add a new worksheet to a workbook's `Worksheets` collection. Assuming myWkBk is a reference to a workbook,

```
Dim MySheet
Set MySheet = myWkBk.Worksheets.Add(Before, After, Count)
```

All of the arguments are optional; if they are omitted, one new worksheet is added before the currently active worksheet. You can use the *Before* or *After* argument to specify the existing worksheet before or after which the new one is to be placed. To add more than one worksheet, specify the desired number in *Count*. If *Count* is more than 1 the Add method returns a reference to the last added worksheet. As always, it is desirable to assign a name to new worksheets, which you can use to refer to the sheet in code later:

```
MySheet.Name = "SalesData"
```

To delete a worksheet, use the Worksheet object's Delete method:

```
MyWkBk.Worksheets(SheetName).Delete
```

SheetName is the name of the worksheet to delete. When you try to delete a worksheet in a script, Excel's default behavior is to display a prompt to the user to verify whether the worksheet should really be deleted. To prevent the prompt from being displayed, set the Application object's DisplayAlerts property to False. Be sure to return this property to True after the worksheet has been deleted:

```
MyXLApp.DisplayAlerts = False
MyXLApp.ActiveWorkbook.Worksheets("SalesData").Delete
MyXLApp.DisplayAlerts = True
```

THE RANGE OBJECT

When working with worksheet contents, the Range object is essential. You use a Range object to specify the target for some action. A range can represent a single cell, an entire row or column in a worksheet, or any rectangular block of cells. A workbook can have multiple ranges defined at the same time, but there is no Ranges collection providing access to all of them.

You can obtain a Range object from the Range property of an Application or a Worksheet object. The way these work are slightly different. The Application.Range property always refers to the currently active worksheet. Thus, after this code executes (assuming that MyXLApp is a reference to the Excel application object)

```
Dim R1
Set R1 = MyXLApp.Range("A2")
```

the range R1 refers to cell A2 in whatever worksheet is active. The Worksheet.Range property differs in that it always refers to a specific worksheet. This code sets R2 to refer to cell B2 in the worksheet SalesData regardless of which worksheet is active:

```
Dim R2
Set R2 = MyWkBk.Worksheets("SalesData").Range("A2")
```

Other properties and methods that return a Range object are listed in Table 18-5. Some of these properties and methods are explained in more detail following the table.

TABLE 18.5 *Other properties and methods returning Range objects.*

Property	Belongs to	Returns a Range object referring to
ActiveCell	Application object	The active cell in the currently active window.
CurrentRegion	Range object	A range bounded by, but not including, the nearest blank rows, blank columns, and worksheet edges.
Selection	Application object	The current selection in the active window.
SpecialCells	Range object	All the cells that match the specified type and value.
UsedRange	Worksheet object	The smallest rectangular region that includes all of the used cells in the worksheet.

MANIPULATING WORKSHEET CONTENTS

When you manipulate the data in a worksheet, you are usually either putting something into worksheet cells or reading something out of worksheet cells. The `Range` object's `Value` property is use to both set and read cell data. For example, the statement

```
SomeRange.Value = data
```

puts *data* (which can be text, a number, or a formula) in the specified range. If SomeRange refers to more than one cell, then *data* is put into each of the cells in the range. Existing data is overwritten without warning. Here are some examples:

```
SomeWorksheet.Range("A1").Value = 12.34
SomeWorksheet.Range("A2").Value = "Sales for March
SomeWorksheet.Range("A3").Value = "=A1 + A2"
SomeWorksheet.Range("A4").Value = "=sum(C1:C10)"
```

To obtain the data in a cell, you use the `Value` property as well. If the specified range refers to a single cell, then the `Value` property returns whatever data — blank, number, or text - that is displayed in the cell. The contents of multiple-cell ranges can also be obtained, but that is beyond the scope of this chapter.

A blank cell's `Value` property appears to return an empty string, but it actually returns the special value `Empty`. You can test for this using the VBScript `IsEmpty` function:

```
If IsEmpty(SomeWorksheet.Range("A1").Value) Then
    ' Cell A1 is empty.
Else
    ' Cell A1 is not empty.
End if
```

If you want to obtain the formula in a cell, use the `Formula` property. While `Value` will return the results of the formula, `Formula` returns the formula itself. For cells that do not contain formulas, `Formula` works just like `Value`.

USING THE CELLS PROPERTY

`Cells` is a property of the `Application`, `Worksheet`, and `Range` objects. It returns a `Range` object that references all of the cells (not just the used cells) in the active worksheet, the specified worksheet, or the specified range, respectively. The usefulness of this property comes from the ability to loop through the cells in a range, examining or performing some action on each cell. This is done using the `Range` object's `Item` property, which has two syntax forms:

```
object.Cells.Item(RowIndex, ColumnIndex)
object.Cells.Item(Index)
```

Object is a reference to the `Application` object or to a `Worksheet` or `Range` object. In the first syntax, *RowIndex* and *ColumnIndex* specify the location of a cell with respect to the top left corner of the range. In the second syntax *Index* is the offset of the cell in the range counting across then down. Suppose that R1 is a range that is four columns wide and three rows high. The following two expressions both return a range that references the first cell in the second row of that range:

```
R1.Item.Cells(2,1)
R1.Item.Cells(5)
```

Because `Item` is the default property for the `Range` object, you can omit the `Item` keyword. The following two statements are exactly equivalent:

```
MyWk3k.Worksheets("Sheet1").Cells.Item(5,5)
MyWk3k.Worksheets("Sheet1").Cells(5,5)
```

Let's look at some examples. This scripts in Listings 18-5 and 18-6 sets the font to Courier New and the font size to 12 for every cell in the worksheet named Sheet1 in the specified workbook.

LISTING 18-5 *Changing formatting in an Excel worksheet (VBScript).*

```
<?xml version="1.0"?>
<?job error="true" debug="true"?>
<!-- List1805.wsf
Demonstrates changing formatting in an Excel worksheet. -->

<job>
<script language="VBScript">
<![CDATA[
```

```
Option Explicit

Dim xlApp
Dim wb
Dim ws

' Create the Excel application.
Set xlApp = WScript.CreateObject("Excel.Application")
' Open the workbook.
Set wb = xlApp.Workbooks.Open("c:\test.xls")
Set ws = wb.Worksheets("sheet1")
With ws.Cells.Font
    .Name = "Courier New"
    .Size = 12
End With

' Close the workbook, saving changes.
wb.Close -1
]]>
</script>
</job>
```

LISTING 18–6 *Changing formatting in an Excel worksheet (JScript).*

```
<?xml version="1.0"?>
<?job error="true" debug="true"?>
<!-- List1806.wsf
Demonstrates changing formatting in an Excel worksheet. -->

<job>
<script language="JScript">
<![CDATA[

var xlApp;
var wb;
var ws;

// Create the Excel application.
xlApp = WScript.CreateObject("Excel.Application");
// Open the workbook.
wb = xlApp.Workbooks.Open("c:\\test.xls");
ws = wb.Worksheets("sheet1");
ws.Cells.Font.Name = "Courier New";
ws.Cells.Font.Size = 12;

// Close the workbook, saving changes.
wb.Close(-1);
]]>
</script>
</job>
```

The scripts in Listings 18-7 and 18-8 create a new workbook and then place the values 1 through 10 in cells A1 through J1. Next, the Excel formula "=sum(A1:A10)" is placed in cell A11 — this formula calculates the total of the values in cells A1 through A10. Then the value in cell A11 (the result of the formula that was placed there) is read out and displayed. Finally, the workbook is saved as TEST2.XLS.

LISTING 18–7 *Working with data in a worksheet (VBScript).*

```
<?xml version="1.0"?>
<?job error="true" debug="true"?>
<!-- List1807.wsf
Demonstrates putting data in and reading data from an Excel worksheet. -->

<job>
<script language="VBScript">
<![CDATA[

Option Explicit

Dim xlApp
Dim wb
Dim ws
Dim i
Dim total

' Create the Excel application.
Set xlApp = WScript.CreateObject("Excel.Application")
' Create a new workbook.
Set wb = xlApp.Workbooks.Add
Set ws = wb.Worksheets("sheet1")
For i = 1 to 10
    ws.Cells(i, 1).Value = i
Next

ws.Cells(11,1).Value = "=sum(A1:A10)"
total = ws.Cells(11,1).Value
WScript.Echo "The total is " & total

' Save the workbook.
wb.SaveAs("c:\test2.xls")
' Close the workbook.
wb.Close
]]>
</script>
</job>
```

LISTING 18-8 *Working with data in a worksheet (JScript).*

```
<?xml version="1.0"?>
<?job error="true" debug="true"?>
<!-- List1808.wsf
Demonstrates putting data in and reading data from an Excel worksheet. -->

<job>
<script language="JScript">
<![CDATA[

var xlApp;
var wb;
var ws;
var i;
var total;

// Create the Excel application.
xlApp = WScript.CreateObject("Excel.Application");
// Create a new workbook.
wb = xlApp.Workbooks.Add();
ws = wb.Worksheets("sheet1");
for (i = 1; i <= 10; i++)
    ws.Cells(i, 1).Value = i;

ws.Cells(11,1).Value = "=sum(A1:A10)";
total = ws.Cells(11,1).Value;
WScript.Echo("The total is " + total);

// Save the workbook.
wb.SaveAs("c:\\test2.xls");
// Close the workbook.
wb.Close();
]]>
</script>
</job>
```

FINDING AND REPLACING DATA

To search a range for data, you use the Range object's `Find` method. This method returns a single cell range that refers to the cell where a match is found, or the special value `Nothing` if no match is found. The syntax is

```
SomeRange.Find(What, After, LookIn, LookAt, SearchOrder, _
    SearchDirection, MatchCase, MatchByte)
```

What is the data to find. This is the only required argument.

After specifies the single cell in the range after which the search is to start. If omitted, the search starts in the top left cell of the range.

LookIn specifies what data is to be searched. Possible values are xlFormula (value = 5), xlValues (–4163, the default), and xlComments (–4144).

LookAt can be either xlPart (2) or xlWhole (1) specifying whether the entire data item or only part of it is to be matched.

SearchOrder can be either xlByColumns (2, the default) or xlByRows (1) specifying the order in which the cells in the range are searched.

SearchDirection is either xlNext (1, the default) or xlPrevious (2) specifying the direction of the search.

MatchCase is True or False (the default) specifying whether the search is case sensitive.

MatchByte is relevant only when double-byte language support is installed. True means that double-byte characters match only double-byte characters, while False means that double-byte characters will match the single-byte equivalents.

When you call the Find method, values specified for the *LookIn*, *LookAt*, *SearchOrder*, and *MatchByte* arguments are saved and will be in effect the next time you call Find unless you explicitly change them.

The procedure for finding data is to start by defining a Range object that references the part of the worksheet you want to search. Then call the Find method, passing it the arguments appropriate for what you want to do. This will locate the first instance (if any) of the data you are searching for. Next, if you want to continue, you can call FindPrevious or FindNext to continue the search either backward or forward. The syntax is

```
SomeRange.FindNext After
SomeRange.FindPrevious After
```

The optional *After* argument has the same meaning as for the Find method. Typically you will pass the range that was returned by the previous Find or FindNext so that the search continues from where it left off. You should be aware that these methods do not keep track of where they have already searched and will loop back and search the range again. It is up to you to write script code that keeps track, which is typically done by storing the address of the first cell where a match is found and comparing subsequent matches with it.

To find and replace data in a range, use the Replace method. The syntax is

```
SomeRange.Replace(What, Replacement, LookAt, SearchOrder,
    MatchCase, MatchByte)
```

What is the string to be replaced, and *Replacement* is the string to replace it with. The other arguments to the Replace method have the same meanings as they do for the Find method. The Replace method always returns True. Here's an example: To replace every instance of "Toronto" with "Montreal" in column A of Sheet1,

```
MyWkBk.Worksheets("Sheet1").Columns("A").Replace
    "Toronto", "Montreal"
```

Let's look at a script that uses the `Find` method. The scripts presented in Listings 18-9 and 18-10 count the number of times the specified text appears in a worksheet and display the result to the user. Note that the JScript version in Listing 18-10 makes use of the same VBScript function as Listing 18-9. This is because JScript does not support the special VBScript value `Nothing` and therefore could not detect the value returned by the `Find` method if there is no match.

LISTING 18–9 *Counting the number of times data is found in a worksheet (VBScript).*

```
<?xml version="1.0"?>
<?job error="true" debug="true"?>
<!-- List1809.wsf
Demonstrates finding data in an Excel worksheet. -->

<job>
<script language="VBScript">
<![CDATA[

Option Explicit

'***********
Function CountData(rng, template)

' In an Excel workbook, returns the number of
' times template is found in rng.

Dim count
Dim r
Dim FirstAddress

count = 0
'Find the first instance.
Set r = rng.Find(template)

' If not found, return 0.
If r Is Nothing Then
    CountStrings = 0
    Exit Function
' If found, loop to find any other instances.
Else
    ' Save the first location's address.
    FirstAddress = r.Address
    Do
        count = count + 1
        ' Find next instance starting where we left off.
        Set r = rng.FindNext(r)
    ' Loop until we return to the first location.
    Loop While r.Address <> FirstAddress

    End If
```

```
CountData = count

End Function
'******************

Dim xlApp
Dim wb
Dim ws
Dim count

' Create the Excel application.
Set xlApp = WScript.CreateObject("Excel.Application")
' Open the workbook.
Set wb = xlApp.Workbooks.Open("c:\test.xls")
Set ws = wb.Worksheets("sheet1")

count = CountData(ws.UsedRange, "Miami")
WScript.Echo "The data was found " & count & " times."

' Close the workbook.
wb.Close
]]>
</script>
</job>
```

LISTING 18-10 *Counting the number of times data is found in a worksheet (JScript).*

```
<?xml version="1.0"?>
<?job error="true" debug="true"?>
<!-- List1810.wsf
Demonstrates finding data in an Excel worksheet. -->

<job>
<script language="VBScript">
<![CDATA[

'***********
Function CountData(rng, template)

' In an Excel workbook, returns the number of
' times template is found in rng.

Dim count
Dim r
Dim FirstAddress

count = 0
'Find the first instance.
Set r = rng.Find(template)
```

```
' If not found, return 0.
If r Is Nothing Then
    CountStrings = 0
    Exit Function
' If found, loop to find any other instances.
Else
    ' Save the first location's address.
    FirstAddress = r.Address
    Do
        count = count + 1
        ' Find next instance starting where we left off.
        Set r = rng.FindNext(r)
    ' Loop until we return to the first location.
    Loop While r.Address <> FirstAddress

    End If

CountData = count

End Function
'******************
]]>
</script>

<script language="JScript">
<![CDATA[

var xlApp;
var wb;
var ws;
var count;

// Create the Excel application.
xlApp = WScript.CreateObject("Excel.Application");
// Open the workbook.
wb = xlApp.Workbooks.Open("c:\\test.xls");
ws = wb.Worksheets("sheet1");

count = CountData(ws.UsedRange, "Miami");
WScript.Echo("The data was found " + count + " times.");

// Close the workbook.
wb.Close();
]]>
</script>
</job>
```

Validating Object References

You have seen that scripting Office applications consists largely of manipulating objects. Clearly, it is essential that your object references be valid or your scripts will not work. Your script might use the wrong object, or it might try to create an object and have the creation fail for one reason or another. Another possibility for run-time errors is when a script references an object that was valid at one time but no longer exists. To guard against this sort of problem, you can use two strategies for verifying the validity of an object reference.

One approach uses the `TypeName` function to obtain the type name of an object. Passed an object reference, this function returns a string giving the name of the object — for example, "Workbook" for an Excel workbook and "Document" for a Word document. Your script code can use the return data of the `TypeName` function to ensure that an object reference is the right type before working with it.

The second approach is to use the global `IsObjectValid` function. You pass an object reference to this function, and it returns True if the reference is value, False if not. For example, the following code checks to see if the reference wdApp is valid. If not, it is set to reference a `Word.Application` object:

```
If IsObjectValid(wdApp) = False then
    Set wdApp = WScript.CreateObject("Word.Application")
End If
```

This function does not provide information about the type of an object, however.

Overview

Word and Excel provide you with a great deal of power and flexibility when it comes to working with text and numerical data. Through their object models, the power of these programs is accessible from your VBScript and JScript scripts. In this chapter we have only scratched the surface of their capabilities. Now that you have an understanding of the fundaments of scripting Office applications, you can explore the topic in more detail on your own as your needs and interests dictate.

N I N E T E E N

Messaging With WSH

Sometimes it seems that electronic mail, or messaging, has taken over the world. While that may be a bit of an exaggeration, it is certainly true that messaging has become a vital part of many enterprises and activities. I don't think many people would want to return to the days where the only options for communication were snail mail, FAXes, and telephone calls! There are various ways for the script programmer to integrate messaging into his or her scripts.

Scripts and Messaging

One way to use messaging in your scripts is by means of Microsoft's Collaborative Data Objects, or CDO. CDO version 1.2.1 is part of Microsoft Outlook 98 and Outlook 2000 (Outlook is the messaging application that is part of Microsoft Office). If you do not have one of these versions of Outlook but have Exchange Client, Inbox, or an earlier version of Outlook, you can download CDO 1.2.1 from http://www.microsoft.com/exchange/downloads/CDO.htm. CDO Version 2.0 is shipping with Windows 2000 and will also be part of the next version of Exchange Server. It expands on the features of CDO 1.2.1 and is clearly influenced by the Internet more than its predecessors. What you learn about CDO 1.2.1 in this chapter should all be applicable to CDO 2.0.

The other approach to script messaging is to control Microsoft Outlook directly from your scripts. Obviously, you must have Outlook installed on your system for this to work. You were introduced to scripting Microsoft Office applications, specifically Word and Excel, in Chapter 18. Scripting Outlook is similar in concept but of course is different in the details.

CDO for NT Server

Another version of CDO is available with NT server version 4. It is known as CDONTS, which stands for Collaborative Data Objects for NT Server. This messaging tool has largely been superceded by CDO and will not be covered here.

Which should you use in your scripts: CDO or Outlook? Your choice may be dictated by what you have available. If you have Outlook 2000 installed, then you have the option of scripting Outlook directly (Outlook 98 can be scripted as well, but the script information presented in this chapter is based on Outlook 2000). If you are running Windows NT, you may have CDO installed already. Windows 95/98 users who do not have Outlook 98/2000 may be able to install CDO, as described previously. Widows 2000 users will have CDO 2.0 at their disposal.

To make things a little easier, you can use the VBScript script in Listing 19-1 to determine if you have CDO installed, and if so the version number.

LISTING 19-1 *Determining if CDO is installed.*

```
' List1901.vbs
' Detecting if CDO is available.

Option Explicit

Dim c
Dim msg

On Error Resume Next

set c = CreateObject("MAPI.Session")
If Err <> 0 then
    msg = "CDO is not installed on this system."
else
    msg = "CDO version " & c.Version & " is available."
end if

WScript.Echo msg
```

Some E-mail Background

While the term *messaging* has a broader meaning than just e-mail, it is certainly the case that e-mail is by far the most popular and important kind of messaging that people use. It will help to have some understanding of e-mail fundamentals before proceeding with the rest of this chapter.

Almost all e-mail is based on two protocols: SMTP, or Simple Mail Transfer Protocol, is used for sending messages, and POP, or Post Office Protocol, is used for retrieving messages. When you click the Send button on your e-mail program, the program uses SMTP to transfer the message to the SMTP server where you have your e-mail account. This server then uses the same protocol to transmit the message over the Internet to the recipient's e-mail account. When you log on to retrieve messages which you have received, your e-mail program connects to your e-mail provider and downloads your messages using POP. In some organizations, POP has been replaced with IMAP, Internet Mail Access protocol, which extends POP to provide additional features such as the ability to organize your messages into folders on the mail server and to share these folders with other people.

Protocols

Don't let the term *protocol* scare you. A protocol is simply a set of rules that specify how something is to be done. In the case of e-mail, a protocol specifies how information is to be formatted and transmitted between computers.

By themselves, SMTP, POP, and IMAP do not permit for message attachments. An attachment is a file that accompanies an e-mail message but is separate from the message content. The recipient of an attachment can save it to disk or open it directly. To deal with the need for attachment support and to provide some other features, the MIME protocol (Multipurpose Internet Mail Extensions) was developed. This standard defines how the various parts of as message — recipient addresses, subject, body, attachments, and so on — are to be arranged.

The next step in the development of e-mail standards was the ability to format messages. Rather than plain text, people wanted to be able to create messages with various types of formatting, such as fonts, text color, graphics, and background images. For this, the language of the Web, HTML (Hypertext Markup Language), was adopted. If your e-mail program supports HTML format you can create messages with the same kinds of formatting you see on Web pages. If the recipient's e-mail program supports HTML, they will see the message will all the formatting you placed in it. (Unfortunately, if their e-mail program does not support HTML, they will see gibberish.)

The last acronym I will ask you to learn is MAPI, which stands for Messaging Application Programming Interface. MAPI is designed to provide a standardized interface between messaging clients and messaging providers. With a wide variety of providers available (Microsoft Exchange, Lotus Notes, and CompuServe are a few examples), each with its own way of doing things, MAPI provides a standardized set of commands and procedures that the client program can call to perform various tasks. MAPI will "translate" these commands into the specific commands required by the provider that was being used. The "translation" also occurs in the opposite direction, when the provider needs to instruct the client to do something. MAPI also introduced the concept of *profiles*, which permit users to keep separate sets of messaging settings for different purposes.

Now you have a broad outline of the various e-mail protocols and standards — SMTP to send messages, POP and IMAP to receive messages, MIME to define the parts of a message, and HTML to format messages.

Scripting CDO

The CDO object model is fairly complex, providing support not only for sending and receiving messages but also for additional features such as address books and message stores. For the scope of this book, however, we will limit ourselves to the most important tasks of sending and receiving messages.

Sending a Message with CDO

The basic steps required to create and send an e-mail message using CDO are as follows:

1. Create an instance of the `MAPI.Session` object.
2. Call the `LogOn` method to log on to the system's installed MAPI messaging system.
3. Use the `Add` method to add a new message to the Outbox. When you call `Add` you can also specify the message's subject and text, or you can do it later.
4. Specify one or more recipients for the message.
5. Call the `Resolve` method to verify that the recipient e-mail address is valid.
6. If desired, add one or more attachments to the message.
7. Call the `Send` method to send the message.

Now let's look at these steps in more detail. The first step, creating an instance of the `MAPI.Session` object, uses the `CreateObject` function that you have seen before. In step 2, the `LogOn` method can be a bit more complicated. The simplified syntax is as follows, where MAPISession is the `MAPI.Session` object that was created in step 1:

```
MAPISession.LogOn(ProfileName, ProfilePassword,
showDialog, newSession)
```

All of the arguments are optional. If you want to log on using a specific user profile, specify the profile name and password in the first two arguments. Note that this password is not the same as the e-mail account password. Most profiles do not have passwords associated with them. To log on to the default profile, omit these arguments.

The *showDialog* argument can be set to True if you want a dialog box to be displayed in which the user can select a profile. The default is False.

Set *newSession* to True if you want a new MAPI session created even if one already exists. The default is False to log on to an existing session if possible.

Once you have logged on to a session, you use the `Add` method to create a new message. Specifically, you want to add a new message to the Outbox's `Messages` collection. The syntax is

```
MAPISession.Outbox.Messages.Add(subject, message)
```

This method returns a reference to the newly created message. Both of the arguments are optional. If you do not specify the message subject and text when you create the message, you can do so later as follows:

```
Set msg = MAPISession.Outbox.Messages.Add()
msg.Subject = "Sales report"
msg.Text = "I received your report, thank you."
```

To specify message recipients, you use the `Recipients` collection's `Add` method. The syntax is (assuming that msg is a reference to a message created as described previously)

```
msg.Recipients.Add(name, address, type)
```

This method returns a reference to the new recipient. *Name* is an optional argument specifying the recipient's display name. If omitted, the address will be used for the display name. *Address* is an optional argument specifying the recipient's e-mail address. You must prefix the actual address with SMTP: to indicate that it is an Internet address. *Type* is an optional argument specifying the type of recipient. Possible settings are `CdoTo` (value = 1, the default) for a regular "to" recipient, `CdoCC` (2) for a carbon copy recipient, and `CdoBcc` (3) for a blind carbon copy recipient.

You may be wondering how both the display name and address arguments can be optional. If you do not specify the *address* argument, you must specify a *name* argument. When you resolve the recipient (which is covered next), the display name you specified will be looked up in the user's address book, and the e-mail address will be obtained in that way.

To resolve a recipient, call the Resolve method. There are no arguments to this method. Here's an example:

```
Set recip = msg.Recipients.Add("Joe Smith", _
    "SMTP:joe_smith@somewhere.com")
recip.Resolve
```

If the address cannot be resolved, an error occurs. Note that successfully resolving an address does not necessarily mean that the address is valid.

The final steps are to send the message, using the Send method, and then to log off the MAPI session using the Logoff method.

Listings 19-2 and 19-3 show examples of how to use CDO to create and send an e-mail message. If you want to test these scripts, replace the dummy e-mail address with a real one.

LISTING 19–2 *Creating and sending an e-mail message with CDO (VBScript).*

```
' List1902.vbs
' Sending mail using CDO.

Option Explicit

Dim MAPISession
Dim msg
Dim recip

' Create the MAPI session object and log on.
Set MAPISession = CreateObject("MAPI.Session")
MAPISession.Logon

' Create a new message.
Set msg = MAPISession.Outbox.Messages.Add()

' Specify the message subject and text.
msg.Text = "Thanks for sending the report."
msg.Subject = "Sales figures."

' Add a recipient to the message and resolve it.
Set recip = msg.Recipients.Add(, "SMTP:someone@somewhere.com")
recip.Resolve

' Send the message and log off.
msg.Send
MAPISession.Logoff
```

LISTING 19–3 *Creating and sending an e-mail message with CDO (JScript).*

```
// List1903.js
// Sending mail using CDO.

var MAPISession;
var msg;
var recip;

// Create the MAPI session object and log on.
MAPISession = WScript.CreateObject("MAPI.Session");
MAPISession.Logon;

// Create a new message.
msg = MAPISession.Outbox.Messages.Add();

// Specify the message subject and text.
msg.Text = "Thanks for sending the reports.";
msg.Subject = "Sales figures";

// Add a recipient to the message and resolve it.
recip = msg.Recipients.Add("", "SMTP:someone@somewhere.com");
recip.Resolve();

// Send the message and log off.
msg.Send();
MAPISession.Logoff();
```

Reading Mail with CDO

Reading mail with CDO is a fairly straightforward task. After creating a `MAPI.Session` object and logging on, you next get a reference to the Inbox's `Messages` collection. You can then loop through the collection, accessing each message in turn. This code fragment shows the basics:

```
Set MAPISession = CreateObject("MAPI.Session")
MAPISession.Logon
Set MyMessages = MAPISession.Inbox.Messages
For Each msg in MyMessages
    ' Process individual messages here.
Next
```

Each individual message has a set of properties, as described in Table 19-1.

There are many other details to working with messages in the Inbox, but they are beyond the scope of this book. The information you have learned will still let you do many useful things. For example, the scripts in Listings 19-5 and 19-6 show how you can search all of the messages in your Inbox for subjects containing a specific word. You could write a similar script to locate messages from a specific person, or with certain text in the body. If

TABLE 19.1 *CDO message properties.*

Property	Description
Recipients	A collection containing one recipient for each message recipient.
Sender	Reference to the message sender. Access the sender's name and e-mail address with `Sender.Name` and `Sender.Address`. Not all messages have senders.
Subject	The message subject.
Text	The text of the message.
UnRead	True if the message has already been read, False otherwise.

you receive loads of e-mail messages, such scripts can help you locate important messages quickly.

LISTING 19-4 *Searching Inbox message subjects (VBScript).*

```
' List1904.vbs
' Searching Inbox message subjects using CDO.

Option Explicit

Dim MAPISession
Dim msg
Dim MyMessages
Dim Count

Dim template

template = "book"

' Create the MAPI session object and log on.
Set MAPISession = CreateObject("MAPI.Session")
MAPISession.Logon

' Get the Messages collection.
Set MyMessages = MAPISession.Inbox.Messages

' Loop through the messages.
For Each msg in MyMessages
    If Instr(1, msg.Subject, template) <> 0 then
        Count = Count + 1
    End If
Next

' Display the result and log off.
WScript.Echo "Your Inbox contains " & Count & " messages with '" _
    & template & "' in the subject."
MAPISession.Logoff
```

LISTING 19–5 *Searching Inbox message subjects (JScript).*

```
// List1905.js
// Searching Inbox message subjects using CDO.

var MAPISession;
var msg;
var MyMessages;
var Count;
var template;
var e;

Count = 0;
template = "book";

// Create the MAPI session object and log on.
MAPISession = WScript.CreateObject("MAPI.Session");
MAPISession.Logon();

// Create an enumeration for the Messages collection.
e = new Enumerator(MAPISession.Inbox.Messages);

// Loop through the messages.
for ( ; !e.atEnd(); e.moveNext())
{
    msg = e.item();
    if (msg.Subject.indexOf(template, 1) > -1)
        Count++;
}

// Display the result and log off.
WScript.Echo("Your Inbox contains " + Count + " messages with '" + _
    template + "' in the subject.");
MAPISession.Logoff();
```

Scripting Microsoft Outlook

Microsoft Outlook is a multipurpose program. While its primary task is e-mail, it also provides a calendar, task list, address book, and notebook. For our purposes. however, the remainder of this chapter is limited to Outlook's e-mail capabilities.

Outlook's basic organization is based on folders and items. An item is an object that holds information, such as a mail message. A folder is a place to keep items. As regards e-mail, Outlook provides several default folders (for example, Inbox for received messages, Outbox for messages to be sent, and

Sent Items for messages that have been sent). The user can create custom folders as well. Note that an Outlook folder is not the same thing as a disk folder.

As with all Office applications, the `Application` object is at the top of the Outlook object model. To script Outlook you always start by creating an instance of the `Outlook.Application` object. One level down from the `Application` object, the `NameSpace` object is used to access Outlook items and folders. Let's look at this object first and then explore the details of working with e-mail messages.

The NameSpace Object

To work with e-mail messages in Outlook, you must use the `NameSpace` object. In theory Outlook can support multiple data sources (and hence multiple `NameSpace` objects), but for the present only MAPI is supported. To obtain a reference to the `NameSpace` object, use the `GetNameSpace` method (assuming that myOLApp is a reference to the `Outlook.Application` object):

```
Set myNameSpace = myOLApp.GetNameSpace("MAPI")
```

Once you have a reference to the `NameSpace` object, you can use it to manipulate Outlook folders and mail messages.

Manipulating Folders and Items

Each Outlook folder is represented by a `MAPIFolder` object. Folders fall into two categories: built-in (default) Outlook folders and user-defined folders. To obtain a reference to a built-in Outlook folder, such as the Inbox, use the `NameSpace` object's `GetDefaultFolder` method. The syntax is

myNameSpace`.GetDefaultFolder(`*itemtype*`)`

Itemtype is a constant identifying the type of item whose default folder you want to retrieve. Possible settings for this argument are described in Table 19-2.

TABLE 19.2 Constants for the GetDefaultFolder method's *itemtype* argument.

Constant	Value	Item
olFolderContacts	10	Contacts (the address book)
olFolderDeletedItems	3	Messages that have been deleted
olFolderDrafts	16	Drafts of not yet completed messages
olFolderInbox	6	Received e-mail messages
olFolderOutbox	4	E-mail messages waiting to be sent
olFolderSentMail	5	E-mail messages that have been sent

Here is an example of VBScript code that obtains a reference to the Inbox folder:

```
Dim MyInbox
Dim MyNameSpace
Set MyNameSpace = MyOLApp.GetNamespace("MAPI")
Set MyInbox = MyNameSpace.GetDefaultFolder(6)
```

References to user-defined folders (folders that are not default Outlook folders) are obtained from the `Folders` collection. Each top-level folder is a member of the `NameSpace` object's `Folders` collection. If there are subfolders defined, then each top-level folder has its own `Folders` collection containing its subfolders. Given that you know a folder's name, you obtain a reference to it by looping through the `Folders` collection until you find it. Note that that folder names in Outlook are case sensitive.

Unfortunately this is not as simple as it seems. Most Outlook installations have only a single top-level folder, often called Outlook Today or Personal Folders. Any folders that have been defined by the user will be subsidiary to this folder and therefore cannot be reached directly through the `NameSpace` object's `Folders` collection. Rather you must obtain a reference to each entry in the `NameSpace.Folders` collection and then loop through its `Folders` collection, looking for the folder you want. The following code fragment shows how to do this. This VBScript code sets `MySalesFolder` to refer to the user-defined folder named Sales, or to the special value `Nothing` if the folder does not exist.

```
Dim MySalesFolder
Dim MyNameSpace
Dim f1
Dim f2
Set MyNameSpace = MyOLApp.GetNamespace("MAPI")
Set MySalesFolder = Nothing
For Each f1 in MyNameSpace.Folders
    For Each f2 in f1.Folders
        if f2.Name = "Sales" Then Set MySalesFolder = f2
    Next
Next
```

Items (that is, e-mail messages) within an Outlook folder are contained in the folder's `Items` collection. For a given folder, the `Items` collection contains one entry for every item in the folder. Individual items can be identified by their index number within the collection or, more usefully, by their default property, which for mail messages is their subject. This VBScript code retrieves a reference to the first message in the Inbox folder where the subject is "Sales Reports":

```
Dim myMessage
Set myMessage = myNameSpace.GetDefaultFolder(olFolderInbox) _
    .Items("Sales Reports")
```

Working with Mail Messages

Individual e-mail messages in Outlook are represented by the `MailItem` object. You will find yourself working with mail messages in two ways: retrieving information from messages that you received, and creating new messages to send.

WORKING WITH RECEIVED MESSAGES

Outlook places received messages in the Inbox folder. You can use the `GetDefaultFolder` method (covered earlier in this chapter) to obtain a reference to the Inbox folder, and then use the `Items` collection to access all the messages in the Inbox. Many scripts loop through all the messages in the Inbox, looking for messages that meet specific criteria. The `MailItem` object has a large number of properties. Those properties that most often used when dealing with received messages are described in Table 19-3. By reading these properties you can determine for each message who sent it and when, the message subject, the message content, and so on. The `MailItem` object also has a set of methods that are used to perform tasks such as deleting, copying, moving, replying to, and forwarding messages. Table 19-4 describes these methods.

TABLE 19.3 *MailItem object properties relevant for received messages.*

Property	Description
Body	Specifies the text of the message (if the message is plain text).
HTMLBody	Specifies the text of the message (if the message is formatted as HTML).
Importance	Returns the importance level of the message. Possible values are `olImportanceHigh` (value = 2), `olImportanceLow` (0), and `olImportanceNormal` (1).
SenderName	Returns the display name of the message sender.
Subject	Returns the message subject.
To	Returns a semicolon delimited list of the message recipients' display names.
UnRead	Returns True if the message has not been opened.

TABLE 19.4 *MailItem object methods.*

Method	Description
Copy	Creates a copy of the message and returns a reference to it.
Delete	Deletes the message (moves it to the Deleted Items folder).
Display	Displays the message.
Forward	Creates a copy of the message for forwarding.
Move(*Destination*)	Moves the message to the indicated folder. *Destination* is a reference to a `MAPIFolder` object representing the destination.
PrintOut	Prints the message.
Reply	Creates a copy of the message preaddressed to the original sender.
ReplyAll	Creates a copy of the message preaddressed to the original sender and all recipients.
SaveAs(*Path*, *Type*)	Saves the message to the file indicated in *Path*. The optional *Type* argument specifies the file format. Values you will use most often are `olDoc` (Word document), `olHTML`, `olMSG` (message format, the default), `olRTF` (rich text format), and `olTXT` (text).

Let's look at an example of working with the messages in the Inbox folder. The scripts presented in Listings 19-6 and 19-7 examine all messages in the Inbox folder looking for messages that were sent by a specific sender. The body text of all matching messages is combined and written to a disk file, and then the individual messages are moved to a different folder. The end result is to create a summary document that contains the text of all the messages from the specified person.

LISTING 19–6 *A script to create a summary of e-mail messages from a particular sender (VBScript).*

```
<?xml version="1.0"?>
<?job error="true" debug="true"?>
<!-- List1906.wsf
Creating a summary document of messages from
a particular sender. It is assumed that at most
100 matching messages will be found, and that the
destination folder exists. -->

<job>
<reference object="Scripting.FileSystemObject" />
<script language="VBScript">
<![CDATA[

Option Explicit
```

```
Dim MyOLApp
Dim MyNameSpace
Dim MyInbox
Dim destFolder
Dim destFolderName
Dim msg
Dim buf
Dim sender
Dim ToMove(100)
Dim Count
Dim f1
Dim f2
Dim i
Dim summaryFileName
Dim summaryFile
Dim fso

' The name of the sender to look for.
sender = "Lewis Smith"
' The folder to which messages are to be moved.
destFolderName = "From Lewis"
' The name of the summary file.
summaryFileName = "c:\summary.txt"
Count = 0

' Create the Outlook application object and get the NameSpace.
Set MyOLApp = CreateObject("Outlook.Application")
Set MyNameSpace = MyOLApp.GetNamespace("MAPI")

' Get a reference to the Inbox folder.
Set MyInbox = MyNameSpace.GetDefaultFolder(6)

' Loop through all messages looking for sender.
For Each msg in MyInbox.Items
    if msg.SenderName = sender then
        buf = buf & msg.Body
        ' Add a separator line between messages.
        buf = buf & vbCrLf & "*************" & vbCrLf
        Count = Count + 1
        ' Put the message in the "to move" list.
        Set ToMove(Count) = msg
    end if
Next

' If no matching e-mails were found, display a message. Otherwise
' Save the summary and move the messages to the specified folder.
```

```
If Count = 0 then
    WScript.Echo "No messages from " & sender & " were found."
else
    ' Get a reference to the destination folder.
    For Each f1 in MyNameSpace.Folders
        For Each f2 in f1.Folders
            if f2.Name = destFolderName Then Set destFolder = f2
        Next
    Next
    ' Move the messages.
    For i = 1 to Count
        ToMove(i).Move destFolder
    Next

        ' Now save the summary to disk.
    Set fso = CreateObject("Scripting.FileSystemObject')
    Set summaryFile = fso.OpenTextFile(summaryFileName, ForAppending, True)
    summaryFile.Write buf
    summaryFile.Close
    WScript.Echo Count & " messages summarized and moved."
end if

]]>
</script>
</job>
```

LISTING 19–7 *A script to create a summary of e-mail messages from a particular sender (JScript).*

```
<?xml version="1.0"?>
<?job error="true" debug="true"?>
<!-- List1907.wsf
Creating a summary document of messages from
a particular sender. It is assumed that at most
100 matching messages will be found, and that the
destination folder exists. -->

<job>
<reference object="Scripting.FileSystemObject" />
<script language="JScript">
<![CDATA[

var MyOLApp;
var MyNameSpace;
var MyInbox;
var destFolder;
var destFolderName;
var msg;
var buf;
var sender;
```

```
var ToMove;
var Count;
var f1;
var f2;
var i;
var summaryFileName;
var summaryFile;
var fso;
var e1;
var e2;

// The name of the sender to look for.
sender = "Lewis Smith";
// The folder to which messages are to be moved.
destFolderName = "From Lewis";
// The name of the summary file.
summaryFileName = "c:\\summary.txt";
Count = 0;

// Initialize the array.
ToMove = new Array(100);

// Create the Outlook application object and get the NameSpace.
MyOLApp = WScript.CreateObject("Outlook.Application");
MyNameSpace = MyOLApp.GetNamespace("MAPI");

// Get a reference to the Inbox folder.
MyInbox = MyNameSpace.GetDefaultFolder(6);

// Loop through all messages looking for sender.
e1 = new Enumerator(MyInbox.Items)
for ( ; !e1.atEnd() ; e1.moveNext())
{
    msg = e1.item();
    if (msg.SenderName == sender)
    {
        buf = buf + msg.Body;
        // Add a separator line between messages.
        buf = buf + "\n*************\n";
        Count++;
        // Put the message in the "to move" list.
        ToMove[Count] = msg;
    }
}

// If no matching e-mails were found, display a message. Otherwise
// Save the summary and move the messages to the specified folder.
```

```
if (Count == 0)
    WScript.Echo("No messages from " + sender + " were found.");
else
{
    // Get a reference to the destination folder.
    e1 = new Enumerator(MyNameSpace.Folders)
    for ( ; !e1.atEnd() ; e1.moveNext())
    {
        f1 = e1.item();
        e2 = new Enumerator(f1.Folders);
        for ( ; !e2.atEnd() ; e2.moveNext())
        {
            f2 = e2.item();
            if (f2.Name == destFolderName)
                destFolder = f2;
        }
    }
    // Move the messages.
    for (i = 1 ; i <= Count; i++)
        ToMove[i].Move(destFolder);

        // Now save the summary to disk.
    fso = WScript.CreateObject("Scripting.FileSystemObject");
    summaryFile = fso.OpenTextFile(summaryFileName, ForAppending, -1);
    summaryFile.Write(buf)
    summaryFile.Close();
    WScript.Echo(Count + " messages summarized and moved.");
}
]]>
</script>
</job>
```

CREATING AND SENDING MESSAGES

Creating and sending messages with Outlook is fairly straightforward, and again the task is made simple by the methods and properties of the objects that Outlook exposes. The required steps are as follows:

1. Create a new `MailItem` object representing the message to be sent.
2. For each person you want to send the message to, add a recipient to the `MailItem` object's `Recipients` collection.
3. Put the message subject in the `Subject` property.
4. Put the message text in the `Body` property.
5. Execute its `Send` method.

Before we look at an example, you need to understand those `MailItem` properties that are relevant when creating and sending messages. They are described in Table 19.5.

TABLE 19.5 *MailItem properties relevant for sending messages.*

Property	Description
BCC	A semicolon-delimited list of display names for the blind carbon copy recipients.
Body	The text of the message for plain text messages.
CC	A semicolon-delimited list of display names for the carbon copy recipients.
HTMLBody	The text of the message for HTML format messages.
ReadReceiptRequested	True to request a read receipt for the message.
Recipients	A collection of `Recipient` objects representing the message recipients.
Sent	True if the message has been sent, False otherwise.
To	A semicolon-delimited list of display names for the message recipients.

WORKING WITH MESSAGE RECIPIENTS

Each recipient of a message is represented by a `Recipient` object in the `Recipients` collection. To add a recipient to the collection, use the `Add` method. The syntax is

```
MyMailItem.Recipients.Add(Name)
```

Name is the display name of the recipient. The display name of the recipient is not necessarily the same as the e-mail address, which is set as the `Address` property of the `Recipient` object. This script fragment illustrates how to add a recipient and specify both its display name and e-mail address:

```
myMessage.Recipients.Add("Joe Smith")
myMessage.Recipients("Joe Smith").Address =
    "jsmith@somewhere.com"
```

If a recipient has an entry in the address book, you can specify the `Name` property only and later obtain the e-mail address from the address book. This process is called *resolving* an address.

The important properties of the Recipient object are described in Table 19-6.

TABLE 19.6 *Properties of the Recipient object.*

Property	Description
Address	The e-mail address of the recipient.
Name	The display name of the recipient.
Resolved	True if the recipient has been resolved, or validated, against the address book.
Type	Specifies the type of the recipient. Possible settings are `olBCC`, (blind carbon copy, value = 3), `olCC` (Carbon copy, 2), `olTo` (to, 1), and `olOriginator` (originator, 0). The default is `olTo`.

To resolve a recipient, use the `Recipient` object's `Resolve` method. The `Resolve` method looks through the address book for a match to the recipient's display name. If a match is found, the corresponding e-mail address is placed in the `Address` property and the `Resolved` property is set to True. The `Resolve` method returns True on success and False on failure. The following code adds a recipient to a message, attempts to resolve the recipient, and, if the resolution fails, displays the message for the user to edit:

```
Set myNewMailItem = myOutlookApp.CreateItem(olMailItem)
Set myNewRecipient = myNewMailItem.Add("Joe Smith")
If Not myNewRecipient.Resolve Then myNewMailItem.Display
```

CREATING A NEW MESSAGE

To create a new mail message, as a `MailItem` object, you call the `Outlook.Application` object's `CreateItem` method. Since Outlook supports various kinds of items besides mail messages, you must specify the type of item to be created by passing the `olMailItem` argument (value = 0) to this method:

```
Set MyMailItem = MyOLApp.CreateItem(olMailItem)
```

Once you have created a `MailItem` object, then you fill in its properties as described previously, resolve its recipient(s), and send it. The scripts in Listings 19-8 and 19-9 show how to do this, sending a message to three recipients.

LISTING 19–8 *Sending an e-mail message. (VBScript).*

```
<?xml version="1.0"?>
<?job error="true" debug="true"?>
<!-- List1908.wsf
Creating and sending an e-mail message using Outlook. -->

<job>
<reference object="Outlook.Application" />
<script language="VBScript">
<![CDATA[

Option Explicit

Dim MyOLApp
Dim Recip
Dim NewMessage

' Create the Outlook application object.
Set MyOLApp = CreateObject("Outlook.Application")
```

```
' Create a new message.
Set NewMessage = MyOLApp.CreateItem(olMailItem)
NewMessage.Subject = "Personnel Evaluations"
NewMessage.Body = "Do not forget to send me your
evaluations by Friday."
' Add and resolve a recipient.
Set Recip = NewMessage.Recipients.Add("Peter G. Aitken")
If Not Recip.Resolve Then NewMessage.Display
NewMessage.Send

]]>
</script>
</job>
```

LISTING 19–9 *Sending an e-mail message. (JScript).*

```
<?xml version="1.0"?>
<?job error="true" debug="true"?>
<!-- List1909.wsf
Creating and sending an e-mail message using Outlook. -->

<job>
<reference object="Outlook.Application" />
<script language="JScript">
<![CDATA[

var MyOLApp;
var Recip;
var NewMessage;

// Create the Outlook application object.
MyOLApp = WScript.CreateObject("Outlook.Application");

// Create a new message.
NewMessage = MyOLApp.CreateItem(olMailItem);
NewMessage.Subject = "Personnel Evaluations";
NewMessage.Body = "Do not forget to send me your evaluations by Friday.";
// Add and resolve a recipient.
Recip = NewMessage.Recipients.Add("Peter G. Aitken");
if (!Recip.Resolve())
    NewMessage.Display
NewMessage.Send();

]]>
</script>
</job>
```

Overview

Many computer users have become heavily dependent on e-mail, and you can often hear them complaining about how much time they spend dealing with messages they receive and send. With scripting, the possibility opens up to automate many time-consuming e-mail tasks. Whether you script Outlook or CDO the possibilities are limitless and can be tailored to meet your specific needs or those of your client. If you explore Windows' e-maile-mail capabilities beyond the introduction presented in this chapter, you will find additional capabilities that can be used in your scripts.

T W E N T Y

Using WSH For Administrative Tasks

While any computer user can get a great deal out of the Windows Scripting Host, it is perhaps the systems administrator, responsible for many computers on one or more networks, who stands to benefit the most. There are numerous tasks that a systems administrator must perform on a more or less regular basis, and many of these tasks are good candidates for scripting. It may seem like a lot of effort to create and debug the scripts for various administrative tasks, but it can often be worth the effort in the long run in terms of time saved and errors avoided. In this chapter I give examples of using WSH for four commonly needed administrative tasks: mapping network drives, automating logon scripts, updating files, and creating folders.

Mapping Network Drives

For computers in a network environment, a commonly needed task is to map one or more network drives. Mapping a drive consists of assigning a local drive letter to a shared network drive. For example, you could map the C drive on a network server named SERVER1 so it is referred to locally as drive P:. Network mapping can also work for folders as well as drives, permitting a specific folder on a server to be mapped to a local drive letter.

The Windows operating system has tools for creating network mappings and for restoring them each time the system boots up. At times, however, you will want the flexibility of scripts to provide different mappings for different purposes. On Windows NT/2000 you can associate a custom mapping with each user by performing the mapping in a script and then assigning a different script as the logon script for a specific user (this technique is explained in the next section). You could also give a single user the option of two or more different mappings depending on the tasks at hand.

Network mapping in a script is performed using the `WScript.Network` object. You learned the fundamentals of this object in Chapter 2. In this section we start by reviewing what was covered in that chapter and then take a more detailed look at using this object to perform drive mappings.

You must, of course, start by creating an instance of the `WScript.Network` object, using the `CreateObject` function. Then, you use the `MapNetworkDrive` method to create the mapping. The syntax for this method is (assuming that WshNetwork refers to an instance of the `WScript.Network` object)

```
WshNetwork.MapNetworkDrive(localname, remotename,
updateprofile, _ username, password)
```

Localname is the local name for the mapped drive, the name by which the drive will be available locally. Typically, drive letters are used (for example, H:). If the local name is already in use, an error occurs.

Remotename is the path to the remote drive; for example, \\Server1\Drive_C. If the path cannot be found, an error occurs.

Updateprofile is an optional argument. Set to True to have the drive mapping saved in the user's profile (so it will be reestablished automatically each time the user logs on). The default is False.

Username is an optional argument for the user's name if you are mapping the drive using someone else's credentials.

Password is an optional argument giving the password, if required.

When you are creating a script to map network drives, you must take into account the possibility of errors. One obvious source of errors is if the network share you are trying to map simply does not exist. There is nothing much a script can do about this situation except to report it to the user. Another source of error is if the requested local name is already in use. This condition can be rectified by removing the existing mapping and then running your mapping script again with a different local name.

To facilitate writing scripts for drive mapping, the procedure in Listing 20-1 includes a procedure named MapNetworkDrive that uses error trapping to verify that a mapping was successful, displaying an error message to the user if there is a problem. This script is presented in VBScript only as the error trapping capabilities of that language are essential. You can, of course, wrap the procedure in a WSF file and call it from a JScript script.

The procedure is written to allow for the need to supply a username and password to perform the mapping. If a username and password are passed as the procedure's fourth and fifth arguments, they are used in the call to `MapNetworkDrive` method. If blank strings are passed, they are ignored. Figure 20-1 shows the message that is displayed when you try to map a local name that is already mapped.

FIGURE 20–1 *An error message displayed by the MapNetworkDrive procedure.*

To use the code in Listing 20-1, you must change the network share names to ones that are actually available to your system.

LISTING 20–1 *Mapping network drives with error checking.*

```
' List2001.vbs
' Network drive mapping with error checking.

Option Explicit

Sub MapNetworkDrive(networkObj, localname, remotename, username, password)

' Maps remotename to localname. Uses the username and
' password if supplied.

Dim msg
Const ERR_DRIVE_IN_USE = -2147024811

On Error Resume Next

if username = "" then
    networkObj.MapNetworkDrive localname, remotename
else
    networkObj.MapNetworkDrive localname, remotename, False, username, password
end if

' No error
If Err = 0 then exit sub

' Error occurred.
If Err = ERR_DRIVE_IN_USE then
    msg = "Mapping " & localname & " to " & remotename & " failed " _
        & "because " & localname & " is already mapped."
else
    msg = "Mapping " & localname & " to " & remotename & " failed " _
        & "from error number " & Err & ": " & Err.Description
end if
WScript.Echo msg

    End Sub
```

```
Dim netObj

Set netObj = CreateObject("WScript.Network")

MapNetworkDrive netObj, "H:", "\\SERVER1\DATA", "", ""
MapNetworkDrive netObj, "H:", "\\SERVER1\USERS", "", ""
```

Automating LogOn Scripts

A logon script is a script that is executed whenever an individual logs on to the system or network. With Windows 2000 and Windows NT, you can specify a script to be executed automatically for each user (Windows 95/98/ME does not support this). Logon scripts can be used for a variety of purposes, such as automating drive mapping, setting environment variables, or starting background processes. Strictly speaking, you can execute any one of a variety of things at logon: a batch file (BAT or CMD) or an executable (EXE) as well as a Windows Scripting Host script. The procedures are similar for Windows 2000 and Windows NT.

For Windows 2000, here are the steps to follow to assign a script to a local user:

1. Open the Control Panel (select Settings, Control Panel from the Start menu).
2. Double click the Administrative Tools icon to open the corresponding folder.
3. Double click the Computer Management icon to open the Computer Management utility.
4. In the left panel, open the System Tools tree and then open the Local users and Groups tree. The right panel will display a list of local users. Figure 20-2 shows the Computer Management window with the local users displayed.
5. Right click the name of the user, and then select Properties from the popup menu. The Properties dialog box for that user will display. Select the Profile tab, as shown in Figure 20-3.
6. In the Logon Script box, specify the name and, if necessary, the path of the script.
7. Click OK.

The default location for Windows 2000 logon scripts is in the NETLOGON share of the domain controller or local computer, or in the *systemroot*\\system32\\repl\\import\\scripts folder on the local computer. If the script

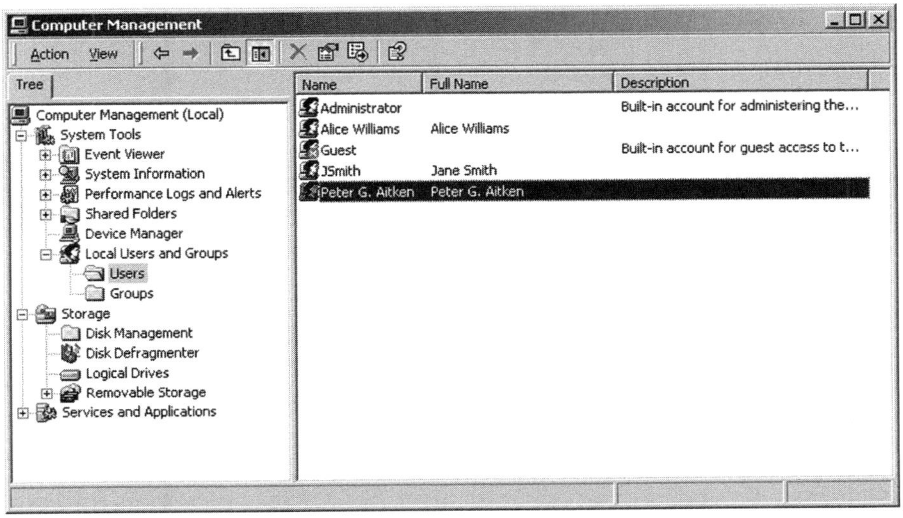

FIGURE 20-2 *The Computer Management window showing local users.*

is located in a subfolder of the NETLOGON share, you must specify a relative path.

For Windows NT, these are the steps to follow:

1. Open the NT User Manager for domains.
2. Select a user and press Enter to display the User Properties dialog box.
3. Click the Profile button to display the User Environment Profile dialog box.
4. In the Logon Script Name box, enter the name and path of the script.
5. Click OK.

The default location for Windows NT scripts is the same as for Windows 2000, as described previously.

Possible Problems with Windows NT

I have seen instances where the Windows NT User Manager is unable to resolve the path to a script file that has been specified as a logon script. This problem can be avoided by calling the script from a batch file and specifying the batch file as the logon script. For example, if your logon script is logon.vbs, here's a batch file to use:

```
@Echo Off
cscript logon.vbs
```

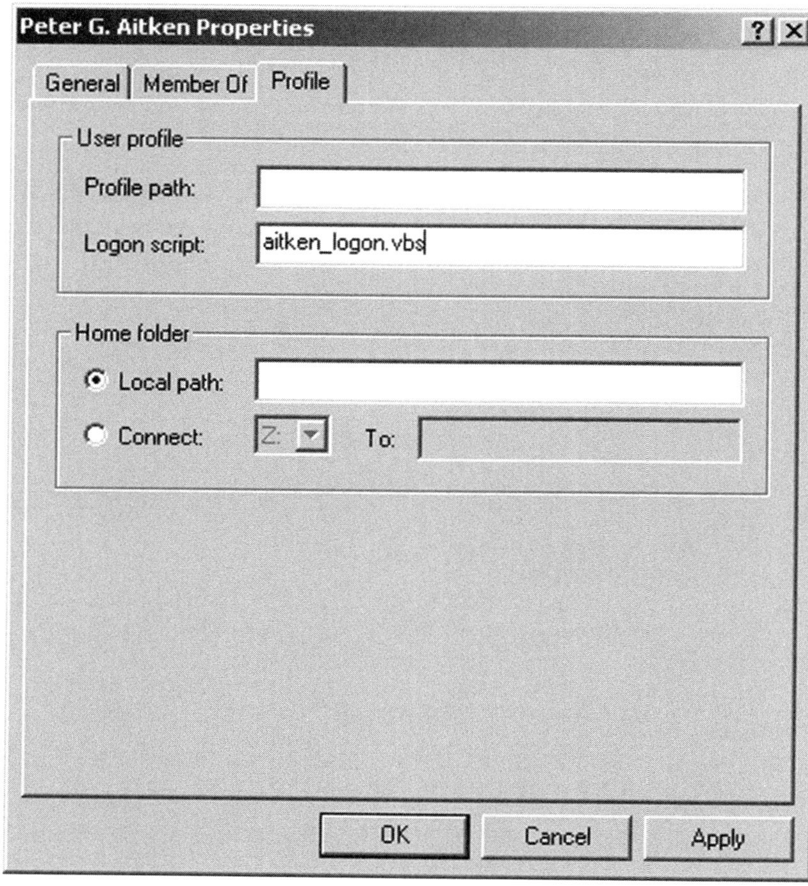

FIGURE 20–3 *Entering a logon script name on the Profile tab.*

Updating Files

If you are a systems administrator, you know how important it can be to keep your users' files up to date, whether they be application files, company policy manuals, Windows database drivers, or what have you. There are commercial utilities for keeping files up to date, but perhaps you do not have such a solution available to you or would rather integrate the file updating into a script. Fortunately the tools available to the script programmer permit file updating to be implemented relatively easily.

The method of using a script for file updating is based on the ability to determine a file's date and time stamp. If you compare the master file with the user's file, then you will know that the user's file needs updating only if its time and date stamp is older. If the user does not have a copy of the file at all, then the "new" file should be copied also.

Comparing file dates is easy in VBScript. The first step is to create a `File` object for the source file and the destination file. Then a simple comparison of the `DateLastModified` property is all that's required:

```
Set fileSource = fso.GetFile(SourceFileName)
Set fileDest = fso.GetFile(DestFileName)
If fileDest.DateLastModified < fileSource.DateLastModified
    Then
    ' File needs to be updated.
Else
    ' File does not need to be updated.
End If
```

Listing 20-2 presents a procedure named UpdateFile for updating files. The procedure takes four arguments:

- An instance of the `FileSystemObject` object.
- The name, without path, of the file being updated (which will be the same in both source and destination locations).
- The path to the source folder — that is, the folder where the new file is located.
- The path to the destination folder — the folder where the file to be updated is located.

Note that both path arguments must end in a backslash. It would be a simple matter to add code that checks for this and adds the \ if needed. It is assumed that both folders exist. The code in the procedure does the following:

1. Verifies that the source file exists. If not, a message is displayed to the user and the procedure terminates.
2. Checks if the destination file exists. If it does not, the source is copied to the destination.
3. If the destination file already exists, its date stamp is compared with the date stamp of the source file. The source is copied over the destination only if it is newer.

Error checking is enabled using the `On Error Resume Next` statement. If an error occurs, an informative message is displayed to the user. If the update proceeds without error, there is no message displayed, permitting the script to run unattended. Listing 20-2 includes several calls to the procedure, for demonstration purposes. You'll need to change this to try the procedure on your system.

LISTING 20-2 *Updating files based on their date and time stamp.*

```
' List2002.vbs
' Updating files based on their date/time stamp.

Option Explicit

Sub UpdateFile(filesystem, filename, sourcepath, destpath)

'Arguments:
'   filesystem: a reference to a FileSystemObject object.
'   filename: the name of the file to update, without path.
'   sourcepath: the path to the source (new) file ending in \.
'   destpath: the path to the destination file ending in \.
'
'The procedure checks to see that sourcefile exists and if not, exits.
'Then:
'    If destfile does not exist, the source is copied to destpath.
'    If destfile exists and is older than source file, the
'        source is copied to destpath.

Dim SourceName
Dim DestName
Dim msg
Dim fs
Dim fd

On Error Resume Next

SourceName = sourcepath & filename
DestName = destpath & filename

' See if the source file exists. If not, display message and exit sub.
If Not filesystem.FileExists(SourceName) Then
    msg = "The source file " & SourceName & " does not exist."
    WScript.Echo msg
    Exit Sub
End If

' See if the destination exists. If not, copy file and exit.
If Not filesystem.FileExists(DestName) Then
    filesystem.CopyFile SourceName, DestName
    If Err <> 0 Then
        msg = "An error occurred while trying to copy: " & vbCrLf
        msg = "Error number " & Err & ": " & Err.Description
        WScript.Echo msg
    End If
    Exit Sub
End If
```

```
' If we reach here we must compare the file dates.
' Get a reference to both files.
Set fs = filesystem.GetFile(SourceName)
Set fd = filesystem.GetFile(DestName)

If fd.DateLastModified < fs.DateLastModified Then
    ' Destination is older, so copy.
    'First release file objects.
    Set fs = Nothing
    Set fs = Nothing
    ' Copy with OverWrite set to True.
    filesystem.CopyFile SourceName, DestName, True
    If Err <> 0 Then
        msg = "An error occurred while trying to copy: " & vbCrLf
        msg = "Error number " & Err & ": " & Err.Description
        WScript.Echo msg
    End If
End if

End Sub

' ***********
' Execution starts here.

Dim fso

Set fso = CreateObject("Scripting.FileSystemObject")
UpdateFile fso, "policy.doc", "c:\master\", "h:\userdocs\company\"
UpdateFile fso, "policy.doc", "c:\master\", "i:\userdocs\company\"
UpdateFile fso, "policy.doc", "c:\master\", "j:\userdocs\company\"
```

Creating Folders

Creating a folder from a script is a simple matter of calling the `FileSystemObject` object's `CreateFolder` method — at least in some situations. The limitation of this method is that it cannot create an entire tree of folders, but only a single folder. For example, suppose you want to create the folder c:\documents\sales\annual. If the path c:\documents\sales already exists, then all you need do is call `CreateFolder` as follows (assuming that fso is a reference to an instance of the `FileSystemObject` object):

```
fso.CreateFolder "c:\documents\sales\annual"
```

If, however, c:\documents\sales does not exist, this method call will fail with an error. It would be a lot more convenient to have a folder creation procedure that does not require the "higher" branches of the path to already exist — in other words, a procedure that will create any and all missing parts of the tree. What this procedure would do is start at the top of the tree and work down, verifying that each folder exists and, if not, creating it. Continuing with the preceding example, the steps would be as follows:

1. Does c:\documents exist? If not, create it.
2. Does c:\documents\sales exist? If not, create it.
3. Does c:\documents\sales\annual exist? If not, create it.

Actually, it will be more efficient to perform step 3 first — in other words, check if the entire tree already exists, in which case nothing needs to be done at all. Only once we know the tree does not already exist will we proceed to verify and create higher-level folders.

The function will start by using the `FileSystemObject` object's `GetAbsolutePathName` method to convert the path passed to the function (which may be a relative path) to a full qualified path. The string returned by this function is guaranteed not to end with the \ character unless it is a reference to the root folder (for example, c:\). Since it is impossible to "create" a root folder, the function will check for this situation and exit with failure when it occurs.

The next step will be to break down the full path into various levels. Using the above example again, this would result in the following "branches" to the tree.

```
c:\documents\sales\annual
c:\documents\sales
c:\documents
```

These individual levels will be stored in a dynamic array, which can be expanded as needed. We will know we have found the final top-most level when the last \ character in the string is at position 3.

The final step will be to go through the list of levels, working backward. For each level, the code will see if it exists and, if not, create it. Listing 20-3 shows the function CreateFolderTree. While written in VBScript, you can call this function from either VBScript or JScript.

LISTING 20-3 *Creating an entire folder tree with one procedure call.*

```
' List2003.vbs
' Creating a folder tree with a single procedure call.

Option Explicit

Function CreateFolderTree(path)

' Creates folders as needed to construct the entire
' tree of folders as specified in path. The argument can
' be an absolute or relative path.
' Returns True on success, False on failure.
```

```
Dim fso
Dim f1
Dim levels()
Dim count
Dim pos
Dim idx

Set fso = CreateObject("Scripting.FileSystemObject")

' Create a full path from the argument.
path = fso.GetAbsolutePathName(path)

' First see if the folder already exists. If so
' do nothing and return True.
If fso.FolderExists(path) then
    CreateFolderTree = True
    Exit Function
End If

' Now make sure it is a path and not the root folder.
If path = "" or Right(path,1) = "\" Then
    CreateFolderTree = False
    Exit Function
End If

' Next we fill the array with the "sublevels".
count = 0
Redim Preserve levels(count)
levels(count) = path

Do
    pos = InStrRev(path, "\")
    path = left(path, pos - 1)
    count = count + 1
    Redim Preserve levels(count)
    levels(count) = path
    If (InStrRev(path, "\") = 3) then Exit Do
Loop While True

For idx = count to 0 Step -1
    If Not fso.FolderExists(levels(idx)) Then
        fso.CreateFolder(levels(idx))
    end if
Next

CreateFolderTree = True

End Function
```

Overview

The many daily or weekly tasks faced by a systems administrator provide plenty of opportunities for script automation. Performing a task with a script, rather than manually, can save time and reduce or eliminate the chance of errors. It can require some investment of time and effort to create and test administrative scripts, but usually it is well rewarded. This chapter presented a few examples of using scripts for administrative tasks, and there are plenty more places where you can put WSH to work.

TWENTY-ONE

A Script Programmer's Library

This final chapter of the book presents several working scripts that perform useful, real-world actions. The three tasks covered are installing files from a CD, obtaining information about a database schema, and printing text files from a script. Admittedly these scripts perform actions that were useful to me, and they may not, at least as written, be quite as useful to you. However, they do serve to demonstrate functional, complete scripts that were written to be used and not to demonstrate a point in the text. Most of the programming principles used in these scripts were covered in the previous chapters. When they were not, I provide enough background material for you to understand how the script works.

Installing Files from a CD

The use of CD-ROMs to distribute files is becoming more and more common. CD "burners" that permit you to make your own data CDs are affordable to most people, and the 650-MB capacity and low cost of the disks makes them a convenient distribution method. When you create a CD to distribute files, it is a professional touch also to provide an installation script that automates the tasks required to perform the installation. There is often more involved than simply copying the files. Let's take a look at what actions may be required.

First, there is the question of where the files will be installed — in other words, the specification of the disk drive and the folder or folders. Some installations let the user specify the installation destination, while other installations always use a preset destination. In the former case your script will need to prompt the user for the destination information, while in the latter case the destination can be hard-coded into the script.

Next is the possibility that backups may be needed. If the destination folder already exists, you certainly do not want to overwrite the user's existing files with the new files. The best approach to this problem is to test for the existence of the destination folder and, if necessary, rename it. Of course, the user must be informed of the new name.

Another potential problem involves disk space. Needless to say, the install process will fail if the destination drive does not have enough free space on it. Any installation script should verify that sufficient space is available before commencing to copy files.

Another matter that may need consideration is the registration of program components. If the files being installed are only data files, then this will not be a concern, but if you are installing an application program there may be program components that need to be registered. This process involves storing certain information about the program in the Windows registry and is accomplished using a utility program called REGSVR32.EXE, which is part of Windows. A full discussion of registering program components is beyond the scope of this book, but if you are planning on creating a program installation CD then you will know what's involved. The sample script presented will show the basics of how registration is done.

The final consideration has to do with the attributes of the files that are copied from the CD. Most CDs are read-only devices, which means that any file on a CD has the read-only attribute set. When the file is copied to a hard disk, this attribute remains set, and the user will not be able to modify the file. In some situations this may be OK, but generally you will want to turn off the read-only attribute after copying the files. You can refer back to Chapter 15 if you need to review information about file attributes.

Listings 21-1 and 21-2 present sample scripts that install a set of project files from a CD to the user's hard disk. This script would be placed in the root folder of the distribution CD, and the user would be provided with instructions on how to run it from that location. Needless to say, you cannot run this script yourself — well, you can but it won't do much of anything as it is designed for a very specific situation. The script also lacks a few safety features that you might want in your situation, such as verifying that the backup folder does not already exist and, if it does, selecting another name for the backup folder. In my situation, however, these features were not needed.

LISTING 21–1 *A script to install files from a CD (VBScript).*

```
' List2101.vbs
' Installs project files to hard disk from CD.

Option Explicit
```

```
Dim fso
Dim fldr1
Dim fldr2
Dim drive
Dim f
Dim msg
Dim dest
Dim shell
Dim spaceNeeded
Dim cmd

' This is the destination folder.
dest = "c:\documents"

' This is the space needed for the install.
spaceNeeded = 2200000

'**************
Sub RemoveReadOnly(folder)
' Removes the read-only attribute from all files
' in the specified folder and its subfolders.

Dim f, fl

for each f in folder.Files
    If f.Attributes And 1 Then
        f.Attributes = f.Attributes - 1
    End If
next

for each fl in folder.SubFolders
    RemoveReadOnly fl
next

end sub
'***************

set fso = CreateObject("Scripting.FileSystemObject")

msg = "This script will copy the  project files to your" & vbCrLf
msg = msg & "hard disk. There will be no indication of " & vbCrLf
msg = msg & "progress but a message will be displayed when done."
Msgbox msg

' Make sure there is enough space on the drive.
Set d = fso.GetDrive("c")
if d.FreeSpace < spaceNeeded then
    msg = "There is not enough free space to install." & vbCrLf
    msg = msg & "Free up some space on drive C: then try again."
    MsgBox msg
```

```
else
    ' See if the destination folder already exists.
    ' If not, create it.
    if not fso.FolderExists(dest) then
        fso.CreateFolder(dest)
    end if
    ' If folder c:\documents\project exists,
    ' rename it.
    if fso.FolderExists(dest & "\project") then
        Set fldr1 = fso.GetFolder(dest & "\project")
        fldr1.Name = "project_old"
        msg = "The existing folder " & dest & "\project has" & vbCrLf
        msg = msg & "been renamed to project_old."
        MsgBox msg
    end if

    ' Now get a reference to the source folder.
    Set fldr2 = fso.GetFolder("\project")
    fldr2.Copy dest & "\project"
    set fldr1 = Nothing
    set fldr2 = Nothing

    ' Remove the read-only attribute from all copied files.
    set fldr1 = fso.GetFolder(dest & "\project")
    RemoveReadOnly fldr1

    ' Now register the DLL
    set shell = CreateObject("WScript.Shell")
    cmd = "c:\windows\system\regsvr32 " & dest
    cmd = cmd & "\project\WBCustomizer.dll"
    shell.Run cmd

    MsgBox "Project files successfully copied."
end if
```

LISTING 21–2 *A script to install files from a CD (JScript).*

```
// List2102.js
// Installs project files to hard disk from CD.

var fso;
var fldr1;
var fldr2;
var drive;
var f;
var msg;
var dest;
var shell;
var spaceNeeded;
var cmd;
```

```
// This is the destination folder.
dest = "d:\\documents";

// This is the space needed for the install.
spaceNeeded = 2200000;

//**************
function removeReadOnly(folder)
{
// Removes the read-only attribute from all files
// in the specified folder and its subfolders.

var e;
var f;
var fl;

e = new Enumerator(folder.Files);
for ( ; !e.atEnd(); e.moveNext())
{
    f = e.item();
    if (f.Attributes & 1)
        f.Attributes = f.Attributes - 1;
}

e = new Enumerator(folder.SubFolders);
for ( ; !e.atEnd(); e.MoveNext())
{
    fl = e.item();
    removeReadOnly(fl);
}

}
//***************

fso = new ActiveXObject("Scripting.FileSystemObject");

msg = "This script will copy the  project files to your\n";
msg = msg + "hard disk. There will be no indication of progress\n";
msg = msg + "but a message will be displayed when done.";
WScript.Echo(msg);

// Make sure there is enough space on the drive.
d = fso.GetDrive("c");
if (d.FreeSpace < spaceNeeded)
{
    msg = "There is not enough free space to complete the install.\n";
    msg = msg & "Free up some space on drive C: then try again.";
    WScript.Echo(msg);
}
```

```
else
{
    // See if the destination folder already exists.
    // If not, create it.
    if (!fso.FolderExists(dest))
        fso.CreateFolder(dest)

        // If folder c:\documents\project exists,
    // rename it.
    if (fso.FolderExists(dest + "\\project"))
    {
        fldr1 = fso.GetFolder(dest + "\\project");
        fldr1.Name = "project_old";
        msg = "The existing folder " + dest + "\\project has been\n";
        msg = msg + "renamed to project_old.";
        WScript.Echo(msg);
    }

    // Now get a reference to the source folder.
    fldr2 = fso.GetFolder("\\project");
    fldr2.Copy(dest + "\\project");

        // Remove the read-only attribute from all copied files.
    fldr1 = fso.GetFolder(dest + "\\project");
    removeReadOnly(fldr1);

    // Now register the DLL
    shell = new ActiveXObject("WScript.Shell");
    cmd = "c:\\windows\\system\\regsvr32 " + dest;
    cmd = cmd + "\\project\\WBCustomizer.dll";
    shell.Run(cmd);

    WScript.Echo("Project files successfully copied.");
}
```

Obtaining Information about a Database

You learned in Chapter 17 how your scripts can access information that is stored in a database. There may be times when you also need to obtain information about the database itself, such as what tables are present in the data source and what fields are defined in a specific table. For this purpose, most database providers support the OpenSchema method. This method's name comes from the fact that the word *schema* is used to describe the internal structure of a database. The simplified syntax for this method is as follows:

```
myCon.OpenSchema(QueryType)
```

MyCon is the `Connection` object that is connected to the data source. *QueryType* specifies the type of schema to obtain. The `OpenSchema` method returns a reference to a recordset that contains the schema information. Once you have this reference, you can loop through the recordset using the techniques presented in Chapter 17 to extract the specific information you need.

The complete details of the arguments to this method are quite complex, and there are also differences between database providers in the schema information that is available. For our purposes, two of the possibilities are most useful:

- An argument of `adSchemaTables` (value = 20) returns a recordset that contains the names and types of the tables in the data source. The fields in the returned recordset that contain this information are named TABLE_NAME and TABLE_TYPE, respectively.
- An argument of `adSchemaColumns` (4) returns a recordset that contains the names of all the tables in the data source and the names of the columns (fields) that each table contains. The fields in the returned recordset that contain this information are named TABLE_NAME and COLUMN_NAME, respectively.

The scripts in Listings 21-3 and 21-4 show how to use the `OpenSchema` method to obtain information about the tables and table types in a database, and also about the fields. These scripts first call `OpenSchema` with the `adSchemaTables` argument and then loop through the returned recordset to create a list of all tables and their type. Next `OpenSchema` is called with the `adSchemaColumns` argument. The resulting recordset is filtered and the fields in the Employees table are listed. The second dialog box displayed by these scripts is shown in Figure 21-1.

LISTING 21-3 *Obtaining information about a database schema (VBScript).*

```
' List2103.vbs
' Obtaining data source information with OpenSchema.

Option Explicit

Dim adoCon
Dim conString
Dim msg
Dim rsTables
Dim TableList
Dim ColumnList

Const adSchemaTables = 20
Const adSchemaColumns = 4
```

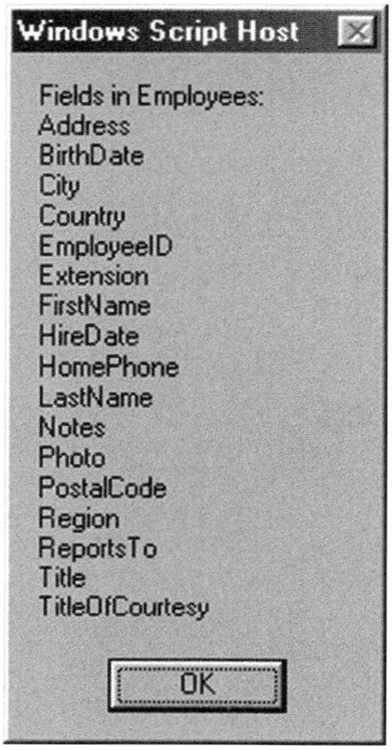

FIGURE 21–1 *The output of the scripts in Listings 21-3 and 21-4.*

```
' Set up the connection string.
conString = "Provider=Microsoft.Jet.OLEDB.4.0;"
conString = conString & "Data Source="
conString = conString & "c:\data\northwind.mdb;"

' Create the Connection object.
Set adoCon = WScript.CreateObject("ADODB.Connection")
adoCon.ConnectionString = conString

' Open the connection.
adoCon.Open

'Test for error and display appropriate message.
If Err <>0 Then
    msg = "An error occurred trying to connect to the Northwinds
database:" & vbCrLf
    msg = msg & "Error number: " & Err & vbCrLf
    msg = msg & "Description: " & Err.Description
    WScript.Echo msg
    WScript.Quit
end if
```

```
' Open the schema and retrieve table names and types.
Set rsTables = adoCon.OpenSchema(adSchemaTables)
' If error, display message then quit.
If Err <> 0 then
    WScript.Echo "Error opening schema."
    adoCon.Close
    WScript.Quit
End If

' Construct the output listing all tables.
Do
    TableList = TableList & rsTables.Fields("TABLE_NAME") & _
       ": " & rsTables.Fields("TABLE_TYPE") & vbCrLf
    rsTables.MoveNext
Loop Until rsTables.EOF

' Display the list of tables and types.
WScript.Echo TableList

' Next get the schema of table and column names.
Set rsTables = adoCon.OpenSchema(adSchemaColumns)
' If error, display message then quit.
If Err <> 0 then
    WScript.Echo "Error opening schema."
    adoCon.Close
    WScript.Quit
End If

' Loop through getting columns for "Employees" table.
ColumnList = "Fields in Employees:" & vbCrLf
Do
    if rsTables.Fields("TABLE_NAME") = "Employees" then
        ColumnList = ColumnList & rsTables.Fields("COLUMN_NAME") & vbCrLf
    end if
    rsTables.MoveNext
Loop Until rsTables.EOF

' Display the fields list.
WScript.Echo ColumnList

' Close the connection.
adoCon.Close
```

LISTING 21–4 *Obtaining information about a database schema (JScript).*

```
// List2104.js
// Obtaining data source information with OpenSchema.
```

```
var adoCon;
var conString;
var msg;
var rsTables;
var TableList;
var ColumnList;
var adSchemaTables = 20;
var adSchemaColumns = 4;

// Set up the connection string.
conString = "Provider=Microsoft.Jet.OLEDB.4.0;"
conString = conString + "Data Source="
conString = conString + "c:\\data\\northwind.mdb;"

// Create the Connection object.
adoCon = WScript.CreateObject("ADODB.Connection");
adoCon.ConnectionString = conString;

// Open the connection.
try {
adoCon.Open();}
//Test for error and display appropriate message.
catch(e) {
    msg = "An error occurred trying to connect to the Northwinds
database:\n";
    msg = msg + e.description;
    WScript.Echo(msg);
    WScript.Quit();
}

// Open the schema and retrieve table names and types.
try {
rsTables = adoCon.OpenSchema(adSchemaTables); }
// If error, display message then quit.
catch(e) {
    WScript.Echo("Error opening schema.");
    adoCon.Close();
    WScript.Quit();
}

// Construct the output listing all tables.
for ( ; !rsTables.EOF ; rsTables.MoveNext() )
{
    TableList = TableList + rsTables.Fields("TABLE_NAME') +  ": " +
rsTables.Fields("TABLE_TYPE") + "\n";
}

// Display the list of tables and types.
WScript.Echo(TableList);
```

```
// Next get the schema of table and column names.
try {
rsTables = adoCon.OpenSchema(adSchemaColumns); }
// If error, display message then quit.
catch(e) {
    WScript.Echo("Error opening schema.");
    adoCon.Close();
    WScript.Quit();
}

// Loop through getting columns for "Employees" table.
ColumnList = "Fields in Employees:\n";
for ( ; !rsTables.EOF ; rsTables.MoveNext() )
    if (rsTables.Fields("TABLE_NAME") == "Employees")
        ColumnList = ColumnList + rsTables.Fields("COLUMN_NAME") +
            "\n";

    // Display the fields list.
WScript.Echo(ColumnList);

// Close the connection.
adoCon.Close();
```

Printing from a Script

WSH has no direct support for sending information to a printer. If you want to print from a script, you must have another application do it for you. If you want to print an application-specific file, such as a Microsoft Word document, you'll need to automate the corresponding application to perform the task. Techniques for doing this with Word and Excel were covered in Chapter 18. For text files, your options are wider because so many applications support this file format. Specifically, the Notepad text editor that is provided with Windows is ideal because it includes an option to print a text file and then automatically close. This option is invoked on the command line as follows:

```
notepad.exe /p filename
```

The /p option tells Notepad to load the specified file, print it to the default printer, and then quit. You can include this functionality in a script, accepting one or more file names as script arguments and using the `WScript.Shell` object's `Run` method to run Notepad as needed. The scripts in Listings 21-5 and 21-6 provide a file printing utility using this technique. To print one or more files, simply call the script with the file names as arguments. For example,

```
list2105.vbs data.txt moredata.txt stillmoredata.txt
```

Remember to use quotes as needed to enclose long file names that contain spaces:

```
list2105.vbs "sales data.txt"
```

You can see that the program uses quotes to enclose the file name argument passed to Notepad, for the same reason.

LISTING 21–5 *A script to print text files (VBScript).*

```
' List2105.vbs
' Priting text files.

' Command line: list2105.vbs file1 [file2 ... filen]

Option Explicit

Dim fso
Dim filename
Dim i
Dim shell

' Create the fso object.
set fso = WScript.CreateObject("Scripting.FileSystemObject")

' Create the shell object.
set shell = WScript.CreateObject("WScript.Shell")

' Make sure there is at least one argument. If not
' display usage message.
if WScript.Arguments.Count < 1 then
    WScript.Echo "Usage: List2105.vbs file1 [file2, ...]"
    WScript.Quit
end if

' Loop for each argument.

For i = 0 to WScript.Arguments.Count - 1
    filename = WScript.Arguments(i)
    ' See if the file exists.
    if fso.FileExists(filename) then
        shell.Run "Notepad /p " & chr(34) & filename & chr(34)
    else
        WScript.Echo filename & " does not exist."
    end if
next

set shell = nothing
set fso = nothing
```

LISTING 21–6 *A script to print text files (JScript).*

```
// List2106.js
// Priting text files.

// Command line: list2105.vbs file1 [file2 ... filen]

var fso;
var filename;
var i;
var shell;

//Create the fso object.
fso = WScript.CreateObject("Scripting.FileSystemObject");

// Create the shell object.
shell = WScript.CreateObject("WScript.Shell");

// Make sure there is at least one argument. If not
// display usage message.
if (WScript.Arguments.length < 1) {
    WScript.Echo("Usage: List2105.vbs file1 [file2, ...]");
    WScript.Quit(); }

// Loop for each argument.
for (i = 0; i < WScript.Arguments.length ; i++) {
    filename = WScript.Arguments(i);
    // See if the file exists.
    if (fso.FileExists(filename))
        shell.Run("Notepad /p  \"" + filename + "\"");
    else
        WScript.Echo(filename + " does not exist.");
}
```

APPENDIX A

VBScript Constants

This appendix lists all of the constants that are defined as part of the VBScript language. They are divided into sections based on their function.

Color Constants

Used to specify display colors.

Constant	Value	Description
vbBlack	&h00	Black
vbRed	&hFF	Red
vbGreen	&hFF00	Green
vbYellow	&hFFFF	Yellow
vbBlue	&hFF0000	Blue
vbMagenta	&hFF00FF	Magenta
vbCyan	&hFFFF00	Cyan
vbWhite	&hFFFFFF	White

Comparison Constants

Used to specify how text comparisons are performed.

Constant	Value	Description
vbBinaryCompare	0	Perform a binary comparison (upper and lower case are different).
vbTextCompare	1	Perform a textual comparison (case does not matter).

Date and Time Constants

Used when working with dates and times.

Constant	Value	Description
vbSunday	1	Sunday
vbMonday	2	Monday
vbTuesday	3	Tuesday
vbWednesday	4	Wednesday
vbThursday	5	Thursday
vbFriday	6	Friday
vbSaturday	7	Saturday
vbUseSystem	0	Use the date format contained in the system's regional settings.
vbUseSystemDayOfWeek	0	Use the day of the week specified for the first day of the week in the system settings.
vbFirstJan1	1	Use the week in which January 1 occurs (this is the default).
vbFirstFourDays	2	Use the first week in the new year that has at least four days.
vbFirstFullWeek	3	Use the first full week of the year.

Date and Time Format Constants

Used when formatting dates and times.

Constant	Value	Description
vbGeneralDate	0	Date and time display is determined by system settings. If there is no fractional part, display a date only. If there is no integer part, display a time only.
vbLongDate	1	Display a date using the long date format specified in the system's regional settings.
vbShortDate	2	Display a date using the short date format specified in the system's regional settings.
vbLongTime	3	Display a time using the long time format specified in the system's regional settings.
vbShortTime	4	Display a time using the short time format specified in the system's regional settings.

Miscellaneous Constants

Constant	Value	Description
vbUseDefault	–2	Use default from computer's regional settings.
vbTrue	–1	True
vbFalse	0	False

MsgBox Constants

The constants in the first table are used to specify options for the `MsgBox` function. Those in the second table are used to identify which button the user clicked to dismiss the dialog box (the function's return value).

Constant	Value	Description
vbOKOnly	0	Display **OK** button only.
vbOKCancel	1	Display **OK** and **Cancel** buttons.
vbAbortRetryIgnore	2	Display **Abort**, **Retry**, and **Ignore** buttons.
vbYesNoCancel	3	Display **Yes**, **No**, and **Cancel** buttons.
vbYesNo	4	Display **Yes** and **No** buttons.
vbRetryCancel	5	Display **Retry** and **Cancel** buttons.
vbCritical	16	Display Critical Message icon.
vbQuestion	32	Display **Warning Query** icon.
vbExclamation	48	Display Warning Message icon.
vbInformation	64	Display Information Message icon.
vbDefaultButton1	0	First button is the default.
vbDefaultButton2	256	Second button is the default.
vbDefaultButton3	512	Third button is the default.
vbDefaultButton4	768	Fourth button is the default.
vbApplicationModal	0	The user must respond to the message box before continuing work in the current application.
vbSystemModal	4096	An application modal message box that always remains on top of any other programs you may have running.

Constant	Value	Description
vbOK	1	OK button was clicked.
vbCancel	2	Cancel button was clicked.
vbAbort	3	Abort button was clicked.
vbRetry	4	Retry button was clicked.
vbIgnore	5	Ignore button was clicked.
vbYes	6	Yes button was clicked.
vbNo	7	No button was clicked.

String Constants

These constants can be used in place of specific characters.

Constant	Value	Description
vbCr	Chr(13)	Carriage return.
VbCrLf	Chr(13) & Chr(10)	Carriage return–linefeed combination.
vbLf	Chr(10)	Line feed.
vbNewLine	Chr(13) & Chr(10) or Chr(10)	Newline character; whatever is appropriate for the platform.
vbNullChar	Chr(0)	Character having the value 0.
vbNullString	String having value 0	Used for calling external procedures.
vbTab	Chr(9)	Horizontal tab.

APPENDIX B

VBScript Keywords

This appendix lists words that are part of the VBScript language and should not be used for other purposes such as variable or function names.

Abs
And
Array
Asc
Atn
Call
CBool
CByte
CCur
CDate
CDbl
Chr
CInt
Class
Clear
CLng
Const
Cos
CreateObject
CSng
CStr
Date
DateAdd
DatePart
DateSerial
DateValue
Day
Dictionary
Dim
Do
Else
Eqv
Eval
Execute
ExecuteGlobal
Exit
Exp
False
Filter
Fix
For
For Each
FormatCurrency
FormatDateTime
FormatNumber
FormatPercent
Function
GetLocale
GetObject
GetRef
Hex
Hour
If
Imp
InputBox
InStr
InStrRev
Int
Is
IsArray
IsDate
IsEmpty
IsNull
IsNumeric
IsObject
Join
LBound
LCase
LoadPicture
Log
Loop
LTrim
Match
Mid
Minute
Mod
Month
MsgBox
Next
Not

Now	Rem	Space	True
Nothing	Replace	Split	TypeName
Null	RGB	Sqr	UBound
Oct	Right	StrComp	UCase
On Error	Rnd	StrReverse	Weekday
Option Explicit	Round	Sub	WeekdayName
Or	RTrim	Tan	Wend
Private	ScriptEngine	Then	While
Public	Second	Time	With
Raise	Select Case	Timer	Xor
Randomize	Set	TimeSerial	Year
ReDim	Sgn	TimeValue	
RegExp	Sin	Trim	

APPENDIX C

ASCII Character Codes

Code	Char	Code	Char	Code	Char
0	□	25	□	50	2
1	□	26	□	51	3
2	□	27	□	52	4
3	□	28	□	53	5
4	□	29	□	54	6
5	□	30	□	55	7
6	□	31	□	56	8
7	□	32	[space]	57	9
8	backspace	33	!	58	:
9	tab	34	"	59	;
10	linefeed	35	#	60	<
11	□	36	$	61	=
12	□	37	%	62	>
13	carriage return	38	&	63	?
14	□	39	'	64	@
15	□	40	(	65	A
16	□	41	)	66	B
17	□	42	*	67	C
18	□	43	+	68	D
19	□	44	,	69	E
20	□	45	-	70	F
21	□	46	.	71	G
22	□	47	/	72	H
23	□	48	0	73	I
24	□	49	1	74	J

Code	Char	Code	Char	Code	Char
75	K	109	m	143	□
76	L	110	n	144	□
77	M	111	o	145	□
78	N	112	p	146	□
79	O	113	q	147	□
80	P	114	r	148	□
81	Q	115	s	149	□
82	R	116	t	150	□
83	S	117	u	151	□
84	T	118	v	152	□
85	U	119	w	153	□
86	V	120	x	154	□
87	W	121	y	155	□
88	X	122	z	156	□
89	Y	123	{	157	□
90	Z	124	|	158	□
91	[	125	}	159	□
92	\	126	~	160	[space]
93	]	127	□	161	¡
94	^	128	□	162	¢
95	_	129	□	163	£
96	`	130	□	164	¤
97	a	131	□	165	¥
98	b	132	□	166	¦
99	c	133	□	167	§
100	d	134	□	168	¨
101	e	135	□	169	©
102	f	136	□	170	ª
103	g	137	□	171	«
104	h	138	□	172	¬
105	i	139	□	173	-
106	j	140	□	174	®
107	k	141	□	175	¯
108	l	142	□	176	°

Code	Char	Code	Char	Code	Char
177	±	204	Ì	231	ç
178	²	205	Í	232	è
179	³	206	Î	233	é
180	´	207	Ï	234	ê
181	µ	208	Ð	235	ë
182	¶	209	Ñ	236	ì
183	·	210	Ò	237	í
184	¸	211	Ó	238	î
185	¹	212	Ô	239	ï
186	º	213	Õ	240	ð
187	»	214	Ö	241	ñ
188	¼	215	×	242	ò
189	½	216	Ø	243	ó
190	¾	217	Ù	244	ô
191	¿	218	Ú	245	õ
192	À	219	Û	246	ö
193	Á	220	Ü	247	÷
194	Â	221	Ý	248	ø
195	Ã	222	Þ	249	ù
196	Ä	223	ß	250	ú
197	Å	224	à	251	û
198	Æ	225	á	252	ü
199	Ç	226	â	253	ý
200	È	227	ã	254	þ
201	É	228	ä	255	ÿ
202	Ê	229	å		
203	Ë	230	æ		

APPENDIX D

VBScript Error Codes

This appendix lists the numerical codes and descriptions of VBScript's runtime errors.

Error Number	Description
5	Invalid procedure call or argument
6	Overflow
7	Out of Memory
9	Subscript out of range
10	This array is fixed or temporarily locked
11	Division by zero
13	Type mismatch
14	Out of string space
17	Can't perform requested operation
28	Out of stack space
35	Sub or function not defined
48	Error in loading DLL
51	Internal error
91	Object variable not set
92	For loop not initialized
94	Invalid use of Null
424	Object required
429	ActiveX component can't create object
430	Class doesn't support Automation
432	File name or class name not found during Automation operation
438	Object doesn't support this property or method

Error Number	Description
445	Object doesn't support this action
447	Object doesn't support current locale setting
448	Named argument not found
449	Argument not optional
450	Wrong number of arguments or invalid property assignment
451	Object not a collection
458	Variable uses an Automation type not supported in VBScript
462	The remote server machine does not exist or is unavailable
481	Invalid picture
500	Variable is undefined
502	Object not safe for scripting
503	Object not safe for initializing
504	Object not safe for creating
505	Invalid or unqualified reference
506	Class not defined
507	An exception occurred
5008	Illegal assignment
5017	Syntax error in regular expression
5018	Unexpected quantifier
5019	Expected ']' in regular expression
5020	Expected ')' in regular expression
5021	Invalid range in character set

APPENDIX E

JScript Reserved Words

JScript's reserved words fall into three categories.

Current Reserved Words

These are words that are currently used in the JScript language. If you try to use one of these as a variable name, an error occurs.

JScript Reserved Words

break	false	in	this	void
continue	for	new	true	while
delete	function	null	typeof	with
else	if	return	var	

Future Reserved Words

These are words that are reserved for future use in the JScript language. If you try to use one of these as a variable name, an error occurs.

JScript Future Reserved Words

case	debugger	export	super
catch	default	extends	switch
class	do	finally	throw
const	enum	import	try

Words to Avoid

Words to avoid are any that are already the names of intrinsic JScript objects or functions, such as `String` and `parseInt`. Strictly speaking, these words are not reserved, as using one of them as a variable name does not cause an error. However, doing so may cause unexpected results when your script runs.

APPENDIX F

JScript Error Codes

This appendix lists the numerical codes and descriptions of JScript's runtime errors.

Error Number	Description
5000	Cannot assign to 'this'
5001	Number expected
5002	Function expected
5003	Cannot assign to a function result
5005	String expected
5006	Date object expected
5007	Object expected
5008	Illegal assignment
5009	Undefined identifier
5010	Boolean expected
5012	Object member expected
5013	VBArray expected
5014	JScript object expected
5015	Enumerator object expected
5016	Regular Expression object expected
5017	Syntax error in regular expression
5018	Unexpected quantifier
5019	Expected ']' in regular expression
5020	Expected ')' in regular expression
5021	Invalid range in character set
5022	Exception thrown and not caught
5023	Function does not have a valid prototype object

Error Number	Description
5024	The URI to be encoded contains an invalid character
5025	The URI to be decoded is not a valid encoding
5026	The number of fractional digits is out of range
5027	The precision is out of range
5028	Array or arguments object expected
5029	Array length must be a finite positive integer
5030	Array length must be assigned a finite positive number

APPENDIX G

WSH Resources on the Internet

This appendix lists various web pages and other Internet resources that may be of interest to the WSH programmer.

Address	Description
http://www.pgacon.com/ScriptHost.htm	The Web page for this book, with updates, corrections, and downloadable source code.
http://msdn.microsoft.com/scripting/	This is the entry page into Microsoft's scripting-related Web pages. You'll find detailed information on WSH, VBScript, JScript, and other related topics.
http://www.windows-script.com/	Created by Ian Morrish, this site contains a WSH FAQ, downloadable code, a discussion group, and other useful information.
http://www.borncity.de/WSHBazaar/WSHBazaar.htm	The Windows Script Host Bazaar, maintained by Günter Born
http://cwashington.netreach.net/	A useful and wide-ranging scripting page maintained by Clarence Washington Jr.
microsoft.public.scripting.jscript*	Microsoft's public newsgroup on the JScript language.
microsoft.public.scripting.vbscript*	Microsoft's public newsgroup on the VBScript language.
microsoft.public.scripting.wsh*	Microsoft's public newsgroup on the Windows Script Host.
http://www.microsoft.com/data/ado/	Not specifically script-related, but useful if you will use ADO in your scripts.
http://www.winscripter.com/	Winscripter, with sample scripts and other resources.

* Microsoft's public newsgroups can be accessed from the server msnews.microsoft.com

INDEX

!=, not equal to 153
! (exclamation point), bang operator 251-252
" (double quotes), as string literals 117
(pound sign), date indicator 129
$ (dollar sign)
  in regular expressions 122
  in variable names 147
%=, assignment operator 152
& (ampersand)
  bitwise And 155
  concatenation operator 95-96
' (single quote), comment indicator 85
*=, assignment operator 152
* (asterisk), in regular expressions 122
+=, assignment operator 152
+ (plus sign), in regular expressions 122
-=, assignment operator 152
. (dot), in regular expressions 122
. (period), in regular expressions 122
/=, assignment operator 152
//, comment indicator 9
/*...*/, comment indicators 9, 145
//? option 58
// (slashes), comment indicators 145
: (semicolon), end-of-line character 15
<=, less than or equal to operator 96, 153
<> (angle brackets)
  is not equal to operator 96
  XML tags 193
<< (left angle brackets), leftward shift 155
< (less than sign), comparison operator 96, 153
= (equal sign), comparison operator 96
== (equal signs), comparison operator 153
>=, greater than or equal to operator 96, 153
> (greater than sign), comparison operator 96, 153
>> (right angle brackets), rightward shift 155
>>> (right angle brackets), Zero-fill rightward shift 155
? (question mark), in regular expressions 122
\ (backslash)
  in a literal string 147
  in regular expressions 122
^ (carat)
  bitwise Exclusive Or 155
  in regular expressions 122
_ (underscore)
  continuation character 15, 85-86
_ (underscore), in variable names 147
| (vertical line), bitwise Or 155

A

Abs function 128
abs function 177
AbsolutePosition property 253
acos function 177
Active Data Objects (ADO) 240-241
ActiveCell property 276
ActiveX object 201
Add method
  Dictionary object 20
  MailItem.Recipients object 303
  MAPI.Session object 289-290
  Workbook object 272
  Worksheet object 274-275
adding worksheets 274-275
addition
  See arithmetic operators
  See number-related functions
  See numeric data
AddPrinterConnection method 50, 51
Address property 303
ADO (Active Data Objects) 240-241
Alert method 186-187
alphabetical order. *See* sorting
ampersand (&)
  bitwise And 155
  concatenation operator 95-96
And operator 97
angle brackets (<>)
  comparison operators 96
  is not equal to operator 96
  XML tags 193
Application object 261
Application property 23
arguments
  collecting 23
  counting 66
  displaying to a screen 66
  versus options 66

passing to scripts 65-66
passing to VBScript procedures 110-111
by reference 111
by value 111
verifying 66-68
Arguments object 66
Arguments property
Wscript object 23
WshShortcut object 36
arithmetic operators
JScript 152
VBScript 95
Array function 94
Array object 150-151
arrays
associative 19-20
as class properties 226
JScript 150-151
named elements. *See* associative arrays
VBScript, in JScript scripts 151
VBScript procedures 112-113
See also VBScript arrays
Asc function 116
ASCII character codes, table of 338-340
ASCII characters, definition 219
ASCII conversions 116
asin function 177
assignment operators
JScript 151-152
VBScript 94-95
associative arrays
definition 19-20
See also Dictionary object
asterisk (*), in regular expressions 122
asynchronous operation 260
AT command, Windows NT 63-64
atan function 177
AtEndOfLine property 220
AtEndOfStream property 220
Atn function 128
attachments, e-mail 288
attributes, returning
files 213
folders 210
Attributes property
Files object 213
Folder object 210
AvailableSpace property 207

B

//B option 58
backslash (\)
in a literal string 147
in regular expressions 122
bang operator (!) 251-252
banner, displaying at startup 58
batch mode, specifying 23, 58
BCC property 303
BeginTrans method 242
bitwise operators 155
Body property 297, 303
BOF property 253
Bold property 264
Boolean data type 148
Boolean object 182
breakpoints 79-80
bugs 75
BuildPath method 217
by reference arguments 111
by value arguments 111

C

Call Stack 81-82
calling VBScript procedures 112-114
capitalization. *See* case sensitivity
carat (^)
bitwise Exclusive Or 155
in regular expressions 122
Case property 264
case sensitivity, JScript
language elements 144-145
and string comparisons 154
in string searches 173
variables 147
case sensitivity, Outlook 296
case sensitivity, VBScript
comparisons 96-97, 103
IgnoreCase property 122
language elements 87
LCase function 120
sorting 96-97
UCase function 96-97, 120
CC property 303
CDO (Collaborative Data Objects) 286-287, 289-294
ceil function 177
Characters property 264
charAt method 170
charCodeAt method 170
Chr function 116-117
Class statements 224-225
classes
default properties 231-232
defining 224-225
example 233-234
instances, creating 225
methods, defining 226-228
versus objects 225
private class information 228
procedural class properties 228-231
properties, defining 225-226
sharing across scripts 232-233
ClearAllFormatting method 267
client-side scripting 70

Close method
  Connection object 242
  Document object 262
  TextStream object 221
closing
  databases 242
  documents 262
  text files 221
  workbooks 272-273
CLSIDs 195
coersion 148-149
Collaborative Data Objects (CDO) 286-287, 289-294
Collection object 17
collections
  accessing items in 182-183
  counting elements in 17
  definition 17
  retrieving items from 18
color constants 332
Column property 220
Command object 240
command-line scripting. *See* Cscript
CommandTimeout property 242
comment indicators
  /*...*/ 9, 145
  // 9
commenting out code 85
comments
  JScript 145
  VBScript 85
CommitTrans method 242
CompareMode property 20
comparing two strings 126-127
comparison constants 332
comparison operators
  JScript 153-154
  VBScript 96-97
comparisons, VBScript 96-97, 103
ComputerName property 49
concat method 170
conditional expressions 155
conditional statements
  JScript 157-160
  VBScript 100-103
Confirm method 186-187
connecting to databases 241-243
Connection object 240
ConnectionString property 242
ConnectionTimeout property 242
constants
  JScript 145-147
  See also VBScript constants
continue statements 163
Copy method
  File object 213
  Folder object 211
  MailItem object 298
  Range object 265
CopyFile method 203
CopyFolder method 204
copying
  files 202-204, 213
  folders 204, 211
  text ranges 265
Cos function 128
cos function 177
Count property
  Arguments object 66
  definition 17
  Dictionary object 17
  WshEnvironment object 31
  WshSpecialFolders object 33
CreateFolder method 205, 315-317
CreateItem method 304
CreateObject method
  creating objects 27-29
  definition 23
CreateShortcut method
  creating shortcuts 36-37
  definition 30
CreateTextFile method 218
creating
  database recordsets 247-251
  Dictionary object 21-22
  files 218
  folders 205
  objects 27-29, 195. *See also* Wscript object
  Outlook messages 302-303, 304-305
  popup windows 39-41
  shortcuts 35-39
  workbooks 272
Cscript
  definition 6
  options 58
  running scripts 6-7
  setting as default executable 58
CurrentRegion property 276
cursors (database) 248
Cut method 265

D

//D option 58
data conversion 149
data elements, organizing. *See* collections
data type, determining 89-90
data types, JScript 148-149
database recordsets. *See* recordsets
databases
  access technologies 239
  ADO 240-241
  canceling changes 242
  closing 242
  committing transactions 242

connecting to 241-243
connection strings, creating 243-245
data source information 242
definition 236-237
executing SQL commands 242
flat-file 237
getting information about 324-329
new transactions 242
NOT SQL operator 247-251
permissions 242
relational 237-239
SQL 241
state of the connection object 242
timeout values 242

data-type prefix notation 88
Date function 129
Date object 176-180
date of creation
files 213
folders 210
date of last access
files 213
folders 210
date of last modification
files 213
folders 210
DateAdd function 130-131
DateCreated property
Files object 213
Folder object 210
DateDiff function 133
DateLastAccessed property
Files object 213
Folder object 210
DateLastModified property
Files object 213
Folder object 210
DatePart function 131-133
dates and times, JScript
date methods 178
Date object 176-180
time methods 178-179
UTC 177
dates and times, VBScript
(pound sign), date indicator 129
adding and subtracting 130-131
constants 333
creating 129-130
current, getting 129
Date function 129
DateAdd function 130-131
DatePart function 131-133
DateSerial function 130
DateValue function 129
Day function 133
formatting 133-134
getting parts of 131-133
Hour function 133
Minute function 133
Month function 133
MonthName function 133
Now function 129
representations 129
Second function 133
Time function 129
TimeValue function 130
two-digit years 130
Weekday function 133
WeekdayName function 133
Year function 133
DateSerial function 130
DateValue function 129
Day function 133
debugger. *See* Script Debugger
debugging scripts 72-75
See also Script Debugger
declaring
JScript variables 148
VBScript variables 88-89
decrement operators 152-153
Default keyword 232
defined constants 262
defining VBScript procedures 110
Delete method
File object 213
Folder object 211
MailItem object 298
Range object 265
Worksheet object 275
DeleteFile method 205
DeleteFolder method 205
deleting
files 205, 213
folders 205, 211
worksheets 274-275
Description property 36, 138
dialog boxes 135-137
Dictionary object
creating and using 21-22
definition 19-20
methods 20
properties 20
Dim statement 88
dimensions method 184
DisconnectObject method 23
disk quotas 207
disks. *See* drives
Display method 298
division
See arithmetic operators
See number-related functions
See numeric data
Document object 261-262
documentation. *See* Internet resources
documents, word processor. *See* Word object model

dollar sign ($)
  in regular expressions 122
  in variable names 147
Do...Loop statements 106-108
DOS batch language 2
dot (.), in regular expressions 122
double quotes ("), as string literals 117
do...while statements 163
downloading
  Script Debugger 76
  WSH 3
drive letter, returning
  drives 207
  files 213
  folders 210
Drive object 202, 206-209
Drive property
  Files object 213
  Folder object 210
DriveExists method 205
DriveLetter property 207
drives
  disk quotas 207
  disk size, returning 207
  file system, returning 207
  free space, determining 207
  mapping on a network 307-310
  network 207
  obtaining references to 206
  path, returning 207
  ready status, determining 207
  root folder, returning 207
  serial number, returning 207
  share name, returning 207
  type, returning 207
  verifying existence of 205
  volume name, returning 207
Drives collection 202, 206-209
Drives object 206-209
DriveType property 207

E

//E option 58
e-mail
  attachments 288
  HTML 288
  IMAP 288
  MAPI 289
  MIME 288
  POP 288
  profiles 289
  SMTP 288
  Word documents 271
  workbooks 274
  See also messaging
End Class statements 224-225
End property 264
end-of-file
  recordsets 253
  text files 220
end-of-line condition, text files 220
Enumerator object 182-183
EnumNetworkDrives method 50, 54-55
EnumPrinterConnections method 50, 51
Environment property 30
environment variables, accessing 31-32
EOF property 253
equal sign (=), comparison operator 96
equal signs (==), comparison operator 153
Eqv operator 97
Erase statement 94
Err object 138
error codes. *See* VBScript error codes
error handling
  default error response 75
  JScript 188-191
  VBScript 138-140
Error object 188
Errors collection 240
escape characters 146
Eval function 141
event handling 23
Excel object model
  adding worksheets 274-275
  closing workbooks 272-273
  counting data items 282-284
  creating workbooks 272
  definition 271
  deleting worksheets 274-275
  e-mailing workbooks 274
  finding and replacing data 280-282
  formatting worksheets 277-279
  looping through cells 277
  opening workbooks 272
  printing workbooks 273-274
  ranges of cells 275
  reading cell data 276, 279-280
  saving workbooks 272-273
  setting cell data 276, 279-280
exclamation point (!), bang operator 251-252
Execute method 122, 267
Execute statements 141-142
ExecuteGlobal statements 141-142
executing programs. *See* running programs
executing scripts. *See* running scripts
execution, global *versus* current context 141-142
Exists method 20
exp function 177
ExpandEnvironmentStrings method 30
exponentiation
  See arithmetic operators
  See number-related functions
  See numeric data
expressions, JScript 155

expressions, VBScript
  comparing 96-97
  definition 91
  evaluating 141

F

faxing 270
file access. *See* FileSystemObject
file extensions
  associated actions 8
  .wsf 192
  .wsh 68
file management. *See* FileSystemObject
File object 202, 213-216
file pointers 220
FileExists method 205
files
  absolute paths 204
  ASCII characters 219
  attributes, returning 213
  copying 202-204, 213
  creating 218
  current character position 220
  date of creation, returning 213
  date of last access, returning 213
  date of last modification, returning 213
  deleting 205, 213
  drive letter, returning 213
  end of file 220
  end of line 220
  file pointer 220
  moving 202-204, 213
  name, returning 213
  obtaining references to 206
  opening 47-48, 218
  overwriting 203
  parent folder, returning 213
  path, returning 213
  reading from 218-222
  relative paths 204
  shortcuts to 35-37
  size, returning 213
  spreadsheet. *See* Excel object model
  text *versus* binary 218-222
  type, returning 213
  Unicode characters 219
  updating 312-315
  verifying existence of 205
  word processor. *See* Word object model
  writing to 218-222
Files collection 202, 213-216
Files property 210
FileSystem property 207
FileSystemObject object
  constants 219
  definition 18
  Drive object 202, 206-209
  Drives collection 202, 206-209
  File object 202, 213-216
  Files collection 202, 213-216
  Folder object 202, 209-212
  Folders collection 202, 213-216
  methods 217
  organization of 18-19
  RootFolder property 18
  scripting run-time library 200-201
Filter function 117-118
Find method 280-282
Find object 267
finding and replacing
  spreadsheet data 280-282
  text in a document 267-270
flat-file databases 237
floor function 177
Folder object 202, 209-212
FolderExists method 205
folders
  absolute path, returning 210
  attributes, returning 210
  copying 204, 211
  creating 205, 315-317
  date of creation, returning 210
  date of last access, returning 210
  date of last modification, returning 210
  deleting 205, 211
  drive letter, returning 210
  files in, returning 210
  identifying as root folder 210
  moving 204, 211
  name, returning 210
  obtaining references to 206
  Outlook 295-297
  parent, returning 210, 217
  shortcuts to 35-37
  size, returning 210
  special 217
  special system. *See* special system folders
  subfolders, returning 210
  temporary 217
  type, returning 210
  verifying existence of 205
Folders collection 202, 209-216
Font property 264
For Each...Next statements 105-106
for statements 161-162
formatting worksheets 277-279
For...Next statements 104-105
Forward method
  Find object 267
  MailItem object 298
Found method 267
FreeSpace property 207
FSO. *See* FileSystemObject
FullName property
  Wscript object 23

WshShortcut object 36
WshURLShortcut object 38
Function object 183
function procedures 109
functions
versus methods 149
number-related 127-128
tracking execution of 81-82
See also entries for specific functions
See also JScript functions
See also VBScript procedures

G

GetAbsolutePathName method 217, 316
GetBaseName method 217
getDate method 178
getDay method 178
GetDefaultFolder method 295-297
GetDrive method 206
GetFile method 206
GetFileName method 217
GetFolder method 206
getFullYear method 178
getHours method 178
getItem method 184
getMilliseconds method 178
getMinutes method 179
getMonth method 178
GetObject method, VBScript 30
GetObject method, Wscript
definition 23
getting objects in files 27, 29-30
referencing running instances 27
GetParentFolderName method 217
getSeconds method 179
GetSpecialFolder method 217
GetTempName method 217
getTime method 179
getTimeZone method 179
getUTCDate method 178
getUTCDay method 178
getUTCFullYear method 178
getUTCHours method 178
getUTCMilliseconds method 178
getUTCMinutes method 179
getUTCMonth method 178
getUTCSeconds method 179
getVarDate method 178
getYear method 178
Global property 122
global variables 112-113
GMT 177
greater than or equal to operator (>=) 96, 153
greater than sign (>), comparison operator 96, 153
Greenwich Mean Time 177

H

//H option 58
help. *See* Internet resources
HelpContext property 138
HelpFile property 138
Hex function 128
host information, retrieving 23, 24
HotKey property 36
Hour function 133
HTML (Hypertext Markup Language) 288
HTMLBody property 297, 303

I

//I option 58
IconLocation property 36
if...else statements 157-159
If...Then...Else statements 101-102
IgnoreCase property 122
IMAP (Internet Mail Access) 288
Imp operator 97
Importance property 297
importing WSF files 196-197
increment operators 152-153
indexOf method 170
infinite loops
JScript 162
VBScript 108-109
InputBox function 137
InsertAfter property 265
InsertBefore method 265
InsertParagraphAfter method 265
InsertParagraphBefore method 265
installing files from a CD 319-324
InStr function 119
InStrRev function 119
Int function 128
interactive mode, specifying 23, 58
Interactive property 23
interactivity
definition 25-26
JScript 186-187
VBScript 135-138
Internet Mail Access (IMAP) 288
Internet resources 57, 347
Is operator 97
IsArray function 90
IsDate function 90
IsEmpty function 90
IsNull function 90
IsNumeric function 90
IsObject function 90
IsReady property 207
IsRootFolder property 210
Italic property 264
italic text 264

Item property
- Arguments object 66
- Dictionary object 20
- WshCollection object 18
- WshEnvironment object 31
- WshSpecialFolders object 33

J

Java *versus* JScript 144
//Job option 58
<job> tag 194-195
Join function 119-120
JScript
- arithmetic operators 152
- Array object 150-151
- arrays 150-151
- assignment operators 151-152
- \(backslash), in a literal string 147
- bitwise operators 155
- Boolean data type 148
- case sensitivity. *See* case sensitivity, JScript
- coercion 148-149
- combining with VBScript. *See* WSF files
- comments 9, 145
- comparison operators 153-154
- concatenating strings 155
- conditional expressions 155
- conditional statements 157-160
- constants 145-147
- continue statements 163
- data conversion 149
- data types 148-149
- decrement operators 152-153
- definition 9
- do...while statements 163
- error codes 345-346
- error handling 188-191
- Error object 188
- errors, creating 190-191
- escape characters 146
- if...else statements 157-159
- increment operators 152-153
- infinite loops 162
- interactivity 186-187
- *versus* Java 144
- line continuation 15
- line continuation, messages 146
- lines, breaking 15
- literal constants 145-146
- logical operators 154-155
- loop statements 161-163
- Null data type 148
- Number data type 148
- Object data type 148
- object references 149
- operator precedence 156
- operators, grouping with parentheses 156
- parseFloat function 149
- parseInt function 149
- reserved words 343-344
- rethrowing errors 189
- for statements 161-162
- with statements 164
- String data type 148
- string operators 155
- switch statements 160-161
- symbolic constants 146
- syntax 144-145
- throw statements 190-191
- try...catch statements 188-189
- Undefined data type 148
- var statements 148
- VBArray function 151
- *versus* VBScript 143
- and VBScript arrays 151
- while statements 162-163

JScript functions
- calling 167-168
- defining 165-166
- definition 164
- Function object 183
- variables 166-167
- *See also entries for specific functions;* VBScript procedures

JScript objects
- Boolean 182
- Enumerator 182-183
- Function 183
- summary table of 182
- VBArray 184-186
- *See also entries for specific objects*

JScript string manipulation
- concatenating strings 155
- objects and methods for 169-173
- searching for strings 170
- searching with patterns 172-172
- splitting strings 171, 172
- string operators 155

JScript variables
- $ (dollar sign), in variable names 147
- _ (underscore), in variable names 147
- declaring 148
- definition 147
- naming 147

K

Key property 20
Keys method 20
keywords. *See* VBScript keywords

L

lastIndexOf method 171
lbound method 184
LCase function 120
left angle bracket (<), comparison operator 96
left angle brackets (<<), leftward shift 155

Left function 120
Len function 121
Length property
- Arguments object 66
- WshCollection object 18
- WshEnvironment object 31
- WshSpecialFolders object 33

less than or equal to operator (<=) 96, 153
less than sign (<), comparison operator 96, 153
line continuation, message lines
- JScript 146
- VBScript 137

line continuation, script code
- JScript 15
- VBScript 85-86

Line property 220
lines, breaking. *See* line continuation
literal constants
- JScript 145-146
- VBScript 86

local variables 112-113
locking database records 248-251
Log function 128
log function 177
logic errors 75
logical operators 154-155
//Logo option 58
Logoff method 291-292
LogOn method 289-290
logon scripts, automating 310-312
loop statements
- JScript 161-163
- VBScript 100-109

looping through cells 277
loops, infinite
- JScript 162
- VBScript 108-109

lowercasing strings 120
- *See also* case sensitivity

LTrim function 121

M

MailItem object 297-302
manuals. *See* Internet resources
MAPI (Messaging Application Programming Interface) 289
MAPIFolder object 295-297
MapNetworkDrive method 50, 53, 307-310
mapping network devices
- drives 53-55, 307-310
- printers 51

match method 171
MatchCase method 267
MatchWholeWord method 267
Math object 175-176, 177
mathematical operations. *See* arithmetic operators; numeric data
max function 177
MAX_VALUE property 174
messages (popup), displaying 39-41
messaging
- CDO 286-287, 289-294
- reading mail 292-294
- sending messages 289-292
- *See also* e-mail; Outlook

Messaging Application Programming Interface (MAPI) 289
methods
- default 16
- definition 14-15
- *versus* functions 149
- *See also entries for specific methods*

Mid function 120
MIME (Multipurpose Internet Mail Extensions) 288
min function 177
Minute function 133
MIN_VALUE property 174
Mode property 242, 243
modulus
- *See* arithmetic operators
- *See* number-related functions
- *See* numeric data

monitoring program execution 80-82
Month function 133
MonthName function 133
Move method
- File object 213
- Folder object 211
- MailItem object 298
- Recordset object 252

MoveFile method 203
MoveFirst method 252
MoveFolder method 204
MoveLast method 252
MoveNext method 252
MovePrevious method 252
moving
- files 202-204, 213
- folders 204, 211

MSDN Library 57
MsgBox constants 334-335
MsgBox function 135-137
MS-Office
- *See* Excel object model
- *See* Office object model
- *See* Word object model

MS-Outlook. *See* Outlook
multiplication
- *See* arithmetic operators
- *See* number-related functions
- *See* numeric data

Multipurpose Internet Mail Extensions (MIME) 288

N

Name property
  Files object 213
  Folder object 210
  Recipient object 303
  Wscript object 23
NameSpace object 295
naming JScript variables 147
NaN property 174
NEGATIVE_INFINITY property 174
network devices, mapping
  drives 53-55, 307-310
  printers 51
networks
  EnumNetworkDrives method 50, 54-55
  MapNetworkDrive method 50, 53, 307-310
  printers. *See* printers, network
  RemoveNetworkDrive method 50, 54-55
  user information, retrieving 49-51
  WshNetwork object 49-55
newsgroups about scripting 57
//Nologo option 58
not equal to operator (!=) 153
Not operator 97
NOT SQL operator 247-251
Now function 129
Null data type 148
Null value 89
Number data type 148
Number object 174-175
Number property 138
number-related functions 127-128
numeric data
  Math object 176, 177
  Number data type 148
  Number object 174-175
  Number property 138
  number-related functions 127-128
  See also arithmetic operators

O

Object data type 148
object references
  comparing 97
  definition 12-13
  JScript 149
  to running instances 22, 27, 30
  as VBScript variables 89
<object> tag 195
objects
  versus classes 225
  creating 27-29, 195. *See also* Wscript object
  definition 10
  disconnecting event handling 23
  getting from files 29-30
  JScript. *See* JScript objects
  retrieving from files. *See* Wscript object
  two-part names 13
  See also entries for specific objects
  See also methods
  See also properties
Oct function 128
Office object model
  definition 259-260
  printing 270
  references 268
  sending e-mail 271
  sending faxes 270
  validating object references 285
On Error Goto statements 140
On Error statements 138
Open method
  Connection object 242
  Document object 262
opening
  documents 262
  files 218
  workbooks 272
OpenSchema method 242
OpenTextFile method 218
operators
  JScript 156
  VBScript 98
Option Explicit statement 88-89
options *versus* arguments 66
Or operator 97
Outlook
  case sensitivity 296
  definition 294-295
  folders 295-297
Outlook messages
  creating 302-303, 304-305
  identifying 296-297
  receiving 297-302
  recipients 303-304
  sending 302-303
overwriting files 203

P

<package> tag 194-195
ParagraphFormat property 264
Paragraphs property 264
Parameters collection 241
ParentFolder property
  Files object 213
  Folder object 210
parse method 179
parseFloat function 149
parseInt function 149
Paste object 265
Path property
  Drive object 207
  Files object 213
  Folder object 210

Wscript object 23
paths
absolute 204, 210
BuildPath method 217
drive, returning 207
file 204, 213
folder 210
GetAbsolutePathName method 217, 316
relative 204
script, retrieving 23
ShortPath property, Files object 213
ShortPath property, Folder object 210
TargetPath property, WshShortcut object 36
TargetPath property, WshURLShortcut object 38
Pattern property 122
patterns. *See* RegExp object
period (.), in regular expressions 122
permissions for databases 242
plus sign (+), in regular expressions 122
POP (Post Office Protocol) 288
PopUp method
definition 30
displaying popup messages 39-41
popup windows
creating 39-41
Popup method 30
POSITIVE_INFINITY property 174
Post Office Protocol (POP) 288
pound sign (#), date indicator 129
pow function 177
printers, network 50-52
printing
Office object model 270
sample script 329-331
workbooks 273-274
PrintOut method
MailItem object 298
Word object 270
Workbook object 273-274
Private keyword 228
procedures. *See* JScript functions; VBScript procedures
profiles, e-mail 289
ProgIDs 195
programs
running. *See* running programs
shortcuts to 35-37
Prompt method 186-187
properties
class default 231-232
default 16
defining for classes 225-226
definition 13-14
procedural class properties 228-231
reading values of 228
read-only 230
script, viewing 69
setting values of 228
See also entries for specific properties
Property Get procedure 228-231
Property Let procedure 228-231
property procedures 228-231
Property Set procedure 228-231
protocols 288
Public keyword 225-226

Q

question mark (?), in regular expressions 122
Quick Launch toolbar 59
Quit method 23
quote ('), comment indicator 85
quotes ("), as string literals 117

R

random function 177
Randomize function 128
Range method 263-266
Range object 263-266
ranges
document text 263-266
spreadsheet cells 275
Read method 221
ReadAll method 221
reading from files 218-222
ReadLine method 221
ReadRecipientRequested property 303
ReadReg method 44, 45-46
Recipient object 303
Recipients property 293, 303
RecordSet object
definition 241
methods 252
properties 253
recordsets
! (exclamation point), bang operator 251-252
accessing field data 251-252
beginning-of-file condition 253
creating 247-251
criteria for exclusion 246
criteria for selection 245-247
current position 252-255
current record 251-252
cursors 248
definition 241
empty, detecting 253
end-of-file condition 253
locking records 248-251
looping through records 253-255
modifying 255-257
moving through 252-255
recursion 212
<reference> tag 195-196
references. *See* object references

RegDelete method 30, 45-46
RegEdit program 43
RegExp object 121-125, 172-173
registry 42-46
Registry Editor. *See* RegEdit program
RegRead method 30
regular expressions. *See* RegExp object
RegWrite method 30, 44, 45-46
relational databases 237-239
Remove method
  Dictionary object 20
  WshEnvironment object 31
RemoveAll method 20
RemoveNetworkDrive method 50, 54-55
RemovePrinterConnection method 50, 52
Replace method 122
replace method 171
Replacement method 267
Reply method 298
ReplyAll method 298
Resolve method 304
Resolved property 303
right angle bracket (>), comparison operator 96
right angle brackets (>>), rightward shift 155
right angle brackets (>>>), Zero-fill rightward shift 155
Right function 120
Rnd function 128
RollbackTrans method 242
RootFolder property 207
Round function 128
round function 177
RTrim function 121
Run method
  definition 30
  opening data files 47-48
  running programs 46-47
running programs 30, 46-48
running scripts
  with Cscript 6-7
  from Quick Launch toolbar 59
  script options 58-59
  from shortcuts 59
  with Wscript 7-8
  from a WSH file 69
run-time errors 74-75

S

Save method
  Workbook object 272
  WshShortcut object 36
  WshURLShortcut object 38
SaveAs method
  MailItem object 298
  Workbook object 272
saving
  e-mail messages 298
  script options in preference files 68-69
  shortcuts 36, 38
  workbooks 272-273
scheduling scripts with
  Task Scheduler 60-63
  Windows NT AT command 63-64
Script Debugger
  breakpoints 79-80
  Call Stack 81-82
  conflicts with other debuggers 78
  definition 76-77
  downloading 76
  function execution, tracking 81-82
  monitoring variables 80-81
  single stepping 79
  starting 58, 77-79
  Step Into 79
  Step Out 79
  Step Over 79
  Wscript object support 77
script information, retrieving. *See* Wscript object
script options 68-69
script preference files 68-69
<script> tag 193
ScriptFullName property 23
scripting engines
  definition 4
  displaying option information 58
  specifying 58
scripting languages
  history of 2-3
  WSH support 4
  See also JScript; VBScript
scripting on the Web 70-71
scripting program version, retrieving 23
scripting run-time library 200-202
Scripting Start Page 57
scripting utilities. *See* Cscript; Wscript
ScriptName property 23
scripts
  file names, retrieving 23
  interactive *versus* batch, specifying 23, 58
  interactivity 25-26
  organizing 6
  paths, retrieving 23
  quitting 23
  running. *See* running scripts
  scheduling with Task Scheduler 60-63
  scheduling with Windows NT AT command 63-64
  setting timeouts 26-27
  suspending execution 23
  terminating 26
  testing. *See* debugging scripts; Script Debugger
  timeouts. *See* timeouts
search method 171

Second function 133
Select Case statements 102-103
Selection property 276
semicolon (;), end-of-line character 15
Send method 291-292
Sender property 293
SenderName property 297
SendFax method 270
SendMail method
  Word object 271
  Workbook object 274
Sent property 303
Sentences property 264
SerialNumber property 207
server-side scripting 71
setDate method 178
SetDefaultPrinter method 50, 52
setFullYear method 178
setHours method 179
setMilliseconds method 179
setMinutes method 179
setMonth method 178
SetRange object 265
setSeconds method 179
setTime method 179
setUTCDate method 178
setUTCFullYear method 178
setUTCHours method 179
setUTCMilliseconds method 179
setUTCMinutes method 179
setUTCMonth method 178
setUTCSeconds method 179
Sgn function 128
ShareName property 207
shortcuts
  to programs, files, and folders 35-37
  for scripts 59
  to URLs 38-39
ShortName property
  Files object 213
  Folder object 210
ShortPath property
  Files object 213
  Folder object 210
Simple Mail Transfer Protocol (SMTP) 288
sin function 177
single quote ('), comment indicator 85
single stepping program execution 79
Size property
  Files object 213
  Folder object 210
Skip method 221
SkipLine method 221
slashes (//), comment indicators 145
Sleep method 23
slice method 171
SMTP (Simple Mail Transfer Protocol) 288
sorting, VBScript 96-97
Source property 138
Space function 126
spawning programs. *See* running programs
special folders 217
special system folders, accessing 32-35
SpecialCells property 276
SpecialFolders property 30
Split function 126
split method 171, 172
spreadsheets. *See* Excel object model
SQL (Structured Query Language) 241
Sqr function 128
sqrt function 177
SRL. *See* scripting run-time library
Start property 264
State property 242
Step Into 79
Step Out 79
Step Over 79
stepping through program execution 79
StoryLength property 264
StoryType property 264
StrComp function 127
string constants 335
String data type 148
String function 126-127
string manipulation. *See* JScript string; VBScript string
String object 169-170
string operators
  JScript 155
  VBScript 95-96
Structured Query Language (SQL) 241
subcommand procedures 109
subfolders, returning 210
SubFolders property 210
Subject property 293, 297
substr method 171
substring method 171
subtraction
  See arithmetic operators
  See number-related functions
  See numeric data
switch statements 160-161
symbolic constants
  JScript 146
  VBScript 86
syntax errors 72-73

T

//T option 58
Tan function 128
tan function 177
TargetPath property

WshShortcut object 36
WshURLShortcut object 38
Task Scheduler 60-63
temporary folders 217
Test method 122
testing scripts. *See* debugging scripts; Script Debugger
text data. *See* JScript string; VBScript string
text editors 73
Text method 267
Text property 264, 293
TextStream object 202, 218-222
throw statements 190-191
time data. *See* dates and times
Time function 129
TimeOut property 23
timeouts
setting 26-27
//T option 58
TimeOut property 23
for unattended scripts 41
TimeValue function 130
To property 297, 303
toGMTString method 179
toLocaleString method 179
toLowerCase method 171
toString method
Number object 175
String object 171
TotalSize property 207
toUpperCase method 171
toUTCString method 179
Trim function 121
True/False comparisons
See Boolean
See comparison operators
See logical operators
try...catch statements 188-189
two-digit years 130
Type property
Files object 213
Folder object 210
Recipient object 303

U

UBound function 91-92
ubound method 184
UCase function 96-97, 120
Undefined data type 148
Underline property 264
underscore (_)
continuation character 15, 85-86
in variable names 147
Unicode characters 219
Universal Coordinated Time 177
Universal Coordinated Time (UTC) 177
Unix scripting 2
UnRead property
CDO object 293
MailItem object 297
uppercasing strings 96-97, 120
See also case sensitivity
URLs, shortcuts to 38-39
UsedRange property 276
user interaction. *See* interactivity
UserDomain property 49
UserName property 49
UTC method 179
UTC (Universal Coordinated Time) 177
utilities. *See* Cscript; Wscript

V

valueOf method
Number object 175
String object 171
var statements 148
variables
VBScript. *See* VBScript variables
VBScript procedures 112-113
VBA (Visual Basic for Applications) 260
VBArray function 151
VBArray object 184-186
vbCrLf constant 137
VBScript
arithmetic operators 95
assignment operator 94-95
case sensitivity. *See* case sensitivity, VBScript
combining with JScript. *See* WSF files
commenting out code 85
comments 85
comparison operators 96-97
conditional statements 100-103
dates and times. *See* dates and times, VBScript
definition 9
dialog boxes 135-137
Dim statement 88
Do...Loop statements 106-108
For Each...Next statements 105-106
Err object 138
error codes 341-342
On Error Goto statements 140
error handling 138-140
On Error statements 138
Eval function 141
Execute statements 141-142
ExecuteGlobal statements 141-142
execution, global *versus* current context 141-142
For...Next statements 104-105
If...Then...Else statements 101-102
infinite loops 108-109
InputBox function 137
versus JScript 143

keywords 336-337
line continuation 85-86
loop statements 100-109
MsgBox function 135-137
operator precedence 98
operators, grouping with parentheses 98
Option Explicit statement 88-89
Select Case statements 102-103
string operators 95-96
uppercasing strings 96-97
user interaction 135-138
versus Visual Basic 84
While...Wend statements 108

VBScript arrays
associative 90
determining size of 91-92
dynamic 92-94
reinitializing 94
static 90-92
variant 94

VBScript constants
color constants 332
comparison constants 332
date and time constants 333
literal constants 86
MsgBox constants 334-335
names 86
string constants 335
symbolic constants 86

VBScript expressions
comparing 96-97
definition 91
evaluating 141

VBScript procedures
arrays 112-113
calling recursively 112-113
calling sequentially 113-114
defining 110
definition 109
function procedures 109
global variables 112-113
local variables 112-113
passing arguments to 110-111
by reference arguments 111
subcommand procedures 109
types of 109
by value arguments 111
variables 112-113
See also JScript functions

VBScript string functions and objects
Asc function 116
Chr function 116-117
Filter function 117-118
InStr function 119
InStrRev function 119
Join function 119-120
LCase function 120
Left function 120
Len function 121
LTrim function 121
Mid function 120
RegExp object 121-125
Right function 120
RTrim function 121
Space function 126
Split function 126
StrComp function 127
String function 126-127
Trim function 121
UCase function 96-97, 120

VBScript string manipulations
" (double quotes), as string literals 117
arrays of strings, subsetting 117-118
ASCII conversions 116
characters, inserting 126-127
comparing two strings 126-127
extracting part of a string 120
finding strings within strings 119
joining strings 119-120
length, determining 121
lowercasing strings 120
regular expression searches 121-125
spaces, inserting 126
spaces, removing leading/trailing 121
splitting strings into substrings 126
uppercasing strings 120

VBScript variables 88-90
version of the scripting program, retrieving 23
Version property 23
vertical line (|), bitwise Or 155
Visual Basic for Applications (VBA) 260
Visual Basic *versus* VBScript 84
VolumeName property 207

W

Web scripting 70-71
Weekday function 133
WeekdayName function 133
while statements 162-163
While...Wend statements 108
Windows Environment variables, accessing 31-32
Windows NT, and logon scripts 311
Windows NT AT command 63-64
Windows Script Host. *See* WSH; WSH (Windows Script Host)

Windows scripting
history of 3
See also Wscript

Windows Scripting Clinic 57
Windows shell access. *See* WshShell object
WindowStyle property 36
with statements 164

Word object model
Application object 261
bold text 264

character formatting 264
characters in a range 264
closing a document 262
copying a range 265
cutting a range 265
Document object 261-262
document ranges 263-266
finding and replacing text 267-270
formatting text 265-266
inserting text 265
italic text 264
opening a document 262
paragraphs 264
pasting text 265
range start/end 264, 265
selecting text 263
sentences 264
stories 264
text case 264
text in a range 264
underlining text 264
words in a range 264
word processor documents. *See* Word object model
Words property 264
Workbook object 272-274
workbooks. *See* Excel object model
WorkingDirectory property 36
worksheets. *See* Excel object model
Write method 221
WriteBlankLines method 221
WriteLines method 221
writing to files 218-222
Wscript
associating with file extensions 8
definition 6
options, specifying at run time 58
running scripts 7-8
setting as default executable 58
Wscript object
definition 22-23
host information, retrieving 23, 24
methods 23
properties 23
Script Debugger support for 77
script interactivity 25-26
.wsf file extension 192
WSF files
definition 192
importing 196-197
<job> tag 194-195
<object> tag 195
<package> tag 194-195
<reference> tag 195-196
<script> tag 193
XML compliance 197-198
XML errors and debugging 198
XML tags 193-196
.wsh file extension 68
WSH files 68-69
WSH object model, online resources for 57
WSH (Windows Script Host)
capabilities of 3-4
downloading 3
history of 2-3
online FAQ 57
scripting language support 4
WshCollection object 17-18
WshEnvironment object 31-32
WshNetwork object 49-55
WshShell object 30
WshShortcut object 35-37
WshSpecialFolders object 32-35
WshURLShortcut object 38-39

X

//X option 58
XML, and WSF files
compliance 197-198
errors and debugging 198
tags 193-196
Xor operator 97

Y

Year function 133